Statistics for Social Workers

FIFTH EDITION

Statistics for Social Workers

Robert W. Weinbach
The University of South Carolina

Richard M. Grinnell, Jr.
Illinois State University

Allyn and Bacon
Boston • London • Toronto • Sydney • Tokyo • Singapore

Senior Editor, Social Work and Family Therapy: *Judy Fifer*
Editor in Chief, Social Science: *Karen Hanson*
Editorial Assistant: *Alyssa Pratt*
Executive Marketing Manager: *Lisa Kimball*
Editorial Production Service: *Chestnut Hill Enterprises, Inc.*
Manufacturing Buyer: *Julie McNeill*
Cover Administrator: *Linda Knowles*
Electronic Composition: *Omegatype Typography, Inc.*

Internet: www.abacon.com

Between the time Website information is gathered and published, some sites may have closed. Also, the transcription of URLs can result in typographical errors. The publisher would appreciate notification where these occur so that they may be corrected in subsequent editions.

Library of Congress Cataloging-in-Publication Data

Weinbach, Robert W.
    Statistics for social workers / Robert W. Weinbach, Richard M. Grinnell, Jr.—5th ed.
      p. cm.
    Includes bibliographical references and index.
    ISBN 0-8013-3312-1
    1. Social sciences—Statistical methods. 2. Social service—Statistical methods. 3.
  Statistics. I. Grinnell, Richard M. II. Title.

HA29 .W45 2000
519.5'024'362—dc21

                                      00-026661

Printed in the United States of America

10 9 8 7 6 5 4 3 2 1   05 04 03 02 01 00

Contents

Preface   xiii

1 Introduction to Statistical Analysis   1

USES OF STATISTICAL ANALYSIS   2

GENERAL METHODOLOGICAL TERMS   3
   Data   3
   Information   3
   Variables and Constants   3
   Conceptualization   5
   Operationalization   5
   Reliability   7
   Validity   7
   Research Hypotheses   8

LEVELS OF MEASUREMENT   9
   Nominal   10
   Ordinal   11
   Interval   13
   Ratio   13

OTHER MEASUREMENT CLASSIFICATIONS   14
   Discrete Variables and Continuous Variables   14
   Dichotomous, Binary, and Dummy Variables   14

LEVELS OF MEASUREMENT AND ANALYSIS OF DATA   15

CATEGORIES OF STATISTICAL ANALYSES   16
   Number of Variables Analyzed   16
   Descriptive and Inferential   16

CONCLUDING THOUGHTS   17

STUDY QUESTIONS   17

2   **Frequency Distributions and Graphs**   **20**

FREQUENCY DISTRIBUTIONS   20
   Absolute Frequency Distributions   22
   Cumulative Frequency Distributions   22
   Percentage Frequency Distributions   23
   Cumulative Percentage Distributions   24

GROUPED FREQUENCY DISTRIBUTIONS   24

USING FREQUENCY DISTRIBUTIONS TO ANALYZE DATA   26

MISREPRESENTATION OF DATA   28
   Example: An Administrator's Efforts to Hire
   More Women   28

GRAPHICAL PRESENTATION OF DATA   29
   Bar Graphs   30
   Pie Charts   30
   Histograms   32
   Frequency Polygons   32
   Pareto Charts   34
   Stem-and-Leaf Plots   34

A COMMON MISTAKE IN DISPLAYING DATA   35

CONCLUDING THOUGHTS   36

STUDY QUESTIONS   37

3   **Central Tendency and Variability**   **39**

CENTRAL TENDENCY   39
   The Mode   40
   The Median   42
   The Mean   43
   Which Measure of Central Tendency to Use?   45

VARIABILITY   48
   The Range   48
   The Interquartile Range   49
   The Mean Deviation   50
   The Variance   51
   The Standard Deviation   51
   Reporting Measures of Variability   55

CONCLUDING THOUGHTS   56

STUDY QUESTIONS   56

4 Normal Distributions 58

SKEWED DISTRIBUTIONS 58

NORMAL DISTRIBUTIONS 60

CONVERTING RAW SCORES TO z SCORES AND PERCENTILES 64
Practical Uses of z Scores 69
Example: Student Anxiety 70

DERIVING RAW SCORES FROM PERCENTILES 72

CONCLUDING THOUGHTS 74

STUDY QUESTIONS 74

5 Introduction To Hypothesis Testing 76

ALTERNATIVE EXPLANATIONS 76
Rival Hypotheses 77
Design Bias 77
Sampling Error 79

PROBABILITY 79

REFUTING SAMPLING ERROR 82
Replication 82
Statistical Analyses 83

RESEARCH HYPOTHESES 83
The One-Tailed Research Hypothesis 84
The Two-Tailed Research Hypothesis 84
The Null Research Hypothesis 85

TESTING THE NULL HYPOTHESIS 85

STATISTICAL SIGNIFICANCE 88
p-Values 88
Rejection Levels 88

ERRORS IN DRAWING CONCLUSIONS ABOUT RELATIONSHIPS 90
Avoiding Type I Errors 91

STATISTICALLY SIGNIFICANT RELATIONSHIPS AND
MEANINGFUL FINDINGS 92
Assessing Strength (Effect Size) 92
Is the Relationship Surprising? 94
Complex Interpretations of Statistically
Significant Relationships 95

CONCLUDING THOUGHTS   95

STUDY QUESTIONS   96

6   Sampling Distributions and Hypothesis Testing   **98**

SAMPLE SIZE AND SAMPLING ERROR   98

SAMPLING DISTRIBUTIONS AND INFERENCE   100
Comparing an Experimental Sample
with Its Population   100
Comparing a Nonexperimental Sample
with Its Population   101

SAMPLING DISTRIBUTION OF MEANS   102
Samples Drawn from Normal Distributions   105
Samples Drawn from Skewed Distributions   110

ESTIMATING PARAMETERS FROM STATISTICS   111
Constructing a 95 Percent Confidence Interval   112
Constructing a 99 Percent Confidence Interval   112

OTHER DISTRIBUTIONS   114

CONCLUDING THOUGHTS   114

STUDY QUESTIONS   115

7   Selecting a Statistical Test   **116**

THE IMPORTANCE OF SELECTING THE CORRECT STATISTICAL TEST   116

FACTORS TO CONSIDER WHEN SELECTING A STATISTICAL TEST   118
Sampling Method(s) Used   118
Distribution of the Variables within
the Population   119
Level of Measurement of the Independent
and Dependent Variables   120
Amount of Statistical Power That Is Desirable   121
Robustness of Tests Being Considered   124

PARAMETRIC AND NONPARAMETRIC TESTS   125

MULTIVARIATE STATISTICAL TESTS   126

GENERAL GUIDELINES FOR TEST SELECTION   127

GETTING HELP WITH DATA ANALYSES   129

CONCLUDING THOUGHTS   130

STUDY QUESTIONS   132

8   Correlation   **134**

USES OF CORRELATION   135
   Scattergrams   135

PERFECT CORRELATIONS   138

NONPERFECT CORRELATIONS   140

INTERPRETING LINEAR CORRELATIONS   142
   The Range of Correlation Coefficients   143
   Interpreting Very Strong Correlations   143
   The Coefficient of Determination   144
   Correlation Is Not Causation   145

COMPUTATION AND PRESENTATION OF PEARSON'S *r*   146

USING PEARSON'S *r* FOR INFERENCE   148
   Example: Verbal Participation among Female
   Group Members   149
   Example: Worker Experience and Error Rates   152

NONPARAMETRIC ALTERNATIVES   154
   Spearman's rho and Kendall's tau   154
   Example: Caregiver Attitudes and Longevity
   of Hospice Patients   154

USING CORRELATION WITH THREE OR MORE VARIABLES   155
   Partial *r*   155
   Multiple *R*   156

OTHER MULTIVARIATE TESTS THAT USE CORRELATION   159
   Factor Analysis   159
   Cluster Analysis   161

CONCLUDING THOUGHTS   162

STUDY QUESTIONS   162

9   Regression Analyses   **164**

WHAT IS PREDICTION?   164

WHAT IS SIMPLE LINEAR REGRESSION?   167
   Formulating a Research Question   168
   Limitations of Simple Linear Regression   168

COMPUTATION OF THE REGRESSION EQUATION   169

MORE ABOUT THE REGRESSION LINE   172
  The Least-Squares Criterion   172
  The Regression Coefficient (b)   174
  The y-Intercept (a)   174
  Predicted Y (Y')   175
  Interchanging X and Y Variables   176

INTERPRETING RESULTS   176
  Presentation of Y' 177
  The Standard Error   177

USING REGRESSION ANALYSES IN SOCIAL WORK PRACTICE   177
  Example: Socializing with Family Members
  and Life Satisfaction   177
  Example: Worker's Case Load Size and Number
  of Sick Days Taken   179

REGRESSION WITH THREE OR MORE VARIABLES   180

OTHER TYPES OF REGRESSION ANALYSES   182
  Discriminant Analysis   182
  Logistic Regression   183

CONCLUDING THOUGHTS   184

STUDY QUESTIONS   185

10 Cross-Tabulation   187

THE CHI-SQUARE TEST OF ASSOCIATION   187
  Observed Frequencies   189
  Expected Frequencies   191
  Degrees of Freedom   193
  Computation of Chi-Square   196
  Presentation of Chi-Square   197
  Interpreting the Results of a Chi-Square
  Analysis   197
  Meaningfulness and Sample Size   198
  Related Indicators of the Strength of a
  Relationship   200
  Restrictions on the Use of Chi-Square   201
  An Alternative to Chi-Square: Fisher's
  Exact Test   202

USING CHI-SQUARE IN SOCIAL WORK PRACTICE   202
    Example: Discharge Planning and Readmission   202
    **Example: Legislators' Voting Patterns
    and Tax Issues   205**

CHI-SQUARE WITH THREE OR MORE VARIABLES   206
    Problems with Sizes of Expected Frequencies   207
    Effects of Introducing Additional Variables   208

SPECIAL APPLICATIONS OF THE CHI-SQUARE FORMULA   209
    McNemar's Test   209
    Median Test   211

CONCLUDING THOUGHTS   213

STUDY QUESTIONS   214

11   *t* **Tests and Analysis of Variance**   **215**

THE USE OF *t* TESTS   216

THE ONE-SAMPLE *t* TEST   218
    **Comparing a Sample's Mean to
    a Population's Mean   218**
    Hypothesis Testing   220
    Presentation of Findings   221
    **A Nonparametric Alternative: The Chi-Square
    Goodness-of-Fit Test   221**

THE DEPENDENT *t* TEST   224
    **Use with Two Connected (or Matched) Samples
    Measured Once   224**
    Use with One Sample Measured Twice   224
    **A Nonparametric Alternative: The Wilcoxon
    Sign Test   225**

THE INDEPENDENT *t* TEST   227
    Example: Study Guide for the State Merit Exam   228
    Example: Treatment of Marital Problems   229
    Example: Staff Turnover   232
    Nonparametric Alternatives: *U* and K-S   235

SIMPLE ANALYSIS OF VARIANCE (ONE-WAY *ANOVA*)   238
    Computation   239
    **A Nonparametric Alternative:
    The Kruskal-Wallis Test   240**

MULTIPLE ANALYSIS OF VARIANCE   240

CONCLUDING THOUGHTS   241

STUDY QUESTIONS   241

References and Further Reading   243

Glossary   245

Index   262

Preface

The fifth edition of *Statistics for Social Workers* contains some important revisions. However, our assumptions about the readers of this book have not changed. We continue to believe that professional social workers possess a wide range of mathematical backgrounds and react in a variety of ways, including terror, to the mention of the word *statistics*. They share one common characteristic, however—they all are people oriented. Most have selected the profession of social work because they prefer to work with people rather than with numbers or abstract concepts. We believe, nonetheless, that once they see how statistical analyses can help them become more effective practitioners, they will approach the topic with less apprehension.

AUDIENCE

As in the previous four editions, the fifth edition is intended for undergraduate or graduate social work students and practitioners who have little or no backround in statistical analysis. Although some knowledge of research methods is desirable, it is not essential. We have presented the material in the most straightforward, unintimidating way possible, using simple language and avoiding highly technical words and convoluted phrases. The text is easy to teach from and to learn from. Figures and case examples have been used extensively to provide visual representations of the concepts presented.

GOAL

Social workers often rely on logic, common sense, and/or practice experience to draw conclusions and make decisions. In this book, we examine more scientific ways to perform the same tasks. Statistical analyses of research data or, in some cases, of data collected for other purposes (e.g., case record data) rely on mathematics and often on the laws of probability. Thus, they are less vulnerable to the biases and distortions that can cloud decision making when we rely exclusively on less scientific methods.

The topics addressed in this book are more than what students often refer to colloquially as statistics. The book is about a process, a widely-accepted systematic way of analyzing data and making sense of it. This book is designed to successfully introduce today's people-oriented social work students and practitioners to a topic they might not choose to study. Readers are likely to possess diverse mathematical backgrounds. Consequently, this book is as unmathematical as we dare make it, while still introducing the core concepts needed for beginning statistical literacy.

Our goal is not to make mathematicians out of social workers. It is to enable students and practitioners to make decisions about when a statistical analysis is necessary to address theoretical or practice-based social work problems, to determine which type of analysis is most appropriate to use, to interpret statistical results, and to communicate the statistical results and interpretations in terms that are meaningful to others. In short, this book is designed to help social workers appreciate, interpret, use, and integrate statistical analyses in their professional practices.

RELIANCE ON COMPUTERS

As in previous editions, we have avoided the inclusion of unnecessary formulas and mathematical computations. We have done this in part because we know how page after page of numbers and mathematical symbols can quickly turn off the reader. We also included few formulas because we think they are no longer needed by most readers. The cost of personal computers and statistical software packages have continued to decline in price to the point where most students and practitioners now have easy access to them. Their availability within schools and departments of social work as well as most human service agencies allows social workers to perform data entry and analyses without having to resort to tedious mathematical computations. It is highly unlikely that social workers in the 21st century will have to perform statistical analyses by hand.

The current state of computer technology suggests an analogy to taking a trip on an airplane. Do we have to know the laws of aerodynamics to fly in an airplane? Or do we just have to know how to select the flight that best meets our needs, make a reservation, and trust that the people who build and fly the planes know those laws well? Do we need to know how to perform all the mathematical calculations of a statistical test just to use it correctly? Or do we just have to know how to select the correct test and how to instruct the computer to perform it on a data set?

This book will help the reader choose the correct statistical analysis. It will offer little to help the reader perform the calculations. We leave that up to the computer.

We know that there is a downside to not providing formulas for most statistics in this book and of not showing how the formulas are used in their calculations. Some readers may not totally understand and appreciate a statistical analysis unless they are shown how its formula is derived. To return to our earlier analogy, we admit readily that an airplane passenger who knows the laws of aerodynamics will unquestionably have a greater understanding and appreciation of the achievement of flight than a passenger on the same flight who does not. However, both passengers will accomplish their goal—both will arrive at the same destination at the same time.

Very few of us would fly if we were required to know the laws of aerodynamics before we entered an airplane. In the same vein, very few of us would use statistical analyses if we were required to know how to perform the complicated mathematical calculations that they require. If a reader of this book wishes to further develop statistical literacy by studying the formulas on which a statistical analysis is based, there are many more advanced books and courses that can assist in this undertaking.

We have also deliberately chosen not to include sample computer printouts, even though we acknowledge that social workers are most likely to receive the output of their data analyses in this format. At the present time, there are too many different statistical software packages in use; there is no standard software that all students or even most of them are likely to see. We believe that seeing a printout from a different software package than the one used might be more confusing than helpful. When there is one package that is more widely used than others (and we believe that may happen soon), sample printouts will be a useful addition to a future edition.

CONTENTS

The contents of this edition have been selected and arranged so that the book can be used as a supplementary text for a social work research methods course or as the primary text in an introductory course on statistical analyses of research or agency records data:

- Chapter 1 introduces basic concepts and definitions that are necessary to understanding statistical analyses.
- Chapters 2–4 contain a discussion of the most basic form of statistical analyses—that designed to summarize and display the distribution of a single variable within a research sample or population.
- Chapters 5–7 introduce readers to the related topics of inferential statistical analyses and hypothesis testing.
- The four remaining chapters (Chapters 8–11) present a wide array of statistical tests commonly used by social workers to attempt to seek support for hypotheses about relationships between and among variables. Along with the most commonly used bivariate tests, multivariate and nonparametric alternatives are also introduced.

We have once again used numerous examples from micro and macro social work practice to illustrate the use of basic statistical concepts. Through these examples, we have tried to demonstrate that statistical analyses can help answer everyday social work questions. The answers, in turn, can be used to enhance our effectiveness as practitioners.

CHANGES IN THIS EDITION

Over the years, we have received hundreds of comments and suggestions from students, instructors, and reviewers who have read the first four editions. With their comments in mind, we determined the specific topics to cover, the depth of coverage, and the sequence of material in this edition of the book.

While retaining the basic organization of earlier editions, we have done some reorganization to make the book more functional, practical, and manageable for students and instructors alike. We also have added a few figures and some new examples and addressed what some of our critics pointed out as important omissions in the earlier editions.

A quick glance at the table of contents reveals the most obvious change—11 chapters instead of 12. In response to reviewers, the content on selected nonparametric tests and some commonly used multivariate procedures that were previously in the last chapter has been integrated into the first 11 chapters. This made these chapters a little longer, but the logic of placing these tests alongside related ones, instead of in a final add-on chapter, is undeniable.

We added content on a second practical use of z-scores—determining what score on a standardized test corresponds to a given percentile. Reliability, an important bridge between research methods and statistical analyses, is discussed in greater detail. There is new content on regression (logistic regression) and expanded discussion of t tests.

The content on sampling distributions in Chapter 6 was new to the fourth edition. We have added a considerable amount of new content to clarify this important concept and created some new figures to demonstrate graphically the relationship between sample size and sampling error.

Earlier editions, like most other books on statistical analyses, focused almost exclusively on the issue of statistical significance and avoiding Type I errors. In this edition, we have provided additional content on statistical significance, but we provide a more balanced approach to statistical decision making with much more content on Type II errors. Specifically, we have added all new content on statistical power analysis and the related concept of effect size and provided broader coverage of measures of association.

We have omitted very little from previous editions and focused instead on deleting unnecessary redundancy and on restating some material in a more succinct way. We believe that this has made for a more readable, crisp approach to the topic.

This edition is organized in a way that makes good sense to us for teaching this content. Since other sequences might make more sense to other instructors, however, the chapters in this book were consciously planned to be self-contained and largely independent of one another. They can be read out of the order in which they are presented, or they can even be selectively omitted. They will probably make the most sense to students, however, if they are read in the sequence presented because each builds on the preceding one to some degree.

ACKNOWLEDGMENTS

Many people have contributed to the completion of this book. Hundreds of students, through questions and challenges posed during class sessions over the past decades, have served to shape our thinking about how a topic that is often intimidating can be taught in a meaningful and user-friendly manner. A number of colleagues have kindly shared their expertise by commenting on what they perceived as strengths and weaknesses of the coverage in the earlier editions.

The following people may take partial credit for the achievements and improvements this edition represents; as always, we alone must accept responsibility for its shortcomings:

- Hailv Abatena, University of Nevada–Las Vegas
- William E. Berg, University of Wisconsin–Milwaukee
- Gil Choi, University of South Carolina
- Joe Crymes, University of Maryland–Baltimore
- Peter A. Gabor, The University of Calgary
- Leon Ginsberg, University of South Carolina
- Arnold L. Greenfield, Michigan State University
- Bud Hanson, University of Windsor
- Stuart P. Hanson, University of California, Berkeley
- Kenneth L. Hobby, Harding University
- Miriam Johnson, University of South Carolina
- J. M. Kapoor, Indiana University
- Keith M. Kilty, Ohio State University
- Paul Kim, University of South Carolina
- Judy L. Krysik, Phoenix, Arizona
- Sally Mason, University of Illinois–Chicago
- Grant McDonald, York University
- Suzanne McMurphy, University of New Hampshire
- Steven L. McMurtry, University of Wisconsin–Milwaukee
- Paul R. Raffoul, University of Houston
- Cleora Roberts, University of South Florida
- Allen Rubin, The University of Texas at Austin
- Bibhuti K. Sar, University of Louisville
- Michael J. Sheridan, Virginia Commonwealth University
- Jackie D. Sieppert, The University of Calgary
- Glenn Stone, Indiana University
- Althea J. Truitt, Benedict College
- Yvonne A. Unrau, Illinois State University
- Roland M. Wagner, San Jose State University
- Alex Westerfelt, University of Kansas

If the material presented in this book helps readers develop or expand their knowledge and assists them in preparing for more advanced courses, our efforts will have been more than justified. If it also encourages them to appreciate the place of statistical analysis in professional social work practice, our task will have been fully rewarded.

Robert W. Weinbach

Richard M. Grinnell, Jr.

Introduction to Statistical Analysis

This book is about building knowledge in a systematic, objective way. The statistical analysis process (hereafter referred to as *statistical analysis*) does nothing more than analyze and make sense of data. The data can come from many sources, which can range from a complex and sophisticated research study to a simple agency client intake form. Most importantly, statistical analysis is a process that can help social workers make practice-related decisions.

Both the National Association of Social Workers (NASW) and the Council on Social Work Education (CSWE) take the position that competent social workers need to understand statistical analyses. There are three interrelated reasons why it should be studied:

1. *Social workers conduct research studies.* A knowledge of statistical analysis enhances our ability to design research studies and to draw justifiable conclusions from their findings. Thus, we need to know how to perform statistical analyses in order to gather, sort, organize, and draw conclusions from research data.

We contribute to the profession's knowledge base by disseminating the findings of research studies. To have credibility, we must demonstrate that the data we gathered were generated, analyzed, and interpreted according to accepted methodological and statistical procedures. Fortunately, these procedures are based on logic that we already use in many social work practice situations. We apply the procedures not only to interpret the findings derived from research studies but also when we collect and analyze data to assist us in making practice decisions.

2. *Social workers rely on others' research findings.* We use the results of others' statistical analyses of their research data to inform our practice decision making. As we read journal articles and other professional literature, we must be statistically literate. Unless we know whether a particular statistical analysis was performed correctly, we cannot know whether the findings are credible. Understanding the results of a statistical analysis increases the likelihood that we will use the most effective and efficient practice interventions with our clients and helps us avoid those that lack adequate statistical support.

3. *Social workers need to evaluate their practice effectiveness.* We evaluate the effectiveness of our individual practice methods and our social service programs not only for our own feedback but also to justify that we are accountable in the use of the resources we receive to carry out our mission. To do this, we must rely on more than our own personal insights, past experiences, intuitions, or feelings that we are or are not being effective. Increasingly, both single-system research designs and program evaluations rely on statistical analyses to determine whether an individual intervention and/or program is accomplishing its objectives.

Using any statistical analysis neither guarantees the generation of "true knowledge" by a research study nor guarantees positive client outcomes in practice interventions. However, the use of a statistical analysis can increase the likelihood of these two events and, at the same time, helps us move toward the goal of becoming knowledge-based professional social work practitioners.

USES OF STATISTICAL ANALYSIS

Whether we are evaluating our own practice effectiveness or conducting a research study to generate new knowledge, a good statistical analysis can be a useful tool. It is of great assistance, for example, when we select, design, evaluate, and fine-tune our data collection instruments. It can also help us make decisions about how large a research sample we need for a given research study or whether a measurement instrument is likely to produce valid and reliable data.

Once data are collected, a statistical analysis can help us

- Summarize the characteristics of a specific research sample or population
- Estimate the characteristics of the population from which our sample was drawn
- Determine if any patterns of relationships found within a research sample can safely be generalized back to the population from which the sample was drawn

A statistical analysis can produce useful information only when sound methods for measurement and data collection have been used. To put it another way, even a good statistical analysis can be useless or, worse yet, misleading if the data that were collected were flawed in some way.

GENERAL METHODOLOGICAL TERMS

Many terms used in the research enterprise have specific meanings. Eight of the most important ones are (1) data, (2) information, (3) variables and constants, (4) conceptualization, (5) operationalization, (6) reliability, (7) validity, and (8) research hypotheses.

Data

In the previous pages, we have used two terms: *data* and *information*. While these terms are sometimes used interchangeably in everyday conversation, in this book, an important distinction is made between them. *Data* refers to the measurements (numbers, scores, and so forth) collected in a research study before they have been analyzed in any way. (The term *data* is plural; the singular is *datum*.) For example, the group of scores obtained by administering a client satisfaction scale to 100 clients is *data*. (An individual client's satisfaction score on the same measuring instrument is referred to as *datum*.)

Social workers engage in many types of data-gathering activities and data-collection methods. We conduct in-depth interviews, content analyses, participant observations, and direct observations of behaviors in natural settings. We also conduct surveys, group experiments, case experiments, meta-analyses, historical research, and so forth.

Data usually consist of measurements that we take ourselves, but they may also be measurements taken previously for some other purpose, (such as, by other researchers seeking to answer another research question or by other practitioners for client record-keeping purposes.) When data collected for some other purpose are statistically analyzed, we refer to the process as *secondary data analysis*.

Whatever method is used to acquire data, measurements must be highly accurate. Conclusions based on a research study's findings are never any better than the quality of the data that formed the basis for those conclusions.

Information

Data, when analyzed, produce *information*. Information is the interpretation we give to collected data after we analyze them. The research conclusion based on a data analysis that "Treatment Intervention A is more successful than Treatment Intervention B in reducing substance abuse among research participants" is information. Similarly, if the outside temperature measured by a thermometer is 102 degrees Fahrenheit, the 102 degrees is *datum*. The interpretation that it is very hot is *information*.

Variables and Constants

There is always a limit to how much data we can collect and use in any given practice or research situation. Like a social work practitioner conducting an intake interview, a social work researcher does not need to know everything about the people (or objects) studied. Thus, we limit data collection activities to measuring only those variables that are considered useful for the specific research study.

What exactly is a variable? A *variable* is a characteristic or attribute that differs in quantity or quality among the people (or objects) studied. All research studies focus on variables. Among human beings, examples of variables are educational level, gender, sexual orientation, ethnicity, motivational level for treatment, stress level, and self-esteem level. The list is practically endless.

In comparison to variables, *constants* are traits or characteristics that do not differ in quantity or quality among people (or objects). An example of a constant among all human beings is mortality. Life expectancy, on the other hand, is a variable, since it differs among human beings. We want to learn why variations occur among people (or objects) and what other variables may relate (or not relate) to these variations in some way.

We may study, for example, a sample of female adolescents addicted to crack cocaine. We would attempt to learn how some other variables, such as education level and income level, might relate to different patterns of drug addiction within the research sample. In this example, adolescence, gender and addiction to crack cocaine are constants (characteristics of all research participants), but the research participants' different educational and income levels, along with their patterns of drug use addiction, are variables.

Value Categories and Values of Variables.

The different measurements that a variable can assume can be expressed in words (e.g., homeless, not homeless) or in numbers (e.g., 1, 2, 3). When measurements are expressed in words, they are called *value categories* and simply describe different forms that the variable can take. The variable *gender,* for example, can be measured by classifying people into two value categories that can be expressed in words—male and female.

When the different measurements of a variable are expressed in numbers that reflect some quantifiable difference, they are called *values* and reflect more precise measurement than value categories. We can measure the variable *age,* for example, by using actual numerical values (e.g., 23, 35, 67) to reflect the actual ages of people on their last birthdays.

Frequencies of Value Categories and Values.

More often than not, a given value category or value occurs more than once in a group of people (or objects). The number of times that it occurs within a group of cases is called its *frequency.* Frequencies for the different value categories or values of variables tend to vary within data sets. Within a research sample of 28 agency clients, for example, the frequency for the value category *female* might be 16 for the variable *gender,* while the frequency for the value category *male* might be 12.

The following example of a questionnaire item can be used to summarize the relationship between a variable, its value categories, and the frequencies of each value category.

What is your highest social work degree completed? (*variable*)

Value Category	Frequency
Associate degree	9
BSW	22
MSW	19
PhD/DSW	3

In the above example, the variable *highest social work degree completed* has four value categories (i.e., Associate degree, BSW, MSW, PhD/DSW) and each value category has a frequency (i.e., there are 9 people who have an Associate Degree, 22 people who have a BSW, 19 people who have a MSW, 3 people who have a PhD/DSW).

Conceptualization

Often, when a research study begins, we do not know which variables will need to be measured and which will not. We need to narrow down the list of potential variables by identifying those that must be measured in an attempt to arrive at answers to our research question. But this is only the first step in an important four-step process known as *conceptualization,* which takes place with the help of a thorough review of the available professional literature. The four steps in the conceptualization process are:

1. Select the most important variables to study.
2. State exactly what is meant by each variable.
3. Specify how each variable is to be measured.
4. State the value categories or values that each variable can assume.

After we have selected the variables to measure, we need to define exactly what each one means. Let us say, for example, that we wish to test the following research hypothesis:

Among 3-year-old children who are diagnosed as autistic, Treatment Intervention A will decrease autistic behavior more than Treatment Intervention B.

The research hypothesis reflects the belief that the two different treatment interventions (A and B) affect autistic behavior differently. In order to examine the relationship between the two treatment interventions used and their relationship to the rate of decrease in the autistic behavior of 3-year-old children, we must clearly state the meaning of both variables (the type of intervention and the amount of autistic behavior). We must also state the value categories or values that each variable can assume as well as the nature of the relationship that we believe to exist between them.

What exactly constitutes autistic behavior? What exactly are Interventions A and B? Without first delineating the meaning of all variables, it would be futile to attempt to establish a relationship between or among them. Note that age and a diagnosis of autism are constants—they do not vary among the children we are studying. Of course, the severity of autism would vary among the children. It would constitute a third variable that we also might decide to measure so that we can better understand the relationship between the two variables of primary interest, type of intervention and amount of autistic behavior. If so, we would also have to conceptualize what exactly we mean by severity of autism.

Operationalization

Specifying exactly how we are going to measure the variables that we have conceptualized is called *operationalization.* Many different indicators may be used to measure the same variable. For example, assertiveness might be operationalized as specific client behaviors observed by medical staff in an inpatient setting, as a subjective diagnosis of clients by the social worker, as self-analyses by clients, or as clients' responses on a standardized self-administered measuring instrument that is believed to measure assertiveness.

More often than not, we need to measure variables that cannot be measured by only one indicator. Several different indicators need to be used in such situations. We might measure, for example, the written and physical responses of research participants to specific stimuli. Suppose we wanted to determine the extent to which computerization in a particular human service agency has affected the job satisfaction of the social workers employed there. The variable *level of job satisfaction of the social workers* could be measured using several different indicators both before and after the computerization takes place. Methods of measurement might include directly asking workers about their current level of job satisfaction and also having them complete a standardized job satisfaction measuring instrument. We could also measure their behaviors, such as job absenteeism, which previous research studies have indicated is directly related to job satisfaction. Each of the three indicators would serve as a kind of check on the other two, thereby increasing the likelihood that our measurement will be accurate.

The specific indicators of a given variable as well as the methods used for measuring it may differ from place to place, time to time, person to person, and study to study. Specifying exactly how a variable is to be operationalized is just as important to good measurement as conceptualization. If, for example, we want to learn something about the relative effectiveness of two different treatment interventions—individual treatment and group treatment—for people who are depressed, we need to state clearly (1) how we will determine which of the two different types of interventions was used and (2) how we will measure level of depression. Will we operationalize depression level as clients' appearances as reported by staff? We would select this indicator only if there is strong evidence in the professional literature of a relationship between depression levels and personal appearance. Even if there were, when used alone to measure depression levels, staff observations of appearance would not be expected to yield valid measurements because appearance is a subjective judgment. Another, better indicator might be each person's score on a standardized self-report measurement instrument that has been shown to measure the variable *depression.*

However we decide to operationalize the variable *depression,* we would hope that a pattern would emerge from our measurements. Perhaps clients who received individual treatment would appear to be less depressed than clients who received group treatment. However, on the basis of an apparent pattern of this nature, we should not conclude that treatment effectiveness and treatment methods are really related. To come to such a conclusion would require a good statistical analysis of the data. For example, the result of statistical testing could help us to determine if it was the type of treatment or something else that might have produced different depression levels. The result of statistical testing depends on the accuracy of the measurements. Statistical tests perform mathematical operations with data; they have no way of knowing whether the measurements that produced the data were good or bad.

Reliability

Two terms are used in research to describe the quality of measurement of variables—reliability and validity. In the simplest of terms, *reliability* is the degree of consistency of a measurement. Reliability addresses the question: To what degree does the measurement of a variable produce consistent results? There are several different types of reliability and several different ways they can be demonstrated. They rely heavily on the concept of correlation (Chapter 8).

Few, if any, measurement instruments produce perfect reliability. But some are more reliable than others. For example, a measuring instrument that proposes to measure the variable *depression* may produce very consistent measurements in a wide variety of situations with a wide variety of people. Therefore, it can be considered to be relatively reliable. Another measuring instrument that also claims to measure depression may be more easily influenced by who is performing the measuring, what specific group of people are being measured, the time of day or year that the measurement takes place, and so on. Thus, it would be considered less reliable than the first measurement.

Validity

Even if a measuring instrument has a high degree of reliability, that does not guarantee that the procedure used to measure the variable is a good one. A measuring instrument can be very consistent in producing the same measurements, but the measurements can be consistently wrong. In other words, the measurement lacks validity. This means that it is not measuring what it is believed to be measuring. Only valid measurement of variables produces data that, when statistically analyzed, can generate valuable knowledge about the variables and the possibility of relationships between and among them.

A reliable measuring instrument or measurement procedure may be biased or distorted in some way. A measuring instrument believed to measure the variable *depression,* for example, may produce consistent results when measuring the depression level of the same group of people in a variety of research situations. But if the measuring instrument really is measuring some variable other than depression (e.g., self-esteem, self-concept, self-worth), it is not producing an accurate measurement of depression and is not an appropriate instrument for measuring that variable.

If measurement of a variable is both reliable (consistent) and truly measuring what it is believed to be measuring, then the measuring instrument is said to be *valid.* There cannot be validity without reliability. As we have seen, however, there can be reliability without validity. Thus, reliability can be regarded as a necessary but not sufficient indication of the presence of validity.

There are several different indicators (often referred to as types) of validity. Demonstrating that one or more of them was present in the measurement that was used is often critical to the credibility of the findings of a research study. Thus, researchers may report on the *face validity,* the *content validity,* the *predictive validity,* the *concurrent validity,* or some aspect of the *construct validity* of their measurement. A detailed discussion of each of these terms is beyond the scope of this book; they are discussed in social work research methods texts.

Research Hypotheses

A *research hypothesis* is a statement of a relationship between or among variables. It is stated in the future tense because it predicts what will be found when the data derived from the research study are analyzed. It expresses what we believe will be found to be true.

The way a research hypothesis is stated allows it to be supported—or not supported—by a statistical analysis. We might state a research hypothesis about the two variables *depression* and *sleep patterns,* for example, as follows:

> *People who are depressed will have different sleep patterns than people who are not depressed.*

We can test this hypothesis by measuring the sleep patterns of people who are diagnosed as depressed and comparing these patterns with those of people who are identified as not depressed. Sleep patterns could be operationalized in relation to sleep phases or simply as number of hours of sleep.

This research hypothesis proposes a relationship between two variables—sleep patterns and depression—but it says little about the nature of the relationship between them, only that one variable is related to the other. If we find statistical support for the research hypothesis that the two variables are related, it doesn't tell us whether depression influences sleep patterns, sleep patterns influence depression, or neither. It could simply mean that the two variables co-vary—that certain value categories (or values) of one variable tend to be found with certain value categories (or values) of the other.

Suppose that, based on a review of the professional literature, we had stated our research hypothesis in a slightly different way:

> *Disturbed sleep patterns cause depression.*

To understand this research hypothesis, we need to discuss the difference between two labels that are applied to variables within research hypotheses, independent and dependent.

Independent Variable.   Unlike the first research hypothesis, the second research hypothesis proposes a direct, causative relationship between sleep patterns and depression—disturbed sleep patterns cause depression. In other words, one variable is predicted to influence the other variable. The variable that is predicted to do the influencing can be referred to as the *independent variable.* In experimental research designs, the independent variable is either manipulated or introduced. If we wanted to see whether disturbed sleep patterns cause depression, for example, we could disturb the sleep patterns of a number of people to see if they became depressed. (In reality, there are ethical reasons why we would do nothing of the sort.) Theoretically, however, sleep patterns would be the independent variable—the one that is manipulated.

Dependent Variable.   The second variable, depression, is the dependent variable. A *dependent variable* is believed to be influenced by the independent variable: People's depression levels are believed to be influenced by their sleep patterns.

The research hypothesis could be turned around:

Depression will cause disturbed sleep patterns.

Here, depression is believed to do the causing and is therefore the independent variable. What is being influenced—sleep patterns—is the dependent variable. Of course, other variables such as drugs taken to treat depression (called *intervening* or *extraneous* variables) may help cause the variation in the dependent variable or may affect the relationship between the independent and dependent variables in other ways.

Independent Variables and Dependent Variables or Predictor Variables and Criterion Variables.   The same variable (depression or sleep patterns in our example) can be considered independent or dependent according to the way the research hypothesis is stated. In the second research hypothesis, depression was the dependent variable. In the third research hypothesis, it was the independent variable. Similarly, sleep patterns was the independent variable in the second research hypothesis and the dependent variable in the third research hypothesis.

The terms *independent variable* and *dependent variable* are nothing more than convenient labels to aid in the communication process. They are used to indicate the presumed direction of influence between or among variables, based on logic. They generally are used in reference to research hypotheses that suggest that one variable is believed to affect the other.

Social work research often does not seek to demonstrate that one variable directly influences another variable. Researchers wish only to find support for the belief that two variables co-vary so that they might be able to predict the value of one variable by knowing the value of the other variable. When demonstration of covariance between variables is our study's main goal, two other terms are used to describe the relationship between variables. The variable that is used for prediction is called a *predictor variable.* The variable whose values we hope to predict is called a *criterion variable.* To make it easier for the beginning student of statistics, and to be consistent with how other books have used the terms, we use *predictor variable* and *criterion variable* in discussing statistical analyses that do not imply causality but rather focus on covariance (Chapters 8 and 9). We use *independent variable* and *dependent variable* throughout the rest of the book.

LEVELS OF MEASUREMENT

The conceptualization and operationalization processes provide a necessary and orderly method for selecting and measuring variables. Formulation of research hypotheses and identification of variables within them as independent, dependent, predictor, or criterion provide further clarification of the study's focus and purpose. Before a statistical analysis can occur, however, we need to make another determination: We must judge how precisely the variables have been measured.

Some variables are difficult to measure with a high degree of precision. Others can be measured precisely, but, through choice or accident, they are measured in a way that provides less precise data than could have been produced. We generally want to select a measuring instrument that yields the highest level of precision possible. But, sometimes, this is neither desirable nor necessary because of either ethical or practical concerns. For example, we may elect to provide income intervals for research participants to check rather than to directly ask them their exact earned income for the previous year. We would do this in the interest of confidentiality and in order to increase the likelihood of a higher response rate.

Determination of a variable's level of measurement (along with other factors discussed in Chapter 6) provides direction as to the most appropriate type of statistical analysis to use. A variable can assume four levels of measurement: (1) nominal, (2) ordinal, (3) interval, and (4) ratio. Table 1.1 provides a brief summary of each level of measurement and the requirements that must be met for each level.

Nominal

The first, and least precise, level of measurement is the *nominal* level. Its value categories are discrete—which means that they are distinct from each other. The nominal level categorizes variables into discrete subclasses—nothing more, nothing less. The different value categories it uses reflect only a difference in kind. There is no implication of a quantifiable difference among the value categories; therefore, no rank-ordering of the value categories is possible. Variables, such as gender, race, ethnicity, referral source, diagnosis, occupation, sexual orientation, marital status, and political party affiliation, are considered by their very nature to be at the nominal level of measurement since the value categories used with them tend to be little more than simple labels reflecting qualitative differences. The following is an example of a question that would produce nominal-level data:

> *Do you believe the government should provide national health care insurance?*
>
> *1. Yes*
> *2. No*
> *3. Undecided*

A nominal-level variable must have two or more value categories, and the value categories must be distinct, mutually exclusive, and mutually exhaustive. This means

TABLE 1.1   Levels of Measurement and Numerical Values

Level	Numerical Value Requirements
Nominal	None: uses value categories.
Ordinal	Values must preserve rank order.
Interval	Values must preserve rank order and unit differences.
Ratio	Values must preserve rank order, unit differences, and fixed zero point.

that each case (each research participant or object studied) must appropriately fit into only one of the value categories and that there must be an appropriate value category for each case. There are only two value categories, for example, for the nominal-level variable *life status*—living or deceased. These two value categories are clearly exhaustive and mutually exclusive, as every person can be classified into one of the categories (exhaustiveness), but only one (exclusiveness).

In nominal-level measurement, numerals (1, 2, 3) or letters (A, B, C) are sometimes assigned for convenience. Suppose we have divided the nominal-level variable *type of treatment intervention* into three value categories: individual treatment, group treatment, and family treatment. We could assign numbers to the three types of intervention, but the numbers would be just labels for value categories. For example:

1. Individual treatment
2. Group treatment
3. Family treatment

The numbers serve only to classify—to reflect a difference in kind. We could have assigned letters to the three types of intervention:

A. Individual treatment
B. Group treatment
C. Family treatment

Nothing would change. It would be incorrect to say that the value category of 1 (or A) is more or less treatment than 2 (or B) or 3 (or C), or to make any other statement that implies that the three value categories have any quantitative meaning. For this reason, value categories are usually used when measuring nominal-level variables since they reflect only differences in kind.

Ordinal

In *ordinal* level measurement, not only do variables assume different value categories (and, sometimes, values), but the different value categories or values also have distinct quantitative meaning. With ordinal measurement, it is possible to rank-order values in such a way that they range from high to low or from most to least. Examples of variables that often are measured at the ordinal level are social class, occupational prestige, educational degrees received, ratings of client change, ratings of treatment effectiveness, ratings of clients' satisfaction with treatment, and rankings of problem severity. Below are some of the more common groupings of value categories that usually suggest that a variable is at the ordinal level of measurement:

1. Considerable
2. Some
3. Little
4. None

1. High
2. Moderate
3. Low

1. Very effective
2. Somewhat effective
3. Somewhat ineffective
4. Very ineffective

1. Very severe
2. Severe
3. Mild
4. Very mild

The following are examples of research questions that would produce ordinal measurement:

How would you rate your social work supervisor? (Circle one number below.)

1. Very good
2. Good
3. Fair
4. Poor
5. Very poor

How satisfied are you in your current job? (Circle one number below.)

1. Very satisfied
2. Somewhat satisfied
3. Somewhat dissatisfied
4. Very dissatisfied

It is important to note that these value categories do not indicate absolute quantities or assume equal intervals between the categories. We might, for example, ask all social workers in North America who hold a social work degree to answer the following question:

What is your highest social work degree completed?

1. Associate Degree
2. BSW
3. MSW
4. PhD/DSW

Since the intervals between the four value categories are not and cannot be equal, we cannot say that a person who has an Associate Degree is exactly two units lower than a person with an MSW or that this interval is exactly the same as the one that separates a person with a PhD/DSW from a person who has a BSW. If we could say this, we could claim that the variable *highest social work degree completed* meets the criteria for the next level of measurement, interval-level measurement.

Interval

Like ordinal-level measurement, *interval-level measurement* also classifies and rank-orders properties of variables. It has one important added criterion—it places the values for the variable on an equally spaced continuum. Thus, unlike ordinal measurement, interval measurement has a uniform unit of measurement, such as one year or one degree of temperature. Therefore, the values indicate exactly how far apart one value is from another. With an interval-level variable, we can say that a research participant has more or less of a given property than another participant, and we can specify exactly how many units more or less.

With equal distances between the values, a measurement of 1 for a variable will be the same distance from a 4 (4 − 1 = 3) as a 6 is from a 9 (9 − 6 = 3). On a measuring instrument that is designed to measure intelligence, which is generally assumed to be an interval-level variable, the difference between IQ scores of 100 and 105 (105 − 100 = 5) should reflect the same difference in intelligence as between IQ scores of 115 and 120 (120 − 115 = 5). On another test, two individuals with achievement scores of 60 and 50 respectively should differ from each other in achievement as much as two other individuals with scores of 90 and 80 respectively. An example of a question that would produce interval-level data is:

What was your score on your most recent state licensure examination?

Interval-level measurement does not have an absolute zero point. This means that we cannot identify a point at which *no* quantity of the variable exists. Thus, we cannot say that a 2 is twice as much as a 1—only that it is 1 standard unit more. Since a reading of 0 degrees on a Fahrenheit thermometer does not coincide with the absence of heat, a temperature of 60 degrees does not mean that it is twice as hot as a temperature of 30 degrees. Thirty-two degrees Fahrenheit is nothing more than an arbitrarily chosen point to signify the temperature at which water freezes.

Ratio

The existence of a fixed, absolute, and nonarbitrary zero point constitutes the only difference between interval-level and ratio-level measurement. Therefore, values at the ratio level of measurement indicate the actual amounts of the property being measured. With such measurement, we can say not only that one person has so many units more of a variable than a second person, but also that the first person has so many times more or less of the variable. Examples of variables that can be measured at the ratio level of measurement are birth, death, and divorce rates; number of children in a family; and number of times that a client attended group treatment over a 6-month period.

The absolute zero point in ratio measurement permits all arithmetic operations—addition, subtraction, multiplication, and division. It also allows for the valid use and meaningful interpretation of ratios formed by two or more measurements. It would be correct to say, for example, that a country with an average birth rate of 4 children per couple has twice as high a birth rate as a country with an average birth rate of 2 children per couple. Following is an example of a question that would produce ratio-level data. It should be obvious that a response of 0 would reflect no personal contact with the social worker.

How many times did you see your social worker during the past month?

————

One way to test for the existence of ratio measurement is to think about the possibility of negative values for the variable being measured. If negative numbers can logically be assigned (e.g., a temperature of –25°F), then the measurement of the variable cannot be considered to be more than interval. With ratio measurement, a zero is assigned to the point at which no measurable quantity of the variable exists.

OTHER MEASUREMENT CLASSIFICATIONS

Like the levels of measurement discussed above, other classifications of variables also guide the selection of the most appropriate statistical analysis to use when analyzing data.

Discrete Variables and Continuous Variables

Discrete variables can take on only a finite number of values, such as the number of correct answers on the Scholastic Achievement Test (SAT) or the number of siblings a person has. Note that there are only a limited number of SAT scores that people can receive. They can score 1000 or 1010, but not 1002.5. Also, people can have 2 or 3 siblings but not 2.16 siblings. By contrast, *continuous variables* can theoretically take on all numerical values. Height of social work students and grade point averages are examples of continuous variables. If we take any two measurements of a continuous variable, it is theoretically possible that there could be one or more other measurements between them. The number of different values a continuous variable can take is unlimited, assuming that we can use measuring instruments capable of measuring the values with ever-increasing precision.

Dichotomous, Binary, and Dummy Variables

A *dichotomous variable* is a specific type of discrete variable that only has two value categories. Examples are gender (male *or* female) or the result of an election (win *or* lose). We could take a more precisely measured variable—such as age of voters, which is at the interval or ratio level—divide its range of values into two groups (top half and bottom half), and convert it into a dichotomous level variable with value categories of older voters and younger voters. However, such an activity would be wasting the precision of measurement that is available for the variable *age.*

A special type of dichotomous variable is a *binary variable.* With binary variables, we assign numerical value categories of 1 or 0 to indicate the presence (1) or absence (0) of the variable. For the variable *car ownership,* for example, we could assign a value category of 1 for people who own a car and a value category of 0 for those who do not own a car.

Another special type of dichotomous variable is called a *dummy variable.* Suppose, for example, we wanted to take the variable *gender,* a nominal level dichotomous variable, and make it more quantitative in order to perform a statistical analysis that requires more precise measurement. We could convert the variable *gender* into one of two binary variables—either *femaleness* (female = 1; not female = 0) or *maleness* (male = 1; not male = 0). These two newly created variables are called dummy variables—variables created from the data already collected, but presented in another format.

LEVELS OF MEASUREMENT AND ANALYSIS OF DATA

Determining whether a variable is ordinal, interval, or ratio can be difficult. There is an ongoing debate, for example, about whether certain measurement instruments produce data that should be regarded as ordinal or interval. A few people suggest that certain measurement scales should be regarded as interval for purposes of data analyses. Others strongly disagree, insisting that only standardized measuring instruments that have undergone extensive testing and revision have any claim at all to interval-level measurement.

Because of the way some variables are measured, they may appear to be interval or ratio but should be treated as ordinal. Suppose, for example, we are measuring the variable *driving skill.* We can operationalize, or measure, driving skill by recording the number of traffic accidents that people have had over the past 10 years. Should driving skill be regarded as ratio? No, even though the number of traffic accidents has a true zero point and equal intervals, the underlying variable, *driving skill* lacks measurement precision. We cannot say that the difference in driving skill between a person who had four accidents and a person who had three ($4 - 3 = 1$) is exactly the same as the difference between a person who had one accident and a person who had none ($1 - 0 = 1$). When data are analyzed, it might be best to form grouped values for the number of traffic accidents (e.g., 0–2 accidents, 3–5 accidents), to treat the variable at the ordinal level of measurement, and to select a statistical analysis created for use with ordinal-level data.

Making a judgment about the variable's level of measurement is important in determining what forms of statistical analyses to use. As discussed in later chapters, sometimes even if we conclude that we have, say, an interval-level variable, that in itself may not be enough to justify the use of a certain form of statistical analysis. Most analyses require other assumptions about variables and the way in which their values are distributed (see Chapter 7). If these assumptions cannot be met, statistical analyses normally designed for higher levels of measurement (interval or ratio) should not be used. Statistical analyses designed for use with ordinal or even nominal data should then be substituted.

While it may be necessary to use a statistical analysis designed for lower-level data, we generally cannot move in the other direction. If, for example, a variable is measured in a way that produces only nominal-level data, the variable cannot be treated as if it were ordinal level. It would be equally incorrect to use a statistical analysis intended for use with interval-level or ratio-level variables with nominal-level or ordinal-level data unless the nominal or ordinal variables are first converted into one or more dummy variables.

CATEGORIES OF STATISTICAL ANALYSES

There are numerous ways in which statistical analyses can be categorized. Two of these are the number of variables being analyzed and the primary purpose for their use.

Number of Variables Analyzed

Statistical analyses can be categorized as univariate, bivariate, or multivariate:

- *Univariate* analyses examine the distribution of value categories (for nominal- and ordinal-level data) and values (for interval- and ratio-level data) for a single variable.
- *Bivariate* analyses examine the relationship between two variables.
- *Multivariate* analyses simultaneously examine the relationship among three or more variables.

Descriptive and Inferential

A second way of grouping statistical analyses uses two broad categories, descriptive and inferential. These two categories simply reflect the purpose, or use, of the analysis.

Descriptive Analysis. After data are collected, the large number of measurements or scores (called *raw data*) frequently is overwhelming. A way must be found to summarize and communicate the most important, salient characteristics of the data. We use certain forms of descriptive analyses to accomplish this. They are described in the early chapters of this book.

A descriptive analysis summarizes the actual measurements of variables within a data set. Our concern does not extend beyond the particular sample (or population) studied. Descriptive analyses generally consist of compiling graphs, tables, and descriptive numbers, such as means and percentages, which are easier to comprehend and interpret than a long list of data reporting the results of measurement of each variable for every case.

Descriptive analyses are also known as data reduction. Its main purpose is to reduce the whole collection of data to simple and more understandable terms without distorting or losing too much of the valuable information collected. Of course, any summary sacrifices some detail. Descriptive statistical analyses are no exception.

Data may have been collected from a *population*—that is, all individuals or events that meet certain criteria. Such a population, for example, might be all full-time students currently enrolled in accredited schools of social work in North America. Descriptive summaries of the measurements of populations are called *parameters.* Descriptive analyses also are used to summarize the measurements taken of certain variables within research samples. When samples are used, the summaries of their measurements are called *statistics.*

Sometimes descriptive statistical analyses are preliminary to other types of statistical analyses (inferential). In some types of research studies—surveys and some qualitative research designs, for example—a descriptive analysis is the primary focus of the data analysis.

Inferential Analysis.   *Inferential analyses* are used when we have access to only a sample drawn from a population rather than to the total population. Inferential analyses refer to a group of procedures for determining how safe it is to make generalizations about the distribution of measurements of variables within a population (parameters) based on the measurements taken of the variable within a sample drawn from that population (statistics). Sample statistics are merely estimates of population parameters; they thus are more or less accurate.

Unless specifically indicated, our discussion of statistical analyses in the pages that follow assumes that the tasks of constructing a study's research design have been performed well (perhaps with the help of certain types of statistical analyses) and have generated valid and reliable measurement of certain variables.

CONCLUDING THOUGHTS

This chapter briefly examined the relationship between good measurement and meaningful statistical analyses of research data. It reviewed some of the basic terms that are especially important to understanding the statistical analyses of data.

As suggested in this chapter and demonstrated in the chapters to follow, statistical analyses involve methods for gathering, organizing, summarizing, and evaluating data. They are not a mysterious mathematical process. In fact, a statistical analysis is little more than the application of the same logic and common sense that are applied elsewhere in good social work practice.

STUDY QUESTIONS

1. Discuss why good measurement is essential to a meaningful statistical analysis. Use an original example in your discussion.

2. Discuss how a variable differs from a constant. Provide an original example of each in your discussion.

3. In a research hypothesis, what do we call the variable whose variations we are most interested in explaining? What do we call the variable that we believe may affect these variations? Which other terms are substituted if we are primarily interested in studying only their covariance or in predicting the value category (or value) of one variable through knowing the value category (or value) of the other? Provide original examples to illustrate your understanding of these terms.

4. What characteristic does a valid measuring instrument possess that an instrument that is merely reliable does not?

5. Suggest three different possible indicators of the variable *motivation to attend a graduate school of social work.*

6. What does the term *value category* mean when referring to a nominal-level variable? What does the term *value* mean when referring to an ordinal-, interval-, or ratio-level variable? Provide one original example of each in your discussion.

7. What additional criterion must be met for a variable to be considered ordinal that is not a requirement for nominal-level measurement? Provide an original example in your discussion.

8. What is required for ratio-level measurement that is not required for interval-level measurement? Provide an original example in your discussion.

9. Operationalize the variable *educational level* so that its measurement would produce nominal-level measurement, ordinal-level measurement, interval-level measurement, and ratio-level measurement.

10. In your own words, discuss the differences between descriptive statistical analyses of data and inferential statistical analyses. Describe some social work research situations where the use of each would be appropriate. What do inferential analyses attempt to determine that descriptive analyses do not? What other methods are used to classify different types of statistical analyses?

11. Construct a research hypothesis with one nominal-level independent variable and one nominal-level dependent variable. Explain how you would measure the dependent variable to produce the desired level of measurement.

12. Construct a research hypothesis that has one nominal-level independent variable and one ordinal-level dependent variable. Explain how you would measure the dependent variable to produce the desired level of measurement.

13. Construct a research hypothesis that has one nominal-level independent variable and one interval-level dependent variable. Explain how you would measure the dependent variable to produce the desired level of measurement.

14. Construct a hypothesis that has one nominal-level independent variable and one ratio-level dependent variable. Explain how you would measure the dependent variable to produce the desired level of measurement.

15. What level of measurement is the variable *highest social work degree received?* Justify your response. What other ways of operationalizing the variable would produce different levels of measurement? Explain.

16. Find a research-based article in a professional social work journal that is of some interest to you. Answer the following questions in relation to the article:
    a. How much of the article is a report of statistical analyses per se (as opposed to theory, ideas, implications, research design, sampling, data collection, and so on)?

b. Was the study conducted using a sample or population? If a sample was used, how was it selected? Do you believe the findings generated by the sample can be generalized to the population from which it was drawn? Why? Discuss.

c. Do you feel the author conceptualized the study's key variables correctly? Why? How could the author have conceptualized them differently? Provide examples.

d. Do you feel the author operationalized the dependent (or criterion) variable correctly? Why? How could the author have operationalized it differently? Provide examples.

e. What were the study's independent (or predictor) and dependent (or criterion) variables? What level of measurement were they? Justify your response.

f. What methods of statistical analyses were used in the article? Did each appear to be descriptive or inferential?

g. Do you think the measurements of the study's key variables were reliable and valid? Why?

h. Did the author use a standardized measuring instrument to measure the dependent (or criterion) variable? If so, which one was used? Do you feel the instrument measured what it was supposed to measure? Why?

2

Frequency Distributions and Graphs

After research data have been collected, they need to be organized and summarized in a systematic way. Two simple formats are used for this purpose: (1) frequency distributions and (2) graphs. Both formats are helpful in visualizing the distribution of the value categories of a nominal-level or ordinal-level variable and the values of an interval-level, or ratio-level variable within a data set drawn from a research sample or population. Frequency distributions and graphs may show trends in a data set, which can then be analyzed more extensively, as will be discussed in later chapters.

Even when another, more sophisticated type of data analysis is used, frequency distributions and graphs may be appropriate to include in research reports. They can provide clear and dramatic evidence of a point made less effectively in words or in the numerical results of a statistical analysis.

FREQUENCY DISTRIBUTIONS

One of the first questions often asked after data have been collected relates to how many persons or objects fell into each value category or value for the variables that were measured. (For the sake of simplicity, throughout the remainder of this chapter, the generic term *value* will be used to refer to the different measurements of all vari-

TABLE 2.1   Raw Data: Clients' Names and Ages

Name	Age	Name	Age	Name	Age
Rashad	32	David	69	Clarisse	37
Rosina	27	Herb	26	Karen	26
Brad	26	Vincent	31	Elwin	49
Chuck	21	Rosemarie	37	Tony	21
Shanti	37	Marguerite	49	Leon	27
Kathy	31	Raquel	31	Mario	31
Antoinette	32	Peter	27		

ables. We want to know how the research sample or population "broke"—that is, we want to know the *frequency* of each value for each variable. *Frequency distribution* tables are designed to help us answer this question. They also provide additional information on the distribution of values of variables.

If a variable is at the nominal level of measurement, frequency distributions are constructed directly from the raw data. If data are at the ordinal level of measurement or higher, however, it is necessary to first arrange the data into an array based on a ranking of their values. An *array* is an ordering of every value that occurred within the raw data set from the lowest or smallest to the highest or largest.

Suppose that a social work agency administrator, Sharon, wonders whether her agency is truly serving older residents of the community, which the agency has operationally defined as residents 50 years of age or older. Sharon decides to record the ages of all new clients who apply for services during the month of October. Twenty clients apply for services, and Sharon obtains their ages from the agency's intake form. The first new client was Rashad, who was 32 years of age; the second client was Rosina, 27 years of age; and so on. Sharon lists the raw data for these 20 clients in a table (Table 2.1).

Sharon's next step is to place the raw data into an array which is shown in Table 2.2. Note that the array displays the data set from the lowest value (21) to the highest value (69). Every client is represented by a value or number—his or her age. Table 2.2 shows

TABLE 2.2   Array: Clients' Names and Ages

Name	Age	Name	Age	Name	Age
Chuck	21	Leon	27	Shanti	37
Tony	21	Kathy	31	Rosemarie	37
Brad	26	Vincent	31	Clarisse	37
Herb	26	Raquel	31	Marguerite	49
Karen	26	Mario	31	Elwin	49
Rosina	27	Rashad	32	David	69
Peter	27	Antoinette	32		

TABLE 2.3   Absolute Frequency Distribution Table: Clients'
Names and Ages

Name	Age	Absolute Frequency
Chuck + Tony	21	2
Brad + Herb + Karen	26	3
Rosina + Peter + Leon	27	3
Kathy + Vincent + Raquel + Mario	31	4
Rashad + Antoinette	32	2
Shanti + Rosemarie + Clarisse	37	3
Marguerite + Elwin	49	2
David	69	1
Total		20

that 2 of the 20 clients were 21 (low) years of age (Chuck and Tony) and only 1 was 69 (high) years of age (David).

The data in Table 2.2 provide a beginning answer to the research question about clients served. Only one client, David, meets the agency's operational definition of older. Table 2.2 makes it much easier for us to eyeball the data than Table 2.1. If the data set had consisted of 250 cases instead of just 20, an array would have been even more helpful.

Having formed an array, Sharon can now construct frequency distribution tables in order to make the data even more comprehensible. Frequency distribution tables consolidate data taken from arrays.

Absolute Frequency Distributions

To construct an *absolute frequency distribution* table (also known as a *simple frequency distribution*), we count the number of times each value occurred and place the total in a table next to the name of that value. An absolute frequency distribution may be constructed for data at any level of measurement.

The absolute frequency column on the right side of Table 2.3 indicates the number of times each value occurred. For instance, Chuck and Tony were 21 years of age, and as a group they constitute a frequency of 2—that is, the absolute frequency for the value *21* is 2. Similar data are given for each of the other 7 ages that occurred. The clients' ages range from 21 (Chuck and Tony) to 69 (David), and the value most frequently reported is 31 (Kathy, Vincent, Raquel, and Mario). Absolute frequency distributions sometimes are seen in research reports, but, more commonly, they appear as just one column within one of the other frequency distributions discussed next.

Cumulative Frequency Distributions

A *cumulative frequency distribution* table, such as Table 2.4, can be constructed if the data generated for a variable are at least at the ordinal level of measurement (i.e., if an array can be formed as in Table 2.2). As Table 2.4 shows, 2 clients were 21 years of

TABLE 2.4 Cumulative Frequency Distribution Table: Clients' Names and Ages

Name	Age	Absolute Frequency	Cumulative Frequency
Chuck + Tony	21	2	2
Brad + Herb + Karen	26	3	5
Rosina + Peter + Leon	27	3	8
Kathy + Vincent + Raquel + Mario	31	4	12
Rashad + Antoinette	32	2	14
Shanti + Rosemarie + Clarisse	37	3	17
Marguerite + Elwin	49	2	19
David	69	1	20

age, and 3 clients were 26. Thus, the cumulative frequency of clients' age 26 and under is 5 (2 + 3). A total of 17 clients (2 + 3 + 3 + 4 + 2 + 3) were 37 years of age and under. In a cumulative frequency distribution, the last number in the cumulative frequency column is the same as the total number of cases, indicating that all case values have been included.

Percentage Frequency Distributions

A third type of frequency distribution table, the *percentage distribution* table, adds an absolute percentage column on the far right-hand side (see Table 2.5). Since there are 20 clients in the sample, each client represents 5 percent of the sample (100%/20 = 5%). The number in the percentage column for each age that occurred within the sample of clients represents the absolute percentage of the entire sample. As Table 2.5 indicates, 2 people (Chuck and Tony) were 21 years of age, and together they represent 10 percent of the total number of clients (5% for Chuck + 5% for Tony). Similarly,

TABLE 2.5 Percentage Distribution Table: Clients' Names and Ages

Name	Age	Absolute Frequency	Cumulative Frequency	Absolute Percent
Chuck + Tony	21	2	2	10
Brad + Herb + Karen	26	3	5	15
Rosina + Peter + Leon	27	3	8	15
Kathy + Vincent + Raquel + Mario	31	4	12	20
Rashad + Antoinette	32	2	14	10
Shanti + Rosemarie + Clarisse	37	3	17	15
Marguerite + Elwin	49	2	19	10
David	69	1	20	5

Brad, Herb, and Karen together represent 15 percent of the total sample (5% for Brad + 5% for Herb + 5% for Karen). Of course, the total for all the clients should equal 100 percent.

If the number of cases in a data set is not a number that can be divided cleanly into 100 to obtain the percentage that each case represents, the percentages in the row alongside a value may have to be rounded up or down to either whole numbers or numbers containing decimals. When this is done, the total for all cases may not be exactly 100 percent. It may be slightly more or less than 100. A notation at the bottom of the table is then used to explain why the total is something other than 100 percent.

Cumulative Percentage Distributions

A fourth type of frequency distribution table is the *cumulative percentage distribution* table. It combines features of the cumulative frequency and percentage distribution tables, but it adds a column that reports cumulative percentages for each value. In Table 2.6, two clients (Rashad and Antoinette) are 32 years of age. Together, they represent 10 percent of all clients (5% for Rashad + 5% for Antoinette). Additionally, 70 percent (14/20 = .7 = 70%) of all clients (including Rashad and Antoinette) are 32 years of age or younger.

GROUPED FREQUENCY DISTRIBUTIONS

Sometimes it is difficult to interpret frequency distribution tables because of the unequal spread of the values. In the example, the variable age is distributed in such a way that there are differently sized gaps (e.g., 21 to 26, 27 to 31, 49 to 69). It is sometimes easier to visualize and comprehend the meaning of values that are distributed this way if they are condensed into a smaller number of groupings of values (e.g., 20 to 29, 30 to 39, and so on). These groupings could then be displayed using any of the frequency distributions such as Tables 2.3 to 2.6 or using only those columns from Table 2.6 that are of special interest.

TABLE 2.6   Cumulative Percentage Distribution Table: Clients' Names and Ages

Name	Age	Absolute Frequency	Cumulative Frequency	Absolute Percent	Cumulative Percent
Chuck + Tony	21	2	2	10	10
Brad + Herb + Karen	26	3	5	15	25
Rosina + Peter + Leon	27	3	8	15	40
Kathy + Vincent + Raquel + Mario	31	4	12	20	60
Rashad + Antoinette	32	2	14	10	70
Shanti + Rosemarie + Clarisse	37	3	17	15	85
Marguerite + Elwin	49	2	19	10	95
David	69	1	20	5	100

In creating a grouped frequency distribution, we can use the age groupings in the first column instead of using the clients' actual ages. We then adjust the numbers in the other columns accordingly. Table 2.7 is a *grouped cumulative percentage distribution* table of the data. It does not contain the actual frequency for any exact age, but it nevertheless provides a good overview of how the data are distributed.

Grouped frequency distributions are especially useful when there are too many different values to individually list each of them. This often occurs when there are a large number of cases with many different values and when forming frequency distributions for variables that are at the interval or ratio levels of measurement. The number of miles driven to class by students in a school of social work, for example, would make for a lengthy list, especially if the miles were measured in fractions or tenths of a mile. Transforming the data into meaningful groupings makes it easier for the reader to visualize the distribution of the data.

What is a meaningful grouping? It is a grouping that reduces the number of values to a reasonably small number that can be easily understood while not losing any more measurement precision than is necessary. When the values are fairly evenly distributed, it is desirable to have groupings that each encompass an equal number of potential case values. If the values are not evenly distributed, the groupings should be set up to reflect homogeneity. This means that the groupings should use value intervals of a size that allows cases within them to be similar in relation to the variable. In grouping students based on the number of miles they travel to class, for example, five meaningful value groupings could be as follows:

1. 3 miles or less
2. 4–10 miles
3. 11–50 miles
4. 51–100 miles
5. 101 miles or more

What makes the previous value groupings homogeneous? Note that all students in the 3 miles or less category share a similar characteristic—they all live close to the university. Those in the 4- to 10-mile grouping live fairly close, but they may not walk to class or ride bicycles, may not feel they are a part of the university community, and

**TABLE 2.7   Grouped Cumulative Percentage Distribution
Table: Clients' Ages**

Ages	Absolute Percentage	Cumulative Percentage
20–29	40	40
30–39	45	85
40–49	10	95
50–59	0	95
60–69	5	100

so forth. Those commuting more than 100 miles may be involved in some form of distance education, may have extreme difficulty participating in student activities on campus, and so on.

There is a logic to the groupings—students within a specific grouping share some similarities with the other members and are likely to be different in important ways from students in the other groupings. Obviously, the students cannot be similar to others in their grouping in all respects. Which characteristics matter the most? Here we must rely on judgment and a review of professional literature to suggest areas where homogeneity should be taken into consideration when forming groupings.

Every case should fall cleanly into one and only one grouping. In the above five groupings, a consistent method would have to be devised for assigning those students on the edge of the different value groupings (e.g., 10.6 miles) into a group. A customary way to do this, for example, is to consider 11 miles as really representing the interval 10.50 to 11.49 miles. A student who drives 10.6 miles would fall into the grouping 11 to 50 miles.

USING FREQUENCY DISTRIBUTIONS TO ANALYZE DATA

Frequency distributions are very revealing. Cumulative frequency distributions are especially useful when we are interested in knowing approximately where a particular value falls relative to the other values in a data set. Suppose, for example, that an administrator of a large social service organization, Jennifer, wants to study the problem of unauthorized staff absenteeism. She would like to identify whether there are seasonal patterns that could possibly be reduced by creating new vacation and annual leave policies. A cumulative percentage distribution table might reveal such patterns.

Table 2.8 shows that in April there were 30 instances of absenteeism, or 15 percent of the total absenteeism in the 4-month period. Another 40 instances (20%) occurred during May. In all, only 70 instances (35%) occurred during (April and May), while the other 65 percent (100% − 35% = 65%) occurred during June and July. The table seems to suggest that there is a seasonal pattern of absenteeism; Absenteeism increases in the summer months.

TABLE 2.8   Cumulative Percentage Distribution Table: Staff Days Lost by Month at XYZ Agency ($N = 200$)

	Monthly Totals	
Month	*Absolute Frequency*	*Cumulative Percentage*
April	30	15
May	40	35
June	60	65
July	70	100

TABLE 2.9   Grouped Cumulative Percentage Distribution Table: Experimental Group's Scores (*N*= 300)

Scores	Absolute Percentage	Cumulative Percentage
50–59	0	0
60–69	10	10
70–79	40	50
80–89	30	80
90–100	20	100

Frequency distributions also can be helpful for comparing measurements taken from two different groups or two different data sets. If the measurements differ somewhat (e.g., if the actual ages were recorded for one data set and age ranges were recorded for the other one), grouped frequency distributions can be used to make the different data sets comparable.

An example will illustrate how frequency distributions can be used to compare two groups or two different data sets. Sue, a social worker, developed a state merit examination study guide. She wished to get a preliminary indication of whether it was effective. She decided to compare the respective scores of people who used the study guide (experimental group) with those of people who did not use it (control group).

Cumulative distribution tables displaying the differences between the results for the two groups are shown in Tables 2.9 and 2.10. Of the people in the experimental group (Table 2.9), 40 percent scored between 70 and 79 on the examination, and 50 percent scored 79 or lower. Table 2.10 shows that 40 percent of the people in the control group scored between 70 and 79 on the examination, and 60 percent scored 79 or lower.

Cumulative percentages also make it possible to calculate approximate percentile ranks for individuals within the two groups. Percentile ranks indicate the percentage of cases within a group whose value falls below a particular value. Suppose that Clarice, a member of the experimental group, scored a 90 on the merit examination after using the study guide. A review of Table 2.9 would indicate that she scored higher than at least 80 percent of all people in the experimental group, meaning that she scored at

TABLE 2.10   Grouped Cumulative Percentage Distribution Table: Control Group's Scores (*N* = 200)

Scores	Absolute Percentage	Cumulative Percentage
50–59	5	5
60–69	15	20
70–79	40	60
80–89	35	95
90–100	5	100

approximately the 80th percentile. Percentile ranks enable us to put an individual value in perspective relative to the other values in a group.

Also notice that the two groups contained different numbers of cases—300 in the experimental group and 200 in the control group. Using percentages facilitates comparing two or more groups of unequal size. It puts groups of different sizes into the same framework; all percentages are based on 100. This is helpful if two research samples are of unequal size from the beginning of the study or if they begin equal but become unequal because more people are lost from one group than from the other.

MISREPRESENTATION OF DATA

From a statistical perspective, the two groups of 200 and 300 in the previous illustration were fairly comparable in size. Percentage comparisons drawn from them would be appropriate, since they would make the data easier to interpret. But a word of caution is in order: The practice of drawing comparisons between two groups of vastly unequal sizes can distort rather than clarify data. The following example demonstrates how this can happen.

Example: An Administrator's Efforts to Hire More Women

Emma, a human service agency administrator, proudly reported to the board of directors that the results of her efforts to hire more women during the years 1999 and 2000 were outstanding. She took the data from Table 2.11 and presented them to the board of directors as a glowing endorsement of her efforts. She noted that in five of the six job classifications (A, B, C, E, and F), she had hired a higher percentage of women than men. Emma was able to make this statement because she was using percentages with value groupings of very different sizes. The actual data she summarized presented a drastically different picture. In fact, Table 2.11 actually shows that Emma hired 78 percent of all male applicants but only 21 percent of all female applicants.

More often than not, misrepresentations are not deliberate. Emma may have made an honest mistake based on inadequate understanding of the importance of using comparably sized groups when making comparisons using frequency distributions. There is a way to avoid giving the impression that we are attempting to distort the facts in such situations. The actual numbers on which percentages are based can be reported along with the percentages for all groups as presented in Table 2.11.

Percentages help people comprehend large numbers, especially when they are used to report research findings based on odd numbers. For example, 35.5 percent is more easily understood than 146 out of 411. Percentages are generally meaningless, however, if not misleading, in reporting data from small samples. There is little reason to report, for example, that 60 percent of the graduates of an intensive job training program found employment if the 60 percent really means three of five completed the program and found a job (3/5 = .60 or 60%). With a small number of cases, it is best to report only the numbers.

Statements that describe findings based on small numbers are comprehensible by themselves. It is understandable to say that three out of five graduates found work. Re-

TABLE 2.11   1999 and 2000 Hiring Data for XYZ Agency Broken Down by Gender

	Males		Females	
Classification	*Number*	*Percent*	*Number*	*Percent*
A	3 of 6	50	4 of 6	67
B	1 of 3	33	1 of 2	50
C	0 of 1	0	1 of 10	10
D	85 of 100	85	2 of 40	5
E	2 of 3	67	2 of 2	100
F	3 of 7	43	4 of 7	57
Totals	94 of 120	78	14 of 67	21

porting findings based on small numbers as percentages can be misleading. Percentages convey the impression that findings were based on a larger numbers of cases (100 or more).

GRAPHICAL PRESENTATION OF DATA

Sometimes it is difficult to grasp the bigger picture of the distribution of values using frequency distribution tables. A graph, however, often can communicate the bigger picture almost immediately.

Graphical representations generally sacrifice detail in an effort to improve communication. This sacrifice is justifiable and even desirable in many situations. If the intended audience of a research presentation or report is not research astute, the audience may become impatient with the tabular presentation of vast amounts of data. Graphs are more likely to hold everyone's interest. Also, if it is essential to get a point across quickly and dramatically, graphs do the job effectively. They allow readers to obtain a comprehensive picture of the distribution of the values without having to focus on unnecessary detail.

Like all methods of displaying data, graphs can produce misleading statements. It is possible to lie with graphs, just as with other types of statistical analyses. We need to be alert to the dangers inherent in the use of graphs and ask whether they are communicating the findings of a research study accurately. But we should not preclude their use; they can be effective communicators.

Several types of graphs are commonly used to display how many cases have the various measurements (values) of a variable. Both the measurement level of the variable and clarity requirements of data portrayal determine which of the various graphical options is best.

Most graphs are drawn (usually using computer software) with x and y axes. The vertical line, or y axis, is called the *ordinate,* and the horizontal line, or x axis, is called the *abscissa.* The point at which the x axis and the y axis meet (see Figure 2.1) is called

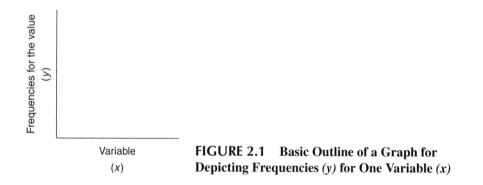

FIGURE 2.1   **Basic Outline of a Graph for Depicting Frequencies *(y)* for One Variable *(x)***

the *point of origin.* In a graph used to present a description of the distribution of values of one variable, the values or value intervals are displayed along the *x* axis. The *x* axis may extend to the left beyond the *y* axis if the data set contains negative values. The *y* axis is used to display the frequencies for each value or value interval.

Bar Graphs

One method of displaying the distribution of frequencies for the values of a nominal-level variable is a *bar graph,* also called a bar chart. Bars of equal width (one for each value) are displayed in any order, since the value categories reflect only qualitative, not quantitative differences. The bars are not allowed to touch. The height of each bar reflects the frequency of the value. A comparison of the frequency for different values is implicit. In other words, if a bar of one length represents the frequency of a value, a bar twice as long represents a frequency twice as large for another value. Figure 2.2a is an example of a simple bar graph.

If lines are used rather than bars, they are also drawn so that their height reflects the frequencies with which given value categories occur. We refer to this type of graph as a *line diagram.* Line diagrams may be constructed so the lines run horizontally, with different nominal values placed along the *y* axis and frequencies reflected in the length of the lines parallel to the *x* axis, as in Figure 2.2b. Bar graphs and line diagrams are used interchangeably.

Pie Charts

If a variable is only at the nominal level, we may choose to use a *pie chart,* also called a pie graph, to represent the distribution of its values. While pie charts are used primarily to display the distribution of nominal-level variables within a data set, they can also be used with variables that are measured more precisely.

Traditionally, pie charts have been constructed to look like pies—that is, as circles divided into two or more wedges, each representing the frequency for a different value. With today's computer software graphic programs, many other pictorial representations of the distribution of a variable are now possible. A pie chart can look like a cartoon figure or almost any object. For example, if we want to show how a client's

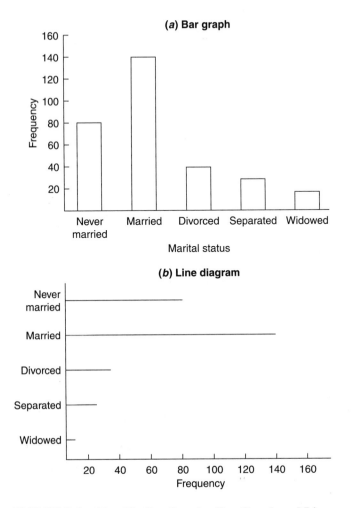

FIGURE 2.2   Two Similar Graphs: Bar Graph and Line Diagram Portraying the Marital Status of Active Clients in XYZ Agency

family budget is divided into sums for food, shelter, clothing, and recreation, the total budget could be displayed as a pie. Portions of the pie could be drawn proportionally to reflect the portion of the total budget represented by each budget item. Or we could portray the same family budget as a cash bag or a paycheck divided to represent the percent of the budget that is spent for each budget items.

Figure 2.3 is a pie chart that portrays the percentages of staff who work at XYZ Agency, broken down by the highest social work degree obtained. Note, for example, that staff members whose highest degree is an Associate Degree (25% of all staff) occupy one-fourth the total area of the circle. The angle in the center of the circle for the Associate Degree segment is 90 degrees (360 degrees × .25 = 90 degrees).

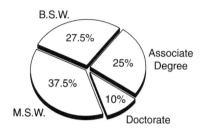

FIGURE 2.3   Distribution of Social Workers at XYZ Agency by Degree (*N* = 100)

Pie charts allow rapid visual appraisal of the distribution of values. Their main limitation is that they cannot easily accommodate many different categories of a variable without becoming too complicated, large, or illegible. Figure 2.3 is comprehensible, but a pie chart that displays, for example, the frequencies of all the academic majors within a large university would be impractical. There would have to be many different slices of the pie, some of them so thin as to be barely visible.

Histograms

A *histogram* is a useful graph for displaying ordinal-, interval-, or ratio-level data. Histograms look like bar graphs, but the bars touch each other. A histogram, like a bar graph, uses the height of the bar to reflect the frequency of a value for a given variable. The rank-order of the variable's values determines the sequence of the values displayed in the graph. The bars of a histogram displaying ordinal-level data are of equal width, such as those in Figure 2.4, which displays four categories of outcome data derived from a review of February case records at XYZ Agency.

When displaying the frequencies for interval- or ratio-level data, and when grouped frequencies of unequal value intervals are used, the bars may be constructed so that their different widths correspond to the size of the different intervals. Figure 2.5 illustrates this variation. The graph accurately portrays frequencies by showing bars of different heights, intervals, and widths. To do this, there must be a degree of measurement precision not present within nominal- or ordinal-level data.

Frequency Polygons

After constructing a histogram with interval- or ratio-level data, we can convert the histogram into a frequency polygon. A *frequency polygon* is a shape that reflects the distribution of values for a given variable. If we were to take a pencil and mark a dot in the middle of the top of each vertical bar in a histogram and then connect the dots with a straight line, we would have a frequency polygon. Lines usually are drawn at each end of the distribution of values to connect the first and last dot with the horizontal axis, thus completing the polygon. Figure 2.6 is a frequency polygon displaying data collected by XYZ Agency at intake.

The data displayed in Figure 2.6 were at the ratio level of measurement when first made. (They were the actual dollars and cents of income reported on clients' most

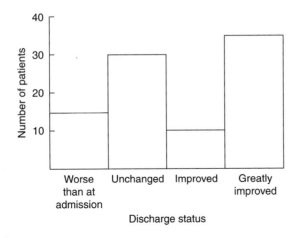

FIGURE 2.4   Histogram: Frequency of Discharge Status at XYZ Agency During February

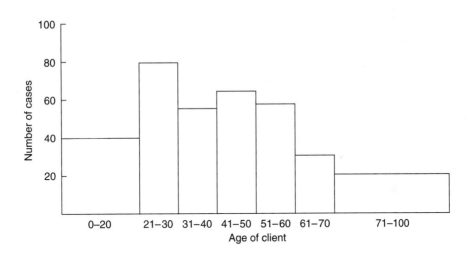

FIGURE 2.5   Histogram: Ages of Clients on Record in XYZ Agency During October

recent federal income tax returns). When they were grouped into income intervals to reduce the number of value groupings, some sacrifice of accuracy (measurement precision) occurred. The data were transformed into ordinal-level measurement. In Figure 2.6, the numbers along the *x* axis are the midpoints of the income groupings that were used. As Figure 2.6 demonstrates, it is possible to plot a frequency polygon for data that are only at the ordinal level of measurement. However, this should be done only when the data are inherently at the interval or ratio level of measurement and have been transformed into ordinal level.

Pareto Charts

A graph that is gaining in popularity as we rely more on computers to create graphics is called a *pareto chart*. It portrays a rank-ordering of values of a variable by frequency in descending order. It also reflects cumulative frequencies and cumulative percentages of cases at any point where cases with new values are added to the graph.

Figure 2.7 displays the education level of 40 residents of an extended care facility. In it, we can see that the greatest number of people (11) completed the 12th grade (highest grade completed). The next greatest number (7) completed fourteen years of school. Only one resident (each) completed 4, 5, 6, 7, 10, and 17 years—each value has a frequency of one within the sample. The curved line displays both cumulative frequencies and cumulative percentages. When those residents who completed 11 years of school are added to the group, there are 30 residents on the left of the chart, representing 75 percent of the sample, and another 10 residents (25 percent) to their right (the values with lower frequencies).

Stem-and-Leaf Plots

Another graph that is easily generated by computer software packages is the *stem-and-leaf plot*. Like the pareto chart, it makes it possible to identify all of the actual case values in the distribution of a variable.

Figure 2.8 portrays the distribution of the ages of the residents of the extended care facility whose education levels were displayed in Figure 2.7. The age of a resident is

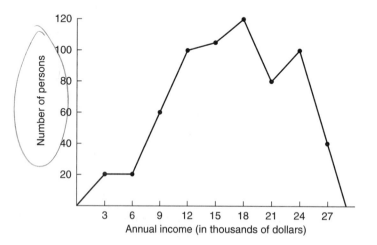

FIGURE 2.6   Frequency Polygon: Annual Income of Families Receiving Family Counseling at XYZ Agency (Rounded to Nearest Category)

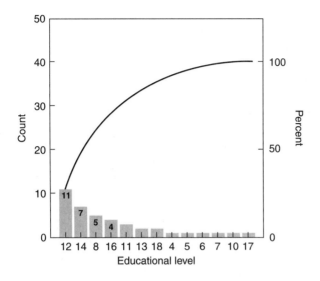

FIGURE 2.7   Pareto Chart: Educational Levels of Residents at XYZ Residential Care Facility ($N = 40$)

displayed as a stem in the middle column (in this case, the first one or two digits of the age) and a leaf in the right-hand column (in this case, the last digit of his or her age). Thus, a resident who is 77 years of age would be represented by one of the sevens in the row where the seven appears under the leaf column. The sample contains 2 residents who are 66 years of age, one who is 80, four who are 84, and so forth. The two oldest residents are 95 and 103. If we were to rotate the graph 90° counterclockwise, with the frequency column on the bottom, and connect the top of the columns of numbers, we would have a frequency polygon for the variable *age of residents.*

A COMMON MISTAKE IN DISPLAYING DATA

As computer graphics become more user-friendly, there is a temptation to display larger and larger amounts of data. Some graphs can become so complex that they are hard to interpret.

Frequency	Stem	& Leaf
1	5	9
2	6	24
6	6	566889
4	7	1144
16	7	5577777777788999
6	8	014444
3	8	558
1	9	5
1	10	3

FIGURE 2.8   Stem-and-Leaf Plot: Ages of Residents at XYZ Residential Care Facility ($N = 40$)

Even relatively simple ways of displaying data, like bar graphs and histograms, can be made complicated. The horizontal bars in bar graphs, for example, may be extended to the left and to the right simultaneously. Figure 2.9 displays data about client problems in a social service agency. It illustrates the percentage of clients who reported problems within one or more of three nominal-level categories of presenting problems—environmental, psychological, and social. A given client may have reported one, two, or all three types of problems. It takes quite a bit of study to be able to understand the data presented in this graph. The *x* axis represents the percentage of clients reporting each problem area (right side) and the percentage not reporting it (left side). Thus, the total number of clients reporting and not reporting each problem equals 100 percent. Figure 2.9 shows that 30 percent of all clients reported psychological problems and 70 percent did not; 50 percent reported social problems, while the other 50 percent did not; and so forth. The data in Figure 2.9 could have been communicated more clearly using three simple bar graphs, one for each type of client problem.

The computer technology that created Figure 2.9 is a mixed blessing. It allows us to communicate more information on a single graph, but it may sacrifice clarity in the process. As we are tempted to use more complex and creative frequency distributions and graphs, we must ask ourselves whether they will really help the reader understand the data. Or will they have the undesirable effect of confusing the reader? Communication is the goal of frequency distributions and graphs. If they confuse the person who is trying to understand how the data were distributed, they have failed to accomplish this goal.

CONCLUDING THOUGHTS

This chapter briefly examined some of the most basic ways of organizing and displaying the distributions of value categories and values of a variable—frequency distributions and graphs. It examined how we can take simple frequencies and convert them

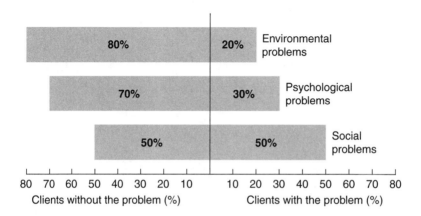

FIGURE 2.9   Bar Graph: Types of Client Problems at XYZ Agency

into tables that portray the percentage of the whole that a given frequency represents. It also introduced the concept *percentile* and its relationship to cumulative frequency distributions.

The chapter examined a few of the most commonly used graphs, in what situations they are appropriate, and how they are constructed. It discussed some of the dangers inherent in the overuse of computer-generated graphs.

STUDY QUESTIONS

1. Discuss how an array differs from raw data. Provide an original example in your discussion.
2. What information is conveyed in a cumulative frequency distribution that is not present in an absolute frequency distribution? Provide an original example in your discussion.
3. What type of frequency distribution would tell us what percentage of the clients of a child protection agency have fewer than four children?
4. In a study attempting to relate type of counseling to success in seeking employment, why would it be inadvisable to group the variable *number of interviews* as 1–10, 11–20, and more than 20?
5. Why is it misleading to report a 50 percent success rate in a treatment program for alcoholics when there were only eight people in the treatment program? Explain in detail.
6. How does a bar graph differ from a histogram? Provide an example of each.
7. If an agency with an $800,000 annual budget allocates $160,000 for travel expenses, what portion (percentage) of a pie chart would be reserved for the travel segment? How many degrees would the angle at the center of the pie chart contain for the travel segment?
8. Why are frequency polygons an accurate portrayal of data only if data are at the interval or ratio level of measurement?
9. Why is simpler usually better when selecting a graph to display data?
10. Describe several ways that we could use graphs to display changes in the ethnic composition of an agency's professional staff between 1999 and 2000.
11. What information contained in frequency distributions is graphically portrayed in a pareto chart?
12. At the University of Twin Peaks, the number of males and females in various major fields of study are as follows:

Major	Males	Females
Social Work	20	80
Humanities	40	40
Business	60	50
Education	90	90
Nursing	10	90

a. What percentage of social work majors are female?
b. What percentage of the total student body are male?
c. Construct a five-slice pie chart for the different female majors.
   Do the same for the males.
d. Construct a bar chart like Figure 2.2a for all males, broken down by major.
   Do the same for the females.
e. What level of measurement is the variable major? Justify your response.

13. The dean of your school of social work has asked you to organize and present data from a one-question (one-variable) survey to determine students' satisfaction in the social work program. There are 220 students in the program; 55 of them (25 percent) were randomly selected to receive the survey. The research question was "How satisfied are you with the social work education you are currently receiving?" Possible responses were
    1. Very satisfied
    2. Satisfied
    3. Somewhat satisfied
    4. Somewhat dissatisfied
    5. Very dissatisfied
        a. At what level of measurement is the variable *satisfaction?*" Justify your response.
        b. Is the variable an independent variable or a dependent variable? Justify your response.
        c. The raw data for the variable were as follows:

           1, 4, 5, 3, 2, 1, 4, 5, 5, 4, 2, 5, 1, 1, 2, 3, 4, 3, 3, 3, 3, 4, 5, 4, 3, 3, 2, 2, 1, 3, 4, 2, 2, 2, 4, 2, 1, 1, 2, 3, 4, 5, 4, 3, 2, 1, 1, 2, 2, 3, 2, 2, 1, 1, 3

        d. How many students completed the survey? Should these students be considered a research sample or a population? Why?
        e. Construct an absolute frequency distribution to display these data.
        f. Construct a cumulative frequency distribution to display these data.
        g. Construct a percentage distribution to display these data.
        h. Construct a cumulative percentage distribution to display these data.
        i. Do you believe that, overall, the students were satisfied with the social work education they were receiving? Justify your response.
        j. The dean took the results to the vice president and said that the social work students were very pleased with their education. Was the dean correct in saying this, given the results of the survey? Why?

3

Central Tendency and Variability

Sometimes we wish to do more than simply display data in tables or graphs. For example, we may wish to summarize the characteristics of the distribution of a variable within a data set by reporting on what was found to be a "typical" value or how much the value of a variable differed from that "typical value." The methods for summarizing the characteristics of data that are discussed in this chapter are useful for describing the people (or objects) that were studied. As we shall see in later chapters, they are also fundamental to understanding more sophisticated forms of data analyses.

CENTRAL TENDENCY

In everyday speech, we tend to use the word *typical* rather loosely. We speak of typical client or a typical starting salary for MSW social workers, often without stating exactly what is meant by the term. In analyzing a data set, the search for the typical represents an attempt to find a single number, or a series of numbers, that is most representative of the distribution of values. In a data set (e.g., Table 2.1 in Chapter 2), a typical case is the one that best represents all cases within the data set.

Three terms, the *mode, median,* and *mean*, are used to describe what is meant by typical within a data set. They are grouped under the general category of *central tendency.* These terms are not interchangeable; they have specific meanings that differ in important ways. They must be used correctly to avoid confusion and to avoid misrepresenting the characteristics of a data set.

All three measures of central tendency have two basic uses:

1. *They summarize data.* They report one value category or value that tells us something important about the characteristics of the distribution of a variable. A social work agency, for example, may state in its annual report that it processed "an average of 16.4 new client intakes a day during the previous year."

2. *They provide a common reference point for comparing two groups of data.* An agency that hires both MSW and BSW beginning social workers may report, for example, "an average monthly starting salary of $3,112 for MSW level social workers and $2,223 for BSW level social workers." This one number, the average monthly starting salary, helps communicate the agency's policy about financial compensation for beginning MSW and BSW social workers.

The Mode

The *mode* is the value in a distribution of values within a data set that occurs most frequently. In the ages of clients presented in the array below, 42 is the mode because it occurs more frequently than any of the other values—in this case, four times more frequently.

Ages of clients (N = 15):

28, 31, 38, 39, **42, 42, 42, 42,** 43, 47, 51, 54, 55, 56, 60

Sometimes, more than one value will occur most frequently within a data set. If we were to draw a histogram of the distribution of the values, it would have two distinct peaks. When this situation occurs, we report both values as the mode for the data set and describe the distribution of the variable as *bimodal*. In the following example, the values in the bimodal array of years of prior social work experience among all 22 social workers in a family service agency contain two modes—0 and 7. Both values occur five times each.

Years of prior social work experience (N = 22):

0, 0, 0, 0, 0, 1, 2, 2, 3, 4, 5, 5, 6, **7, 7, 7, 7, 7,** 8, 9, 11, 14

When data are available in grouped form, the mode can be reported in one of two ways. We may simply report the grouping that had the largest frequency as the mode, or we can report the actual midpoint of the interval with the highest frequency. Table 3.1 portrays the grouped job satisfaction scores of 50 social workers. For these data, the mode could be reported as the value interval containing the largest frequency, which is 48–50, which includes the values 48, 49, and 50. This three-number range occurred seven times. The mode could also be reported as 49, since the midpoint for interval 48–50 is 49.

Of the three measures of central tendency, the mode is the most unrestricted—that is, it has the fewest requirements for its use. It can be used with all four levels of measurement (i.e., nominal, ordinal, interval, ratio). The mode, however, is not used as often

TABLE 3.1 Grouped Frequency Distribution: Job Satisfaction Scores for Social Workers

Scores	Absolute Frequency	Cumulative Frequency (High-Low)	Cumulative Frequency (Low-High)
81–83	3	3	50
78–80	1	4	47
75–77	5	9	46
72–74	6	15	41
69–71	1	16	35
66–68	5	21	34
63–65	4	25	29
60–62	1	26	25
57–59	1	27	24
54–56	4	31	23
51–53	3	34	19
48–50	7	41	16
45–47	1	42	9
42–44	4	46	8
39–41	2	48	4
36–38	2	50	2

as the other measures of central tendency, as it may not do a good job of describing what is typical in the distribution of a variable. As can be seen in Table 3.2, the most common or frequent value of a distribution of scores is not necessarily the most accurate portrayal of a typical value. The mode is clearly not in the center of the distribution; rather, it is toward the high end of it (the 57–59 group). When data are at the ordinal, interval, or

TABLE 3.2 Grouped Cumulative Frequency Distribution: Job Satisfaction Scores for Social Workers

Scores	Absolute Frequency	Cumulative Frequency (High-Low)	Cumulative Frequency (Low-High)
57–59	10	10	33
54–56	6	16	23
51–53	7	23	17
48–50	3	26	10
45–47	2	28	7
42–44	1	29	5
30–41	4	33	4

ratio level of measurement, we can usually obtain more accurate and representative descriptions by using one or both of the other two measures of central tendency.

The Median

If data can be formed into an array—that is, if they are at least at the ordinal level of measurement—the median can be used to report central tendency. The *median* divides an array of values into two equal halves. The example in Distribution A below presents an array of 21 values for the variable *number of treatment sessions attended*. The median is 9 sessions because 9 coincides with the point that divides the 21 values into two identical parts. There are just as many values, or cases (10), above 9 as there are below 9.

Distribution A: Number of treatment sessions attended (n = 21):

2, 2, 2, 3, 3, 4, 5, 5, 7, 8, **9,** 10, 11, 11, 14, 14, 15, 16, 18, 20, 41

If there had been an even number of values, the median might be the average of the two most central values as in Distribution B below. Here the median is 4.5.

Distribution B: Number of treatment sessions attended (n = 24):

1, 1, 1, 1, 1, 1, 2, 2, 3, 3, 3, **4, 5,** 6, 6, 7, 8, 11, 11, 13, 14, 15, 17, 20

The median (4.5) in Distribution B does not coincide with specific value in the distribution. It cannot, because with an even number of cases there is no case that falls at exactly the midpoint. This observation underlines a point that is important to understanding the median. Contrary to a common misconception, the median is not synonymous with the value of the middle case in an array of data (although it sometimes works out that way, as in Distribution A).

Even when the array contains an odd number of cases, the median is likely to be a mixed number (a whole number and a decimal) that coincides with no actual case value. That happens because the formula used to compute the median takes various conditions into consideration, such as case values with a frequency of 0 near the center and others with a frequency greater than 1 that occur near the center of the array (but are not centered around it). When these conditions exist, computation involves viewing values as intervals, as in the discussion in Chapter 2 of assignment of cases within grouped frequency distributions. Computation of the median can get quite complicated; fortunately, most statistical computer software packages can compute a median in a matter of seconds once the raw data have been entered.

If we look at Distribution A, we see that one client had been seen many more times than any other—41 times. This atypical value is known as an *outlier.* If a histogram were created for the variable, this value would lie outside the area where most of the other values are found (in Distribution A, between 2 and 20). The frequency polygon that could be formed by connecting the tops of the bars in the histogram would be distorted by the value 41. It would be asymmetrical, or *skewed.* (We will discuss skewness in more detail in Chapter 4.)

Of the three most common measures of central tendency, the median is affected the least by the presence of outliers, such as the client who was seen 41 times. Remember that the median coincides with the midpoint of the values in an array. This client is canceled out by the first client, who was seen only 2 times and is the counterpart at the extreme other end of the array. The client seen 29 times similarly is canceled out by the second client seen only 2 times, and so on. It would not matter whether the client seen the most times was seen 41 times, 100 times, or 410 times—the median would treat any of these values as simply the highest value in the data set.

The Mean

When a variable within a data set is at the interval or ratio level of measurement, the *mean* (also called the arithmetic mean) can be used to represent a typical value of that variable. It is the most easily understood, the best known, and the most useful of the three measures of central tendency. It is nothing more than the sum of all the values in a distribution divided by the total number of values—what we refer to in everyday speech as the average.

A mean can be computed for any interval-level or ratio-level variable. It cannot be computed with nominal-level variables. It also should not be computed with ordinal-level variables, even if numbers have been used for values, as in the case of rankings. For example, students may be assigned rankings based on their grades in each class they are taking. A student may rank number 3 in one class, number 4 in another, and number 2 in a third class. While a mean ranking could be obtained mathematically (the student's mean rank would be 3), to report this could be misleading. A ranking, while it is a number, is still a rather imprecise measurement of student achievement. A mean rank thus might not provide an accurate description of overall student performance relative to that of other students. A student with a mean ranking of 3 could actually be performing less well academically overall than a student with a mean ranking of 3.1! When we see that the mean is used as an indicator of central tendency, we should be able to assume that the measurement of the variable was at least at the interval level.

Another issue must be considered when deciding if it is appropriate to use the mean. Unlike the median, the mean uses all the values within a data set in its computation, not just some of them (the ones near the center of an array). This characteristic of the mean can promote accuracy or distortion when it is used as a measure of central tendency, depending on the degree to which a distribution of values is symmetrical or skewed. Even one or two outliers can easily distort the mean (skew it badly) if the total number of cases is small. With larger data sets, a few outliers cause less distortion.

The Trimmed Mean.   A variation of the mean, the *trimmed mean* is designed to minimize the effect of a few extreme outliers. It combines the best features of both the mean and the median. It still uses most of the actual case values in its computation but, like the median, it allows extreme values on either end to cancel each other out. It works like this: First a small percentage (usually, the top 5 percent and the bottom 5 percent) of values in an array are thrown out. Then, the remaining 90 percent of values are averaged. This average is the trimmed mean.

Even when a mean can be computed, the presence of a few extreme outliers may distort it so that it is either too large or too small to be considered typical for a variable. Then, the trimmed mean, the median, and/or the mode should be considered.

The Weighted Mean.   There is still another variation of the mean that is used in social work research and practice. Sometimes, it is necessary to compute an average for values that are not equally weighted (or of equal importance). Then we should compute a *weighted mean.* Computing a weighted mean entails the "weighting" of numbers in order to arrive at a value that is more meaningful for the data set than either the arithmetic mean or the trimmed mean.

For example, RuthAnn, a social worker working on a case management team in a hospital, was being criticized by her boss for her team's lack of productivity. She decided to compare her team's number of successful hospital discharge placements with those of a widely-praised case management team within the hospital in order to demonstrate that her team had been equally productive during the past week. Unlike RuthAnn's team, all five members of the other team were full-time employees. RuthAnn used the arithmetic mean to determine the other team's mean rate of success. She simply added together all of the workers' successful placements for the previous week and then divided by five to get the mean number of successes (per worker). The other team produced a total of 35 successful placements during the past week, so the mean number for members of the other team was 7 (35/5 = 7).

Computing a comparable indicator for RuthAnn's team was a bit more complicated. Unlike the other team, her team has six workers. Two (including herself) are full-time (5 days per week); three work half-time; and one works one-fourth time. Their number of successful placements for the week were (respectively): 8, 8, 3, 2, 4, and 2. RuthAnn could not simply add the number of successes together and divide by six. (The result would be 4.5, suggesting an unfair and unfavorable comparison.) Since most of the workers on her team are part-time, she needed to compute a weighted mean in order to get a fair description of their success.

How did RuthAnn compute a weighted mean for her team? She set up her data as follows:

Worker Name	Employment Status	# Placed Successfully	× Weighting Factor	= Score
RuthAnn	full	8	1	8
Ralph	full	8	1	8
Joaquim	half	3	2	6
Jerry	half	2	2	4
Ricky	half	4	2	8
Simeon	quarter	2	4	8
Total				42

RuthAnn used a weighting (multiple) for all six team members, based on the time that each worker actually worked. For team workers employed full-time, she used the weighting of 1 (really, equivalent to no weighting). For workers employed half-time, she used the multiple of 2; for the one worker employed one-quarter time, she used the multiple of 4. When she multiplied the workers' actual number of successful placements for the week by their respective weightings, she produced the number of cases that (theoretically) they would have successfully placed if they had been employed full-time and had continued at the same rate of productivity.

RuthAnn then added the scores for all six workers to get a total of 42, the number of placements that (theoretically) would have been made if all six workers had been employed full-time. Dividing by six, the mean worker success rate was 7 discharges, exactly the same as that of the other team.

Weighted means have a variety of uses. Teachers use them to compute final grades of students when averaging scores on assignments and examinations that are given different weights. If Joetta, for example, received a 90 on her midterm exam (¼ of the final grade), 80 on her final exam (½ of the final grade), and 100 on her term paper (¼ of the final grade), her three scores could not simply be added up and divided by 3. (That would produce an arithmetic mean of 90.) Since the graded assignments were not of equal importance, a weighted mean would need to be computed as follows:

Exercise	Score ×	Weighting Factor =	Points
Midterm	90	.25	22.5
Final	80	.50	40.0
Paper	100	.25	25.0
Course grade (weighted mean)			87.5

As the previous two examples clearly demonstrate, a weighted mean (rather than the arithmetic mean) should be used in those situations where not all measurements are of equal weight, or importance. It allows for fair comparisons.

Which Measure of Central Tendency to Use?

With nominal- and ordinal-level variables, the mode is the only measure that should be used. However, it is not always easy to decide which measure of central tendency to use when describing a distribution of values at the interval or ratio level. The final decision is often more a question of judgment and of ethics than of rules. Judgment relates to the issue of what outliers might distort the mean and whether the median or trimmed mean should be used instead. Ethics are involved because we have an ethical obligation as researchers and practitioners to represent our data as accurately as possible.

As with frequency distributions and graphs, we want to use measures of central tendency to provide our readers with an accurate mental image of our data set—a shorthand description of what our data really look like. Yet, in some situations no single measure of central tendency would accurately represent a data set. If so, accuracy dictates that we should report more than one measure of central tendency. An example using data from records of closed cases in a social service agency will help illustrate this point.

An agency administrator wishes to see if the agency really is using short-term crisis intervention treatment, as stated in its mission statement. Data are collected and analyzed for cases closed during the month of December (Table 3.3). Figure 3.1 is a frequency polygon that presents the data from Table 3.3 with the mode, median, and mean indicated.

TABLE 3.3   Frequency Distribution: Number of Interviews for Cases Closed at XYZ Agency during December ($N = 1290$)

Number of Interviews	Number of Cases	Total Number of Interviews (Column 1 × Column 2)
1	55	55
2	35	70
3	55	165
4	40	160
5	25	125
6	15	90
7	10	70
8	20	160
9	5	45
10	35	350
Totals	295	1290

The variable *number of interviews* is at the ratio level of measurement, and there are a large number of cases ($N = 1290$). These conditions suggest that the mean might be the best measure of central tendency to report, but what about outliers? The shape of the frequency polygon indicates that the presence of outliers may produce a distorted mean—it is rather badly skewed.

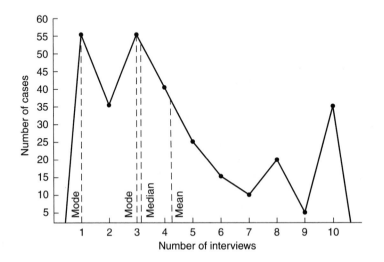

FIGURE 3.1   Frequency Polygon: Number of Interviews for Cases Closed at XYZ Agency during December

The mean number of interviews in Table 3.3 is actually 4.37, primarily because of the fairly large number of cases (outliers) that were seen 10 times ($n = 35$). A trimmed mean (5% off both ends) would be a little lower, about 4.24. Yet, it is apparent from Figure 3.1 that a client interviewed 4 times (rounding down) would not really be a typical client within the agency in some respects. There are actually two other values, both lower (i.e., 1 and 3), that occurred as frequently as or more frequently than 4. Because they are both well to the left of the mean, the mean or trimmed mean appear to be too high to reflect a typical value for the distribution.

If the mean or trimmed mean would not be representative portrayals of the data, what about the median? It falls between the values of 3 and 4, very close to one of the most common values (3). As a choice for a single measure of central tendency to represent the data, it is fairly good. It does not, however, even hint that a fairly sizable group of clients ($n = 35$) were interviewed 10 times, a fact that may be useful to the administrator of an agency whose mission is to provide short-term crisis intervention. It also does not confirm the more predictable finding that a large number of clients ($n = 55$) were interviewed only once. In short, the median may be better in some ways than either the mean or the mode for presenting what is typical, but it has its own problems.

The distribution in Table 3.3 is bimodal, with the two modes falling at 1 and 3 interviews. But if we were to use only the mode, we would be suggesting that either 1 or 3 interviews (both small numbers) is representative of the typical client when, in fact, fewer than half of all clients were seen 4 times or less. As is true of the median, the mode alone provides no hint of the possibility that a sizable percentage of crisis intervention cases were interviewed a fairly large number of times. Besides, the mode is really most appropriate for nominal- and ordinal-level data. It treats different value categories of a variable as if they were differences of kind only. It would not take into account the fact that the value categories in our example reflect quantitative differences, which is critical to an accurate interpretation of the data set.

In our example, as in many data sets, no single measure of central tendency would adequately summarize how the distribution of values for the variable, number of interviews, actually looked. Any one measure of central tendency has the potential to mislead. Yet, the mode, the median, the trimmed mean, and the mean all would help to describe how the data looked. The fact that the data set was bimodal, with modes at 1 and 3 interviews, indicates that short-term treatment occurs quite often within the agency. Perhaps, the median best reflects what is typical. It uses some of the available precision of measurement, more than the mode, but less than the mean. It at least suggests that short-term treatment may not be as typical of the agency as one might believe from reading the agency's mission statement. If the mean or the trimmed mean is also reported, the fact that either is over 4 is even stronger evidence that a sizable number of clients clearly are not the recipients of short-term crisis intervention services.

Any one measure of central tendency can be misleading. When in doubt about which measure of central tendency to use, a good rule is to report all that would be helpful in visualizing the data set. If the mode, median, and mean (and/or trimmed mean) are all reported, an experienced reader of research reports, or even one with just a good understanding of central tendency, will be able to compare them and piece together a reasonably accurate picture of how the data were distributed.

VARIABILITY

A measure of central tendency can tell us much about the distribution of the values of a variable. It can fall short, however, of giving us a complete picture of what a data set looks like. For example, it cannot tell us if most values tend to cluster around a typical value or, if not, how widely they vary from the typical value. To provide a more accurate description of the distribution of the variable, we need to add a summary descriptor called *variability,* which gives us an indicator of the degree of variation that occurred. Variability is also called *dispersion.*

Why is an understanding of variability so important? Suppose that there are two class sections of a graduate social work research course. The ages of the 15 students in each of the sections are as follows:

Ages; Section 1:

21, 22, 24, 24, 26, 29, 30, 31, 32, 33, 36, 38, 38, 40, 41

Ages; Section 2:

27, 28, 28, 29, 29, 30, 30, 31, 32, 32, 33, 33, 34, 34, 35

If we were to report only the mean and median for the variable *age* for each section, both measures of central tendency would be identical. The mean (31) and median (31) are the same for both sections. Only the sections' modes would give us any hint that the distribution of ages within them are quite different.

If a student who was 23 years of age were to register late for the class, the student might feel more comfortable in section 1 than in section 2. A student who is 34 might feel more comfortable in section 2. Neither student would know this based only on central tendency data. If the two students had one or more measures of variability for the two sections, however, they could anticipate how comfortable they might feel in registering for one section or the other.

If a variable is at the nominal or ordinal level of measurement, variability can be communicated best in a frequency distribution or graph, such as a bar chart. If a variable is at the interval or ratio level of measurement, however, measures of variability can help describe the distribution of values. The five measures of variability are (1) range, (2) interquartile range, (3) mean deviation, (4) variance, and (5) standard deviation.

The Range

The range is the distance that encompasses all values within a data set. Expressed as a formula, the range is computed as follows:

Range = maximum value – minimum value + 1

The formula above differs slightly from the way we use the word *range* in common English usage. Why is the range not simply the difference between the maximum value (the value of the case with the largest value of the variable) and the minimum value (the value of the case with the smallest value of the variable)? We add 1 to the difference so that the range reflects the total number of values of the variable that it encompasses.

In a distribution of the variable *age* for example, with a maximum age of 35 and a minimum age of 30, the range is 6 (35 − 30 + 1 = 6). That is because there are potentially 6 different ages (or values) that are included within the range: 35, 34, 33, 32, 31, and 30. Even if we think of values as reflecting equal intervals (Chapter 1), the range would still be 6 since it would include the distance from the lower limit of the interval for 30 (29.50) and the upper limit of the interval for 35 (35.49).

The range for section 2 in our previous example is 9 (35 − 27 + 1 = 9). There are potentially 9 different ages included in the data: 27, 28, 29, 30, 31, 32, 33, 34, and 35. The range for section 1 is 21 (41 − 21 + 1 = 21). The larger range in section 1 indicates a greater variation in the students' ages.

The range can be computed quickly and easily. Calculating the range also suggests the number of intervals to employ in creating grouped frequency distributions (Chapter 2) as well as the most appropriate interval size. Like the mean, however, the range is easily distorted by the presence of outliers. One outlier at either end of an array can greatly increase the range of a data set and suggest much more variability than is actually present. Let us suppose that the student who is 41 years old in section 1 drops out of the research course and is replaced by a student who is 64. The distribution of values would now look like this:

Ages; Section 1:

21, 22, 24, 24, 26, 29, 30, 31, 32, 33, 36, 38, 38, 40, 64

While only one value has changed, the range for section 1 has jumped from 21 to 44 (64 − 21 + 1 = 44). A student considering enrolling in section 1, who was told that the range for the students' ages is 44 would mistakenly assume that the ages of the students are much more diverse than they really are.

The vulnerability of the range to the influence of outliers is an undesirable characteristic, especially when comparing the ranges of two distributions of the same variable. The presence of outliers in one distribution and not in the other can give a misleading impression about the degree of dissimilarity of the two distributions.

The Interquartile Range

One way to handle the problem of outliers is to use a different measure of variability. Instead of using the maximum and minimum values to obtain a range, variability can be reported as the distance (in whole numbers and decimals) between the 75th and 25th percentiles. This distance is known as the *interquartile range.*

The median falls at the 50th percentile, or midpoint, of an array where half the values fall above it and half the values fall below it. In such an array, the 25th percentile theoretically would fall at the point where one-fourth of values in the array would have lower or smaller values and three-fourths would have higher values. The 75th percentile would fall at the point where three-fourths of values in the array would have lower or smaller values and one-fourth would have higher values.

Once an array has been formed and the 75th and 25th percentiles have been determined, the interquartile range is found by subtracting the 25th percentile from the 75th percentile. The interquartile range is a more stable measure of variability than the range for the same reason that the median is a more stable measure of central tendency than the mean. Outliers cannot distort the interquartile range as they distort the range because their actual values are used only in the first step of its computation, forming an array. Once an array is formed, their specific values are not used for computation.

Like the median, the interquartile range is difficult to compute. It is often not a whole number, as it would be with any of the examples of distributions that we have previously used. With the use of computers to analyze data, however, this presents few problems, and computation takes only a few seconds once the data have been entered.

Another, less widely used measure of variability that is a variation of the interquartile range is the *semi-interquartile range.* It is simply the interquartile range divided by 2. Thus, it is a distance that is one-half the distance (in whole or fractional values) between the 75th and 25th percentiles in an array of measurements of a variable.

The Mean Deviation

The range, interquartile range, and semi-interquartile range can all present accurate descriptions of the variability within values of a variable. They are all useful in certain situations. However, the fact that they do not use every case value in their final calculations sometimes results in a distorted picture of the data set. The *mean deviation,* however, is derived from computations involving all the values in a given data set.

The mean deviation is the average amount that the values of a variable differ (or deviate) from the mean. Like other measures of variability, it describes only the amount of variation among values of a variable, not their absolute values. That is the work of frequency distributions and graphs as presented in Chapter 2.

Table 3.4 lists five values (i.e., 1, 2, 3, 4, 5), their mean (3), and the deviation score of each (i.e., -2, -1, 0, 1, 2), which is the difference between each respective value (i.e., 1, 2, 3, 4, 5) and their mean (3).

The formula for the mean deviation is

$$\text{Mean deviation} = \frac{\text{Sum of deviation values (ignoring sign)}}{\text{Number of cases}}$$

TABLE 3.4   Deviations from the Mean

Value	–	Mean	=	Deviation from the Mean
1	–	3	=	-2
2	–	3	=	-1
3	–	3	=	0
4	–	3	=	1
5	–	3	=	2
	Total			0

To compute the mean deviation for the data in Table 3.4, we would proceed as follows:

Mean deviation $= \dfrac{2 + 1 + 0 + 1 + 2 = 6}{5}$

$= 1.2$

While the mean deviation is relatively easy to compute and interpret, it is rarely reported in professional literature. We have chosen to discuss it because the process of subtracting raw scores (values) from the mean is an important step in computing two other, more widely used measures of variability, the variance and the standard deviation.

The Variance

me alue of variability
mean of
variability — *how much do all the other score vary around the mean*

Obtaining the *variance* requires

1. Subtracting the mean of the distribution from each value (getting the mean deviation)
2. Squaring each difference
3. Dividing the sum of the squared differences (called the *sum of squares*) by either the total number of values minus one (for sample data) or simply the total number of values (for population data)

To compute the variance for the population data in Table 3.4, we would proceed as follows:

Variance = Sum of squared deviations from the mean divided by the number of cases

Substituting values for words, we get the following:

Variance $= \dfrac{(-2)^2 + (-1)^2 + (0)^2 + (1)^2 + (2)^2}{5}$

$= \dfrac{4 + 1 + 0 + 1 + 4}{5}$

$= 2$

The variance sometimes is computed merely to describe (in shorthand fashion) the variability of a variable within a data set. It also is a critical component of some of the formulas for other types of statistical analyses discussed in later chapters of this book.

The Standard Deviation

The *standard deviation* is simply the square root of the variance. It appears frequently in quantitatively oriented reports. It is useful for describing the variability of data (when certain conditions are met), and it is used in many other types of statistical analyses as well.

Like the mean deviation and the variance, the standard deviation requires interval-level or ratio-level data. It is most appropriately used with fairly large samples and with variables that, if graphed, would produce a frequency polygon that is relatively symmetrical and bell-shaped (described in Chapter 4). It is not appropriate when the distribution of a variable is badly skewed within the population.

Like the mean deviation and the variance, the standard deviation uses all case values in its computation. It tells us to what degree the values cluster around the mean, which makes it extremely useful. As we shall see in Chapter 4, when used with the mean in appropriate situations, it allows us to determine where a given value falls relative to other values (its exact percentile) and to reconstruct the distribution of all the values of a variable. For the moment, we will concentrate on how the standard deviation is computed from a set of values.

Computing the standard deviation involves eight steps, those discussed in relation to the variance, plus one more (determining the square root of the variance). A convenient way to compute a standard deviation is:

1. List the values in a distribution in column *a*.
2. Compute the mean of the values in column *a*.
3. List the mean in column *b*.
4. Subtract the mean from each value in column *a*, and place this value in column *c*.
5. Square each value in column *c*, and place this value into column *d*.
6. Compute the sum of the squares in column *d*.
7. Divide the sum of squares in column *d* by the total number of values minus one (for sample data) or simply the total number of values (for population data) in column *a*.
8. Compute the square root of the number computed in Step 7 (the variance). The result is the standard deviation of the values in column *a*.

The data in the distribution below give the number of years of employment of the six social workers (the population) who work in Agency A:

Years of Employment; Agency A:

5, 5, 6, 6, 7, 7

Using the data, we can compute the standard deviation using the eight steps described above (see Table 3.5).

Now suppose that agency B also has six social workers, but their years of employment are as follows:

Years of Employment; Agency B:

1, 2, 4, 8, 10, 11

Again, we can compute the standard deviation for the variable *years of employment* (see Table 3.6).

The distribution of years of employment in agency B shows more variation than does the distribution for agency A. This is also reflected in their respective standard

TABLE 3.5   Determining the Standard Deviation of Years of Employment for Agency A

Step 1 (*a*) Value	–	Step 3 (*b*) Mean	=	Step 4 (*c*) Deviation from Mean	Step 5 (*d*) Squared Difference from Mean
5	–	6	=	−1	1
5	–	6	=	−1	1
6	–	6	=	0	0
6	–	6	=	0	0
7	–	6	=	1	1
7	–	6	=	1	1
		Total		0	Step 6 = 4

$$\text{Step 7} = \frac{4}{6}$$

$$= .67 \quad \text{(Variance)}$$

$$\text{Step 8} = \sqrt{.67}$$

$$= .82 \quad \text{(Standard deviation)}$$

TABLE 3.6   Determining the Standard Deviation of Years of Employment for Agency B

Step 1 (*a*) Value	–	Step 3 (*b*) Mean	=	Step 4 (*c*) Deviation from Mean	Step 5 (*d*) Squared Difference from Mean
1	–	6	=	−5	25
2	–	6	=	−4	16
4	–	6	=	−2	4
8	–	6	=	2	4
10	–	6	=	4	16
11	–	6	=	5	25
		Total		0	Step 6 = 90

$$\text{Step 7} = \frac{90}{6}$$

$$= 15 \quad \text{(Variance)}$$

$$\text{Step 8} = \sqrt{15}$$

$$= 3.87 \quad \text{(Standard deviation)}$$

**FIGURE 3.2   Variability of Years of
Employment for Agency A (from Table 3.5)**

deviations—3.87 for agency B and only .82 for agency A. This demonstrates an important point: In comparing two distributions of measurements of the same variable, larger standard deviations reflect more variation, and smaller standard deviations reflect less variation. (The same is true for all of the other measures of variability discussed in this chapter—larger measures of variability correspond to more variation among values, and smaller measures correspond to less variation.)

A pictorial representation of the above data will further demonstrate the meaning of standard deviation. Figures 3.2 and 3.3 each show how the data on length of employment in the two agencies would look if displayed as weights on a scale. Note that Figures 3.2 and 3.3 both balance on 6 years, reflecting the fact that both distributions have a mean of 6 (years of employment). Notice, however, how much more variation is shown in agency B (Figure 3.3) than in agency A (Figure 3.2). This is a graphical portrayal of the greater variability among values of the variable in agency B as reflected in its larger standard deviation.

While adding or subtracting a fixed amount to all values of a distribution will affect the mean by increasing or decreasing it by that amount, it will not affect the standard deviation for that distribution. A standard deviation reflects variation, and the amount of variation does not change. For example, if every employee in the agency in our example above received a $2000 annual raise, the mean annual salary would increase by $2000, but its standard deviation (and its range and interquartile range) would remain exactly the same. Similarly, if we were to repeat our measurement of years of employment 1 year later with the same employees in either agency, the mean would now be 7 years, but the respective standard deviations would be the same as they were a year earlier.

**FIGURE 3.3   Variability of Years of
Employment for Agency B (from Table 3.6)**

Reporting Measures of Variability

Like measures of central tendency, different measures of variability are most appropriate for certain situations. Also like measures of central tendency, it often is desirable to report more than one measure of variability.

The range is generally reported (as a single number) within the text of a research report. Interquartile ranges, semi-interquartile ranges, variances, standard deviations, and, when they are reported, mean deviations often are reported in tabular form, especially when there are many to report.

Since the standard deviation represents the distance between the mean and a certain point on a frequency polygon, it is only natural that the mean is commonly reported along with the standard deviation. Where one is appropriate, the other generally is also. Reporting the two together enables the reader of a research report to get a fuller picture of how the values of a variable were distributed.

When the interquartile range or semi-interquartile range is used instead of the standard deviation or variance because of the presence of a number of extreme outliers (a skewed distribution) within an interval-level or ratio-level data set, it is often reported along with the median. Again, this is logical since all of these measures are designed to counteract the distorting effect of outliers.

To provide an even more complete image of the distribution of the measurements of a variable, we sometimes report what is referred to as a *five-number summary*. It consists of the minimum value, the 25th percentile, the 50th percentile (median), the 75th percentile, and the maximum value.

A graph known as a *box plot* is also sometimes used to display the central tendency and dispersion of the distribution of a variable. In a box plot such as Figure 3.4 (a representation of the ages of the extended care facility residents described in Chapter 2), we can identify the 25th percentile, the median, the 75th percentile, and outliers. The box in the figure contains all cases between the 25th and 75th percentiles (those within the interquartile range). The horizontal line within it is the median. The short

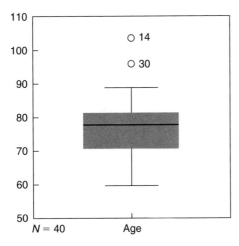

FIGURE 3.4   Box Plot: Ages of Residents at XYZ Residential Care Facility (*N* = 40)

horizontal lines outside the box (above and below a vertical line extending from the box) represent the largest values that would not be regarded as outliers. Values above or below these lines would be regarded as outliers. Their case numbers (14 and 30) appear near the top of the graph.

CONCLUDING THOUGHTS

This chapter briefly discussed basic ways to summarize the distribution of values of a variable within any given data set. We looked at one group of measures that is used to describe what is typical of a data set (central tendency) and another group that is used to summarize the degree to which values differ from each other (variability). We suggested when each measure is most appropriate to use and noted their respective limitations.

As in Chapter 2, this chapter emphasized the importance of honest and clear communication. Frequently, using a single measure of central tendency or a single measure of variability will not accomplish this objective. This is most likely when the distribution of a variable is skewed—that is, it contains outliers that tend to badly distort the distribution. Thus, we should include as many measures of central tendency and dispersion as are necessary insure that the distribution of a data set can be fully visualized.

STUDY QUESTIONS

1. What does a frequency polygon look like when its distribution is described as bimodal? Provide an original example in your discussion.
2. Why is the median more likely to be an accurate description of interval-level data than the mode? Explain.
3. Discuss why the median is a more stable measure of central tendency than the mean. Provide an original example in your discussion.
4. Why do we generally consider the mean to be a more precise measure of central tendency than either the median or the mode?
5. How does a trimmed mean combine the best features of both the median and the mean?
6. In what situations is it necessary to compute a weighted mean? Provide an original example.
7. Why may only one measure of central tendency be an inadequate description of a data set? Provide an original example in your discussion.
8. Discuss why the range is an especially unstable measure of variability and when the inter-quartile range may be preferable if the distribution of a variable is skewed.
9. Which measures of variability consider all values of a variable in their computations? When is this better than using only some of the values in a distribution? When is it not? Explain in detail.
10. How would an extreme outlier tend to distort the mean deviation of a data set?
11. How would a data set containing the values of a variable with a mean of 50 and a standard deviation of 3 compare with another data set containing the same variable but a mean of 50 and a standard deviation of 12?
12. How would adding the number 10 to each of the values of a variable affect its mean and standard deviation? Provide an example.

13. Fifteen students were registered in section 1 and 15 in section 2 of a research course. They took the same midterm exam, and their exam scores were distributed as follows:

    Section 1: 89, 56, 45, 78, 98, 45, 55, 77, 88, 99, 98, 97, 54, 34, 94

    Section 2: 77, 88, 87, 67, 98, 87, 55, 77, 45, 44, 88, 99, 69, 67, 98

    a. Calculate the mode, median, mean, range, variance, and standard deviation for both sections.
    b. Which section did better overall on the exam? Fully justify your answer using the concepts presented in this chapter.

14. Locate an article in a professional social work journal that uses one or more of the measures of central tendency and variability presented in this chapter. Answer the following questions in relation to the article.
    a. Do you feel the author reported the data accurately when referring to the data set used in the research study? Why?
    b. What other measures of central tendency and variability would you have liked the author to report? Why would they have been helpful?

15. Discuss why a mean should not be used with ordinal-level variables.

16. For each of the following, indicate the measure of central tendency that would be most appropriate, and indicate why.
    a. An income distribution in which 97 percent of the cases are in a range of $20,000 to $50,000 and a few cases are between 0 and $5,000.
    b. Data reporting the religious preferences of 100 social work students.
    c. A grouped frequency distribution of the variable *age* that has an open-ended interval of over 65 years of age.

17. The measures of central tendency have been reported for three different social service agencies for the variable *number of years employed in the agency* as follows:

    Agency A: mode 16, median 17, mean 16

    Agency B: mode 4, median 7, mean 10

    Agency C: mode 1, median 3, mean 6

    Use the measures of central tendency to describe and compare the staff of the three agencies.

18. What is a box plot, and what does it portray? Provide an example of a box plot.

Normal Distributions

Chapter 2 presented simple ways that tables and graphs can be used to portray the distributions of values (and value categories) of a variable within any given data set. Chapter 3 illustrated the methods that can be used to summarize two important characteristics of a distribution of values within a data set—central tendency and variability. This chapter will demonstrate how this knowledge can be used to present a more complete description of the distribution of an interval-level or ratio-level variable.

SKEWED DISTRIBUTIONS

A frequency polygon can assume a variety of shapes depending on where the values of an interval-level or ratio-level variable tend to cluster. Some variables contain relatively large numbers of low values and thus, when displayed as a frequency polygon, a large percentage of the area of the polygon is on the left side, where lower values of the variable are displayed; others reflect the opposite pattern.

Suppose, for example, Sue, a hospital administrator, wished to study changes in admission diagnoses over a 6-year period. She wanted to substantiate her impression that the hospital was experiencing a decline in some diagnoses and an increase in others. The data might look like those in Table 4.1 for a diagnosis such as emphysema.

Just by glancing at the data contained in Table 4.1, it is easy to see that the number of emphysema patients admitted to the hospital over the 6-year period has declined

TABLE 4.1   Cumulative Frequency Distribution: Emphysema Patients Admitted to XYZ Hospital by Year (*N* = 210)

Year	Absolute Frequency	Cumulative Frequency
1995	60	60
1996	50	110
1997	40	150
1998	30	180
1999	20	200
2000	10	210

over time. This trend is even more apparent when the data are placed in a histogram, such as the one in Figure 4.1.

The midpoints of the bars in the histogram in Figure 4.1 are connected. The line joining them to form a frequency polygon is called a curve. Distributions like the one shown in Table 4.1 and reflected in the frequency polygon in Figure 4.1 are referred to as skewed, a term we introduced in the previous chapter when we were discussing the presence of outliers in the distribution of a variable. As we noted then, a *skewed distribution* is asymmetrical—that is, its ends do not taper off in a similar manner in both directions. Note that the frequency polygon in Figure 4.1 has a "tail" on the right side (where, normally, the largest case values are displayed). A curve like the one in Figure 4.1, which has a tail to the right, is called a *positively skewed* distribution.

Trends in admissions of HIV-positive cases over the same 6-year period in the hospital might reflect the exact opposite pattern from those with emphysema admissions. Table 4.2 and Figure 4.2 illustrate this point.

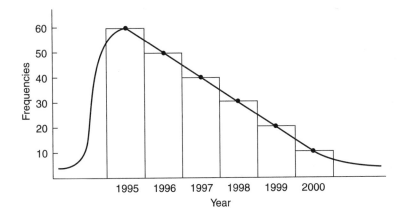

FIGURE 4.1   Positively Skewed Frequency Polygon: Emphysema Patients Admitted to XYZ Hospital by Year (*N* = 210)

TABLE 4.2   Cumulative Frequency Distribution: HIV-Positive Patients Admitted to XYZ Hospital by Year ($N = 210$)

Year	Absolute Frequency	Cumulative Frequency
1995	10	10
1996	20	30
1997	30	60
1998	40	100
1999	50	150
2000	60	210

The distribution in Figure 4.2 is also skewed, but this time the tail of the frequency distribution is to the left. A curve that is skewed to the left, where the smallest case values are displayed, is called a *negatively skewed distribution.*

NORMAL DISTRIBUTIONS

Many interval-level and ratio-level variables contain no or relatively few extreme outliers. In addition, values tend to cluster around the mean with lower and lower frequencies occurring among values farther and farther away from the mean (either smaller than or larger than it). A frequency polygon portraying such a distribution would not be skewed. It would be symmetrical. When such a distribution of the values of a variable occurs, it is called a *normal distribution.* It is of special interest to us in our study

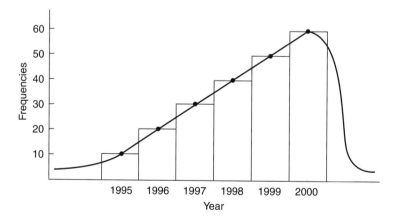

FIGURE 4.2   Negatively Skewed Frequency Polygon: HIV-Positive Patients Admitted to XYZ Hospital by Year ($N = 210$)

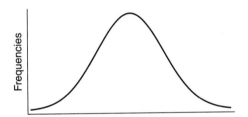

FIGURE 4.3   The Normal Curve

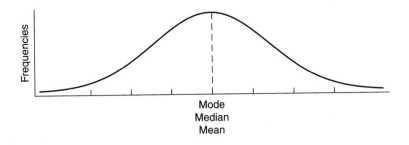

FIGURE 4.4   The Normal Distribution

of statistics. An interval- or ratio-level variable that is normally distributed can be represented by a bell-shaped frequency polygon; the curve thus formed is referred to as the normal curve. One example of a normal curve reflecting a normal distribution is presented in Figure 4.3.

Distributions of all interval- or ratio-level variables that tend to be normally distributed share the same properties. In addition to being symmetrical and bell-shaped, in a normal curve, the mode, median, and mean all occur at the highest point and in the center of the distribution, as in Figure 4.4. Note that in skewed curves, the mode, median, and mean occur at different points, as in Figures 4.5a and b.

The ends of the normal curve extend toward infinity—they approach the horizontal axis (x-axis) but never quite touch it. This property represents the possibility that,

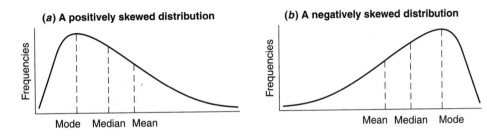

FIGURE 4.5   Skewed Distributions

while the curve contains virtually all values of a variable, a very small number of values may exist that reflect extremely large or extremely small measurements of the variable (outliers). It also reflects the fact that at a higher level of abstraction, a total population of cases (or the universe) is never static because it is always subject to change as cases are added or deleted over time. Thus, populations are always evolving.

The horizontal axis of a normal curve can be divided into six equal units—three units between the mean and the place where the curve approaches the axis on the left side, and three units between the mean and the place where it approaches the axis on the right. These six units collectively reflect the amount of variation that exists within virtually all values of a normally distributed interval- or ratio-level variable. In a normal distribution of any variable, virtually all values (except for .26%) fall within these six units of variation. The larger the units (the more variation among values in the data set), the flatter the curve. The smaller the units (less variation), the higher the curve.

Exactly how much variation does each unit represent for a given variable? Each unit corresponds to 1 standard deviation. How much variation a unit represents within a variable is determined by using the standard deviation formula presented in the previous chapter.

Figure 4.6 shows a typical normal curve with 3 units of standard deviation to the left of the mean and 3 units to the right of the mean. Note that the units are labeled to reflect the number of standard deviations (*SD*) that each falls from the mean. Units to the left of the mean (where values are smaller than the mean) use the minus sign (i.e., –1*SD*, –2*SD*, –3 *SD*), and units to the right of the mean (where values are larger than the mean) use the positive sign (i.e., +1*SD*, +2*SD*, +3*SD*) or no sign at all.

The term *standard deviation* can be a little misleading. *Standard* refers to the fact that once the standard deviation for a variable has been computed, it becomes a standard unit that reflects the amount of variability that was found to exist within the variable. But remember, a standard deviation (or a mean) is specific to a given variable within a given data set. Standard deviations (and means) differ from one variable to another and from one data set to another (even when the same variable has been measured). They differ based on the measurements that were taken and how much they vary from each other. The mean and standard deviation for test scores for males, for example, might be different from the mean and standard deviation for test scores of fe-

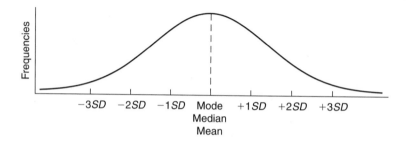

FIGURE 4.6   The Normal Distribution with Standard Deviations Illustrated

males who take the same examination. Or the mean and standard deviation computed from test scores of people who took the examination in 2001 might be different from the mean and standard deviation computed from scores of people who took the examination in 2000.

Different normal curves, therefore, tend to have different means and different standard deviations. Figures 4.7*a, b,* and *c* demonstrate how this occurs by comparing three pairs of normal curves. They also demonstrate the fact that normal curves can be drawn differently to reflect the distribution of data; that is, curves may be high and narrow, low and wide, or anything in between. They are usually drawn to suggest the degree of variation present in the distribution of an interval- or ratio-level variable— that is, the size of its standard deviation. Flatter curves suggest relatively large standard deviations, and higher ones reflect relatively small standard deviations.

Not surprisingly (since it is symmetrical), 50 percent of the total area of the frequency polygon formed by a normal curve falls below the mean, and 50 percent falls above it. Other segments of the frequency polygon similarly reflect standard percentages of its total area. Mathematicians have determined what percentage of the normal curve

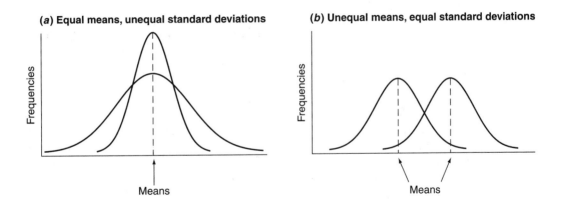

(a) Equal means, unequal standard deviations

(b) Unequal means, equal standard deviations

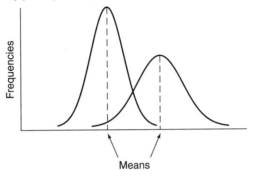

(c) Unequal means, unequal standard deviations

FIGURE 4.7   Variations in Normal Distributions

falls between the mean and the point referred to as +1 standard deviation, between—1 standard deviation and—2 standard deviation, and so forth (see Figure 4.8).

By looking at Figure 4.8, we can see that the area of a normal curve between a point on the horizontal axis (e.g., −2SD) and the mean is equivalent to the area of the curve between the comparable point on the other side of the mean (e.g., +2SD) and the mean. This makes sense because, as we have already noted, a normal curve is symmetrical. If we add up all the percentages within each of the segments of the frequency polygon between −3SD and +3SD, they equal 99.74 percent of the curve.

Thus, almost all the area of the frequency polygon (99.74%) lies between the points −3SD and +3SD. We could also add together other segments of the normal curve to learn that 47.72 percent of it (34.13% + 13.59% = 47.72%) falls between the mean and −2SD and another 47.72 percent falls between the mean and +2SD, or that 68.26 percent (34.13% + 34.13% = 68.26%) falls within ±1SD of the mean.

Now let us look at Figure 4.8 from a different perspective. Up to this point, we have viewed the numbers in the figure as areas or portions of a frequency polygon. But these numbers are also something else. They are the percentage of values (persons, cases, or objects) that fall within the respective distances from the mean of a normally distributed interval- or ratio-level variable. If, for example, Figure 4.8 were a frequency distribution of a normally distributed variable, such as height of female social work students, the figure would tell us that the height of 47.72 percent of all female social work students (34.13% + 13.59% = 47.72%) falls between the mean and −2SD; the height of 68.26 percent of them (34.13% + 34.13% = 68.26%) falls between −1SD and +1SD from the mean, and so on.

If we know that the height of female social work students tends to form a normal distribution (which it probably does), we could compute the mean and standard deviation for their heights and then make very precise statements about the distribution of values of the variable. We could assign actual heights to correspond to the various mean and standard deviation points in Figure 4.8 and make statements like 68.26 percent of the heights of female social work students fall between _____ inches tall and _____ inches tall. Understanding that the percentage of the area under a normal curve is also the percentage of values that fall within a certain distribution area of a normally distributed interval- or ratio-level variable is critical to understanding the material in this chapter and other parts of our discussion of statistics that rely on the normal distribution of values.

CONVERTING RAW SCORES TO z SCORES AND PERCENTILES

When we encounter values of an interval- or ratio-level variable based on measurements taken from two different samples or populations, we are sometimes unable to make direct comparisons between them. Suppose we have two friends, Rita and Miriam, who are in two different sections of a social work practice course. Both take their midterm exams. Rita's raw score is 21, and Miriam's is 85. Who did better on her midterm? Without additional information, we would have no way of knowing.

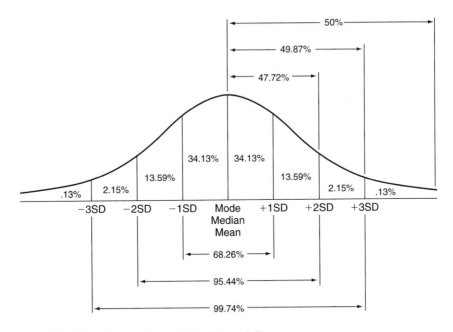

FIGURE 4.8   Proportions of the Normal Curve

If we could learn the maximum score that each could have received on her respective examination, it would help a great deal. Perhaps, Rita's score of 21 was out of a maximum of 25—that would be 84 percent correct. And Miriam's score of 85 was out of a maximum of 100–85 percent correct. Can we thus assume that Miriam is doing better at midterm than Rita? Maybe, maybe not. Perhaps we would learn that Miriam's 85 percent was the lowest grade in her course section and Rita's 84 percent was the highest grade in her section. That might cause us to rethink our initial assumption.

We could conduct a meaningful comparison of our friends' scores if we had a more comprehensive picture of how each score compares with the scores of other students in the respective course section. We can do this by converting the two raw scores, or values (i.e., 21 and 85), to a common standard.

It is possible to use a common standard to compare values of an interval- or ratio-level variable taken from two different populations only if the variable is normally distributed within both populations. Let us assume that the scores in both sections are normally distributed (a pretty big assumption). Now we can use *z scores* (also known as standard scores), which are raw scores converted to standard deviation units. Every raw score in a normal distribution has a corresponding *z* score that reflects how many standard deviation units it falls above or below the mean. Once two raw scores are converted to *z scores,* each *z* score (even if the scores were taken from two different normal distributions) can be compared directly with the other. Or, the *z* scores can be converted to percentiles, and the two percentiles can be compared by seeing where each score fell relative to all other scores in their respective distributions. As suggested in Chapter 2, a percentile is a point below which a certain percentage of the distribution of values lies. Thus, each z score corresponds to both a certain z score and a certain percentile rank.

For example, suppose that Axel received a score of 75 on a research methods exam. By converting his raw score (i.e., 75) first to a z score and then to its corresponding percentile we could determine that approximately 82 percent of the class received a score below his score. Suppose Durshka's score on a research methods exam in a different section was also 75, but by converting her score first to a z score and then determining its percentile we learn that 92 percent of students did not receive as high a score as Durshka. It is now possible to compare Axel's and Durshka's scores (even though they took different exams in different course sections) and conclude that Durshka did better on her exam (at least in one respect) than Axel did on his.

To convert a raw score into a z score, the following formula is used:

$$z \text{ score} = \frac{\text{raw score} - \text{mean}}{\text{standard deviation}}$$

As mentioned above, a z score reflects the number of standard deviation units that a given raw score falls from the mean of the distribution that contains the score. A raw score above the mean has a corresponding positive z score; a raw score below the mean has a corresponding negative z score. The mean of all the z scores of a normally distributed interval- or ratio-level variable is 0.00. To put it another way, if we were to take all the z scores of a normally distributed interval- or ratio-level variable and place them into a frequency polygon, that polygon would have a mean of 0 and a standard deviation of 1.

As long as we know the mean and the standard deviation of a distribution from which any raw score is obtained, we can compute its z score. A figure such as Figure 4.8 could also quickly tell us the corresponding percentile for a raw score that has a z score that is a whole number such as $z = -2.0$ or $z = 3.0$. As we observed earlier and can see from Figure 4.8, 34.13 percent of the area of the curve falls between the mean (the 50th percentile) and +1 standard deviation. Thus, a score with a corresponding zscore of 1.0 would fall at approximately the 84th percentile ($50 + 34.13 = 84.13$). A raw score with a z score of -1.0 would fall at approximately the 16th percentile ($50 - 34.13 = 15.87$). A raw score with a z score of 2.0 would fall at approximately the 98th percentile ($50.00 + 34.13 + 13.59 = 97.72$); A raw score with a z score of -2.0 would fall at approximately the 2nd percentile ($50.00 - 34.13 - 13.59 = 2.28$), and so forth.

As we might expect, z scores usually do not turn out to be whole numbers. More typically, they are fractions or mixed numbers, which we express in the form of decimals, such as $z = 2.11$ or $z = -2.24$. Figure 4.8 cannot be used to accurately determine the percentage of values that would fall between a fractional z score and the mean of the frequency distribution that contains its raw score. We have to use a table like Table 4.3 to convert fractional z scores into percentiles. Table 4.3 shows the area of a normal curve (and the corresponding percent of values) within any normal distribution that falls between a whole or fractional z score and the mean.

In Table 4.3, the whole number and the first decimal of a z score are found in the left-hand column. The second number to the right of the decimal in the z score is found in the column headings that run across the top of the table. The area of the normal curve between a given z score (obtained by using the z score formula) and the mean

TABLE 4.3   **Areas of the Normal Curve**

				Area under the normal curve between mean and z score						
z	.00	.01	.02	.03	.04	.05	.06	.07	.08	.09
0.0	00.00	00.40	00.80	01.20	01.60	01.99	02.39	02.79	03.19	03.59
0.1	03.98	04.38	04.78	05.17	05.57	05.96	06.36	06.75	07.14	07.53
0.2	07.93	08.32	08.71	09.10	09.48	09.87	10.26	10.64	11.03	11.41
0.3	11.79	12.17	12.55	12.93	13.31	13.68	14.06	14.43	14.80	15.17
0.4	15.54	15.91	16.28	16.64	17.00	17.36	17.72	18.08	18.44	18.79
0.5	19.15	19.50	19.85	20.19	20.54	20.88	21.23	21.57	21.90	22.24
0.6	22.57	22.91	23.24	23.57	23.89	24.22	24.54	24.86	25.17	25.49
0.7	25.80	26.11	26.42	26.73	27.04	27.34	27.64	27.94	28.23	28.52
0.8	28.81	29.10	29.39	29.67	29.95	30.23	30.51	30.78	31.06	31.33
0.9	31.59	31.86	32.12	32.38	32.64	32.90	33.15	33.40	33.65	33.89
1.0	34.13	34.38	34.61	34.85	35.08	35.31	35.54	35.77	35.99	36.21
1.1	36.43	36.65	36.86	37.08	37.29	37.49	37.70	37.90	38.10	38.30
1.2	38.49	38.69	38.88	39.07	39.25	39.44	39.62	39.80	39.97	40.15
1.3	40.32	40.49	40.66	40.82	40.99	41.15	41.31	41.47	41.62	41.77
1.4	41.92	42.07	42.22	42.36	42.51	42.65	42.79	42.92	43.06	43.19
1.5	43.32	43.45	43.57	43.70	43.83	43.94	44.06	44.18	44.29	44.41
1.6	44.52	44.63	44.74	44.84	44.95	45.05	45.15	45.25	45.35	45.45
1.7	45.54	45.64	45.73	45.82	45.91	45.99	46.08	46.16	46.25	46.33
1.8	46.41	46.49	46.56	46.64	46.71	46.78	46.86	46.93	46.99	47.06
1.9	47.13	47.19	47.26	47.32	47.38	47.44	47.50	47.56	47.61	47.67
2.0	47.72	47.78	47.83	47.88	47.93	47.98	48.03	48.08	48.12	48.17
2.1	48.21	48.26	48.30	48.34	48.38	48.42	48.46	48.50	48.54	48.57
2.2	48.61	48.64	48.68	48.71	48.75	48.78	48.81	48.84	48.87	48.90
2.3	48.93	48.96	48.98	49.01	49.04	49.06	49.09	49.11	49.13	49.16
2.4	49.18	49.20	49.22	49.25	49.27	49.29	49.31	49.32	49.34	49.36
2.5	49.38	49.40	49.41	49.43	49.45	49.46	49.48	49.49	49.51	49.52
2.6	49.53	49.55	49.56	49.57	49.59	49.60	49.61	49.62	49.63	49.64
2.7	49.65	49.66	49.67	49.68	49.69	49.70	49.71	49.72	49.73	49.74
2.8	49.74	49.75	49.76	49.77	49.77	49.78	49.79	49.79	49.80	49.81
2.9	49.81	49.82	49.82	49.83	49.84	49.84	49.85	49.85	49.86	49.86
3.0	49.87									
3.5	49.98									
4.0	49.997									
5.0	49.99997									

These #'s are the area under the curve

%

Source: The original data for Table 4.3 came from *Tables for Statisticians and Biometricians,* edited by K. Pearson, published by the Imperial College of Science and Technology, and are used here by permission of the Biometrika trustees. The adaptation of these data is taken from E. L. Lindquist, *A First Course in Statistics* (revised edition), with permission of the publisher, Houghton Mifflin Company.

TABLE 4.4   Examples of *z* Scores and Their Corresponding Areas and Percentiles

z Score	Row	Column	Area Included between Mean and z Score	Percentiles
.12	0.1	.02	04.78	54.78
1.78	1.7	.08	46.25	96.25
−2.90	2.9	.00	49.81	.19
1.15	1.1	.05	37.49	87.49
−1.15	1.1	.05	37.49	12.51

would be the number in the body of the table where the appropriate line and column intersect. Note that the number alongside 1.0 in the left-hand column is 34.13, the area of the normal curve between the mean and either −1*SD* or +1*SD* (see Figure 4.8) and the percent of cases that fall between the mean and either −1 or + 1 standard deviations. Also, the number alongside 2.0 in the left-hand column is 47.72, the sum of the numbers 34.13 and 13.59 in Figure 4.8. The 47.72 represents the percentage of values in any normal distribution that falls between the mean and either −2*SD* or +2*SD*.

To find the area of the curve between a raw score and the mean when, for example, the raw score's *z* score computes to 1.55, we would first go down the left-hand column in Table 4.3 to 1.5. Then we would move right across the table to the .05 column (to pick up the second decimal). The number 43.94 appears at the intersection of the 1.5 line and the .05 column. That means that the area of the curve between our raw score and the mean would be 43.94 or, viewing it another way, that nearly 44 percent of all values (or cases) fall between that raw score and the mean.

For positive *z* scores (those to the right of the mean) we would add the area of the curve found in the body of Table 4.3 to 50.00 (corresponding to the area of the curve below the mean) to find the percentile rank where the raw score fell. In our example (using a *z* score of 1.55), we would add 43.94 to 50.00 to get 93.94. The raw score corresponding to a *z* score of 1.55 would fall at approximately the 94th percentile. It is logical to add 50.00 to the number found in Table 4.3 since we know that the raw score fell above the mean—it would thus have to fall above the 50th percentile. With a *z* score of 1.55, all scores below the mean (50% of them in a normal distribution), plus the other 43.94 percent between the mean and the score, fell below it.

As in our earlier example using whole number *z* scores, for negative *z* scores (those to the left of the mean), we would subtract the area of the curve found in the body of Table 4.3 from 50.00 (the percentile of the mean). If the *z* score in our example had turned out to be −1.55, we would subtract 43.94 from 50.00 to get 6.06. The raw score corresponding to a *z* score of −1.55 would fall at approximately the 6th percentile. Table 4.4 provides additional examples of *z* scores and their corresponding areas and percentiles.

It is appropriate to use *z* scores with interval- or ratio-level variables that form normal distributions or at least approximate the normal curve. When a distribution is badly skewed, the areas between, for example,—1*SD* and the mean and between +1*SD* and the mean are not likely to be the same. Then, a *z* score cannot be used to produce a standardized proportion of the distribution from which it was computed. The distribution in Figure 4.9, for example, is positively skewed. Area A is clearly not equal to area B.

Practical Uses of *z* Scores

When used with a normally distributed variable, *z* scores make it possible to take any raw score and gain an accurate understanding of where it falls relative to the other scores. By converting raw scores to percentile ranks, we can put raw scores into perspective. A student receiving a raw score of 57 on a first exam, for example, may become quite alarmed, but learning that the score fell at the 96th percentile would be of considerable comfort, especially if the instructor has promised to "grade on a curve."

In fact the process of grading on a curve is a dubious one, especially in course sections that are not very large. Scores on examinations are often not normally distributed. Because of this and because of the frequent presence of outliers (extremely high or low values), assigning grades based on, essentially, how many standard deviations scores fall from the mean can produce grades that may seem unfair.

Treating scores as if they are normally distributed might lead an instructor to award an A to exam scores that were in the top 16 percent (above +1*SD*) or an F to exam scores below the 2nd percentile (below –2*SD*). Is this fair? What if the class was especially knowledgeable, and the 2nd percentile corresponded with a raw score of 97 out of 100? Should an individual who received a 97 get a letter grade of F, even though mastery of most of the content was demonstrated? Or should a student who answered only 35 percent of questions correctly get an A on an exam, just because all scores were extremely low and the 35 fell at +1*SD* for the class?

Grading on a curve may be desirable if it is unknown whether an exam is too easy or too difficult. It guarantees the distribution of letter grades among class members in a way that not "too many" (whatever that is) will get any one grade, but it is unnecessary

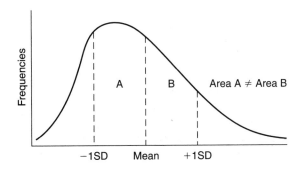

FIGURE 4.9   Comparing Areas of the Curve of a Skewed Distribution

if an instructor can create a fair and rigorous exam and knows what constitutes exceptional, average, or poor performance on it.

A common and more statistically justifiable use of normal distributions can be seen in standardized tests, such as IQ tests or the Scholastic Achievement Test (SAT). Over the years, these tests repeatedly have been refined to the point that the scores of the large numbers of persons taking them tend to fall into patterns with consistent means and standard deviations. In other words, their scores now form normal distributions.

SAT scores were originally designed so that combined verbal and math scores for large numbers of students would form a normal curve with a mean of 1000 and a standard deviation of 200. In addition, all scores would fall between $-3SD$ and $+3SD$ from the mean. The lowest possible score would be $3 \times 200 = 600$ below the mean, or 400. (This is the 400 that one is rumored to get for just showing up or signing one's name.)

The highest possible (or perfect) score (the 100th percentile) would be 1600. SAT scores declined considerably during the 1980s and early 1990s, however. Although scores of 400 and 1600 still occurred, the mean dropped to around 920. In 1994, a decision was made to adjust future test scores upward so that they would again have a mean of approximately 1000 which in turn would better approximate a normal curve.

The results of various IQ tests tend to form normal distributions. They generally have a mean of 100 and a standard deviation of either 15 or 16, depending on the test. If we understand the principles and characteristics that relate to normal distributions, it is possible, given these data, to convert any raw IQ score to its corresponding z score and then to a percentile using Table 4.3. A score with a z score of 1.00 (115 or 116, depending on the test), for example, would fall at about the 84th percentile.

Even when we have little or no knowledge of a standardized measurement instrument other than its mean and standard deviation, we can put a raw score derived from it into a meaningful perspective. Or we can compare a score derived from it with another score on a measuring instrument with which we are more familiar.

Example: Student Anxiety

Deborah is a social worker in a student health center. She leads a treatment group of college students diagnosed as experiencing chronic anxiety. In the past, group members have been selected for treatment on the basis of their scores on Anxiety Scale A, a standardized measuring instrument given to all students as a part of intake screening at the center. The measuring instrument has a mean of 70 and a standard deviation of 10. Only students scoring over 80 on Anxiety Scale A are eligible to join Deborah's group.

A vacancy occurred in the group. Deborah checked the files of active cases and noted that the highest score among potential group members was 78 (Gina). Deborah, however, had just received a referral from a family service agency stating that one of their former clients (Tom) had just enrolled at her university and needed further assistance with his anxiety problems. The referral letter indicated that Tom had received a score of 66 on Anxiety Scale B. The letter further stated that Anxiety Scale B has a mean of 50 and a standard deviation of 12.

Both standardized measuring instruments (Anxiety Scales A and B) are considered to be valid and reliable when used with college students. Based on her knowledge of normal distributions and the information received in the referral letter, Deborah saw no need to have Tom take Anxiety Scale A. She decided to use z scores to determine whether Gina or Tom was a better candidate for the group vacancy. To simplify her decision, Deborah constructed Table 4.5.

Deborah then computed the z score for both potential group members, which allowed her to compute their percentile rank.

$$z \text{ score (Gina)} = \frac{\text{Raw score} - \text{mean}}{\text{Standard deviation}}$$

Substituting values for letters, we get:

$$z = \frac{78 - 70 = 8}{10} = .80$$

.80 (corresponds to area of 28.81; see Table 4.3)

Area between raw score and mean = 28.81 +

Area left of the mean = 50.00

= 78.81

= 79th percentile (Scale A)

$$z \text{ score (Tom)} = \frac{\text{Raw score} - \text{mean}}{\text{Standard deviation}}$$

Substituting values for letters, we get:

$$z = \frac{66 - 50 = 16}{12} = 1.33$$

1.33 (corresponds to area of 40.82 in Table 4.3)

Area between raw score and mean = 40.82 +

Area left of the mean = 50.00

= 90.82

= 91st percentile (Scale B)

TABLE 4.5 Comparative Data: Two Indices and Clients' Scores

Data	Anxiety Scale A (Gina)	Anxiety Scale B (Tom)
Raw score	78	66
Mean	70	50
Standard deviation	10	12

Based on her comparative analysis using *z* scores, Deborah chose Tom for the group. His relatively higher level of anxiety (based on his measuring instrument) made him more appropriate for the group than Gina, whom she assigned to individual counseling. Deborah saw no need to relax the group's admittance criteria, which required a score of 80 (84th percentile), in order to admit Gina (79th percentile).

Figures 4.10 and 4.11 illustrate the comparison that Deborah was able to make using *z* scores. Note that the score of 80 (cutoff point on Scale A) is comparable to a score of 62 on Scale B, because both fall at the point $z = +1$ (the 84th percentile). Tom's score was above this point (Figure 4.11) and Gina's (Figure 4.10) was below it.

DERIVING RAW SCORES FROM PERCENTILES

While the most common use of *z* scores is to gain a better perspective on the meaning of a raw score by determining its percentile, there are occasions when social work practitioners and researchers use them to derive a raw score from a percentile as well. This entails reversing the steps. For example, suppose a social worker, Lauren, wishes to form a treatment group of college students with high anxiety levels using the results of testing with Scale B above (mean = 50; standard deviation = 12). However, she wants to include only those who are very high in anxiety, which she operationalizes as being in the top 10 percent of all students measured by Scale B. She will need to know who to admit or not admit to her group. Lauren can use the *z* score formula to find what she is seeking—the cutoff point (the raw score) that would best coincide with the 90th percentile. Only students who scored at or above that raw score would be admitted to her group.

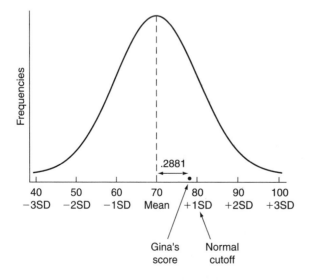

FIGURE 4.10   Distribution of Scores on Anxiety Scale A (Mean = 70; Standard Deviation = 10)

.4082

| 14 | 26 | 38 | 50 | 62 66 | 74 | 86 |
| −3SD | −2SD | −1SD | Mean | +1SD | +2SD | +3SD |

Comparable cutoff

Tom's score

**FIGURE 4.11   Distribution of Scores on Anxiety
Scale B (Mean = 50; Standard Deviation = 12)**

Lauren would begin by subtracting the percentile of the mean (50.00) from 90.00 to determine the area of a normal curve that would fall between the 90th percentile and the mean. It is 40.00. Then she would go to the body of a table such as Table 4.3 to find the area that is closest to 40.00. Note that 40.00 falls between two numbers in the table, 39.97 and 40.15. It is closer to 39.97, which corresponds to a z score of 1.28, so the raw score that Lauren would be seeking had a corresponding z score of about 1.28. Now the z score formula could be used, but this time Lauren would be solving the algebraic equation for the raw score (x) since she already knows the other three parts of the equation, the z score (1.28), the mean (50), and the standard deviation for Scale B (12). The equation would look like this:

$$\frac{1.28 \ (z \text{ score}) = x \text{ (raw score sought)} - 50.00 \text{ (mean)}}{12 \text{ (standard deviation)}}$$

Solving for x algebraically, Lauren would remove the denominator on the right-hand side of the equation (12) by multiplying the z score on the left-hand side by it ($1.28 \times 12 = 15.36$). Now the equation would read:

$$15.36 = x - 50$$
$$x = 50.00 + 15.36$$
$$= 65.36$$

Because the z score was positive (and the percentile was greater than 50.00), Lauren would expect to get a raw score larger than 50.00, which she did (65.36). To play it safe, she would probably round up in this instance, using a raw score of 66 or higher as her cutoff point. Only college students with an anxiety score of 66 or higher would be admitted to her treatment group.

CONCLUDING THOUGHTS

Chapter 4 focused on normal distributions. We described what they are and some ways that they are useful for the social worker.

When the values of an interval- or ratio-level variable form a normal distribution, it is possible to determine where a given value (raw score) falls relative to other values. Using a simple formula, we first convert the raw score into its z score. Then, using a table of areas of the normal curve, we can learn the score's percentile rank. The percentile rank tells us approximately what percentage of scores falls above or below the raw score.

This procedure is especially useful to the social worker practitioner for interpreting the results of standardized testing, a commonly used diagnostic tool in many medical and psychiatric settings. Even if all we know about a standardized test are its mean and standard deviation and the fact that it is believed to provide a valid and reliable measurement of an interval- or ratio-level variable, it is possible to take a client's test score and put it into meaningful perspective. Or, we can reverse the procedure and find the cutoff score (the raw score) that corresponds to any percentile that we wish to select. By using z scores, we can even compare two scores drawn from two different data sets with different means and/or different standard deviations.

This does not conclude our discussion of normal distributions. We will examine other ways in which they are used for analysis of data in Chapter 5 and Chapter 6.

STUDY QUESTIONS

1. How does a positively skewed distribution differ in appearance from a negatively skewed one? Provide examples of social work variables that tend to be positively skewed or negatively skewed.
2. Discuss the characteristics of a normal, or bell-shaped, curve.
3. In a frequency polygon for the variable *number of times married* within the general population, is the distribution likely to be normal, positively skewed, or negatively skewed? Explain.
4. In a positively skewed distribution, where is the median relative to the mean?
5. With a variable that is normally distributed, approximately what percentage of all scores falls within one standard deviation of the mean?
6. What is the z score for a score of 79 when the mean score of all persons who complete a depression scale is 89 and the standard deviation is 5? Is a person with a score of 79 more or less depressed than most other people who complete the scale?
7. In a normal distribution, how frequently would a score occur that is more than 3 standard deviations above or below the mean?
8. On an IQ test with a mean of 100 and a standard deviation of 16, at approximately what percentile will an IQ of 104 fall?

9. Which z score corresponds to a higher value within a distribution of values, -1.04 or 1.00? Explain.

10. If an individual falls at the 16th percentile for weight and the 48th percentile for height, would that individual be considered underweight or overweight? Explain.

11. Discuss several ways in which a social worker can use z scores in social work practice.

12. Assume that a distribution has a mean of 12, a median of 14, and a mode of 13. Should a distribution with these central tendencies be considered normally distributed? Why?

13. Use Table 4.3 to find the following:

    a. The area of the normal curve above a z score of 1.71.

    b. The area of the normal curve between the mean and a z score of -1.34.

    c. The z score that marks the lower limit of the 38 percent of the curve immediately below the mean.

    d. The z scores that mark the upper and lower limits of the middle 42 percent of the normal curve.

14. Explain how to find the raw score that corresponds to the 75th percentile using the formula for the z score.

5

Introduction to Hypothesis Testing

The previous four chapters presented ways to organize, display, and summarize the distribution of the values of a variable. What we have discussed so far is what is often called data reduction. Sometimes it is the only type of analysis that we need—our only intention is to accurately describe the distribution of the values of a variable within a population or sample. This would likely be the case in a research study that is primarily descriptive. But, more often than not, we want to learn more from research data. For example, we may want to determine if two variables that appear to be related within our research sample are truly related within the population from which the sample was drawn. This requires different methods of data analyses—the topic of this and the chapters that follow.

As noted in Chapter 1, the issue of how safe we might be in generalizing findings from a sample to the population from which it was drawn brings us to the concept of inference. Inference requires us to assess the degree of confidence we have when we say that the relationship between two variables that we observed within a research sample is a real one that probably also exists among the cases within the entire population from which the sample was drawn.

ALTERNATIVE EXPLANATIONS

Just because the distribution of variables within a sample of cases drawn from a population makes them appear to be related, we cannot be 100 percent certain that they really are related anywhere but within the sample. In order to make inferences about the relationship between the same two variables within the population from which the sample was drawn, we have to be reasonably confident that what we found to exist within the sample cannot be attributed to alternative explanations, that is, other reasons that might account for the relationship between the two variables.

Many alternative explanations can be attributed to potential problems that our study's research design failed to control. Two likely suspects are (1) rival hypotheses and (2) design bias.

Because rival hypotheses and design bias are both related to problems of research design, they are best addressed before data are collected. Social work research methods texts generally devote considerable space to discussing strategies designed to minimize their existence. Once data are collected, it may be possible to conduct statistical analyses to estimate the amount of effect that they had, or to statistically "control" them in some way. But this is not nearly as desirable as a proactive approach that uses methods to eliminate or at least reduce their effects before data are collected.

Rival Hypotheses

Rival hypotheses are one theoretical explanation for why a relationship between the independent and dependent variables might occur in a research sample, even though the variables are really unrelated. Rival hypotheses really refer to "other variables." They are a recognition of the fact that some other variable(s), unknown to us, may have caused the independent and dependent variables to be related in our sample or made them appear to be more strongly related in the sample than they really are in the population.

In a research hypothesis, we often predict that the independent variable will be found to have produced or at least influenced the values of the dependent variable. But, if in our literature review, we did not identify one or more other variables that, either individually or in concert, help produce the variations within the dependent variable, we could be led to a false conclusion about the true relationship between the independent and dependent variables. Some other variable, for example, may have caused both the independent and dependent variables to co-vary, or it may have produced the relationship between the independent and dependent variables in some other, more complicated way.

Design Bias

A concept that is closely related to rival hypotheses is the concept of *design bias*. It encompasses a wide range of design problems that also can produce an erroneous impression about relationships between variables found within a sample. Two of the most common and troublesome forms of design bias are (1) measurement bias and (2) sampling bias.

Measurement Bias. *Measurement bias* is a consistent, deliberate, or unintentional distortion in the measurement of variables. It can produce measurements that, while perhaps reliable, are not valid. Biased measurement can negatively affect the quality of data we collect and thus can lead to erroneous conclusions when we subsequently interpret them.

There are many ways in which measurement bias can creep into a research study. For example, it might result from the fact that data were collected at an atypical time or that the research study was influenced by some outside event, or to the conscious or unconscious tendency of the person collecting the data to get a less-than-true perception of what was occurring.

If, for whatever reason(s), the measurement of variables is biased, two variables can appear to be related when, in fact, they are not. Like rival hypotheses, measurement bias is best eliminated, or at least minimized, by using sound measurement practices incorporated into a good research design.

Sampling Bias. The second form of design bias, *sampling bias,* refers to the systematic distortion of a research sample. It prevents the sample from being representative of its population in one or more important respects. It can result from such factors as an inappropriate sampling method or the time and place when and where the sample was drawn. A biased sample is characterized by either overrepresentation or underrepresentation of certain values of variables relative to the population from which it was drawn. Simply stated, the sample is not typical of the population in some important ways.

How can we be reasonably certain that sampling bias is not the real explanation for a relationship between variables that occurs within a research sample? Selecting the cases in a sample at random (use of a simple random sample) helps eliminate the potential for sampling bias. Other specific sampling methods that rely on randomization (e.g., cluster sampling, stratified sampling) also help ensure that every case within a population has an equal likelihood of being selected as part of the research sample. We also can pay special attention to how, when, and where a sample is selected.

A true experimental design provides good control of a special kind of sampling bias through random assignment of cases to experimental and control groups. In an experiment, the researcher often hopes to demonstrate that the presence of the independent variable in the experimental group produced a different measurement of the dependent variable than that found in the control group. If sampling bias produces groups that are not comparable to begin with, any such conclusions drawn from the data may be erroneous. But random assignment to experimental and control groups relies on the laws of probability (discussed later in this chapter) to equalize the groups, making them comparable to each other in relation to a wide variety of variables, even some that a literature review failed to identify as important. Other methods (e.g., matching) also are helpful when two or more samples are used. They also increase the likelihood that the samples (experimental and control groups) will be comparable in relation to certain key variables.

No matter what sampling method is used, it is sometimes possible to analyze data in a way that determines whether sampling bias is present. At the point that data have been collected, however, it may be too late to eliminate the negative effects of sampling bias on the quality of a study's findings. Then, all the researcher can do is report the presence of sampling bias (as a possible limitation) within the research report.

Sampling Error

Even if rival hypotheses and design bias can both be successfully dismissed as alternative explanations for an apparent relationship between variables within a sample, there is still another possible alternative explanation—sampling error. The term *chance* is sometimes used to describe this phenomenon. *Chance* and *sampling error* mean the same thing, but we prefer to use the latter term because we think it is more easily understood. *Sampling error* can be defined as the natural tendency of any sample, especially a small one, to differ from its population. Thus, a sample may not be really representative of the population from which it was drawn. It follows then that any relationship between variables within the sample may be just a fluke, a result of sampling error, and the variables may really not be related at all. As we shall see, sampling error is likely to be relatively large in small samples and smaller in larger samples. Chapter 6 will discuss exactly how sampling error works and how the extent of its effect on the representativeness of a sample can be estimated.

We can never totally rule out sampling error as the explanation for an apparent relationship between variables. The only way we could guarantee that sampling error would not exist at all would be to study an entire population. But then, the concept of inference would be irrelevant. To whom would we be able to generalize our findings?

Sampling error also is commonly referred to as the *null hypothesis.* The null hypothesis says, in effect:

> The variables are really unrelated. The relationship between them within the research sample is just a fluke. It occurred because of sampling error, the natural tendency of samples to differ from their populations. The sample must have been very atypical. If the entire population had been studied, no relationship between the variables would have been found.

Sampling error is the third alternative explanation to a true relationship between variables. A researcher must convince the skeptical consumer of a research report that sampling error probably did not produce a relationship between variables within a research sample in order to be able to claim that the relationship is probably a real one that exists within the population. This is accomplished by providing mathematical proof that sampling error was highly unlikely to have produced it.

Solid research designs cannot prevent sampling error from occurring whenever samples are used. However, it is possible to assess the likelihood that sampling error could have produced any relationship between variables that existed within a sample. We can do this by using various types of inferential statistical analyses. They rely heavily on the laws of probability.

PROBABILITY

Probability theory is based on the mathematical likelihood of an event occurring. It relies on certain laws. One basic law of probability, for example, states that the likelihood of any one event occurring can range only from 0 (never) to 1.0 (absolute certainty).

One assumption is central to all probability theory. It is that while certain patterns of events can be seen to exist in many repeated observations over time, individual or short-term observations tend to differ somewhat from these overall long-term patterns. If we flip a fair coin in the air, for example, it has a 50 percent (.50, or 1 out of 2) probability of landing on heads. It also has a 50 percent probability of landing on tails. But these are only theoretical probabilities. They are the percent of heads (or tails) that would occur in an infinite number of flips of the coin, when the law of averages has had an opportunity to take effect. It is not an accurate prediction of what might occur if we flip a coin only a small number of times. The law of averages suggests that in the long run, things will balance out and events will unfold as they theoretically should.

In reality, we know that if we flip a coin only 10 times, we will probably get a different result from the one that is theoretically expected to occur—that is, five heads. We would not be surprised if we obtained four, six, or even three or seven heads. We would simply blame it on sampling error and assume that in the long run, if we repeated the coin tossing many more times, the percent of heads would eventually approximate 50 percent.

What if the 10 coin flips produced eight or nine heads? At this point, we might suspect that something was wrong. The results seem to be so unlikely that they "defy the laws of probability." How could these results have occurred? Could the coin be defective? Could the way in which the coin was tossed have influenced the results? What is going on here? Another way of stating these questions might be, "Is something else (some other phenomenon besides sampling error, perhaps some other variable) influencing the results (the number of heads)?"

The laws of probability can be applied in many areas of life. They have been developed to determine the theoretical likelihood of an event's occurrence. Some of the laws are simple; others are more complicated. They tell us, for example, that the probability that a student will guess correctly on a multiple-choice question with four alternative answers is 25 percent (.25, or 1 out of 4). That is pretty obvious. One law, the multiplication law, states that the likelihood of guessing correctly on two consecutive questions on a multiple-choice exam with four possible responses is $.25 \times .25$ or 6.25 percent (.0625, or 1 out of 16). That may seem less plausible. Still another law, the addition law, states that the mathematical probability of getting only one answer correct is 37.5 percent (.375, or 6 out of 16) and of getting one or both correct is 43.75 percent (.4375 or, 7 out of 16).

We can use these various laws of probability to determine what should happen in various situations, that is, what would happen in the long run (with an infinite number of events). Of course, in the short run strange aberrations can and do occur. For example, we could flip a coin 10 times and get all 10 heads. Or on a single examination, a student might guess on four questions and get all four or none of the four correct.

How do these phenomena relate to our study of inference? Unusual, short-run situations occur in coin tossing, guessing test answers, and an almost infinite number of other life situations, including the drawing of research samples. In all of them, unlikely (but not impossible) events sometimes occur, even though most of the time (in the long run) it would not happen that way.

Variables may appear to be related within a research sample. Often, this can be attributable to the same phenomenon that produces unlikely results in tossing several coins or guessing test answers—sampling error. However, sometimes sampling error is an inadequate explanation for what happens. By using statistical analyses, we can determine the mathematical probability that sampling error might have been responsible for what we observed.

Probability also helps us understand data analyses in another, related way. The percentage of all cases with a given measurement of a variable within a population also can be thought of as a probability. If 20 percent of cases all have the same value—if, for example, all subjects are 23 years old—there is a 20 percent probability that a case drawn at random from that distribution will have the value of 23—that is, the subject will be 23 years old.

If the variable is at least at the interval level of measurement, the frequency distribution of the variable could be portrayed using a frequency polygon. If 10 percent of cases in the population have the lowest value of the variable found within the distribution, then the area to the far left of the polygon (the bottom 10 percent of it) would represent those cases. The probability of randomly selecting a case from the distribution with this lowest value would be 10 percent. If another 10 percent of cases in the population have the highest measurement value of the variable found within the distribution, then the area to the far right of the polygon (the top 10 percent of it) would represent those cases. The probability of randomly selecting a case from the population with this highest value likewise would be 10 percent. And the probability of randomly selecting a case in the range containing all values would be 100 percent.

For example, suppose we collect data on the ages of adolescents who are participating in an anger management program. The 14 adolescents in the program consist of two 12-year-olds, three 13-year-olds, four 14-year-olds, three 15-year-olds, and two 16-year-olds. In this instance, the ages of these adolescents is normally distributed; the mean, mode, and median age are all 14.

If we were to randomly draw one case from the group of adolescents, there would be a 100 percent probability of selecting a client who is between the ages of 12 and 16. That is because all adolescents are represented in the distribution (100 percent of a frequency polygon that would represent it). We can also specify the probability of selecting a case from the distribution within a certain age range.

What if we wanted to know the probability of randomly selecting a 13- or a 14-year-old? The probability would be 21.4 percent (3 chances out of 14) for picking a 13-year-old and 28.6 percent (4 chances out of 14) for choosing a 14-year-old—a total of 50 percent (7 chances out of 14) for randomly selecting either a 13- or a 14-year-old. In other words, we would have a 50 percent probability of randomly selecting a 13- or 14-year-old from our sample.

Like the areas of a normal curve between standard deviation units, intervals encompassing specified values would correspond to areas of a frequency polygon. Narrow intervals (encompassing fewer cases) would correspond to smaller areas of the frequency polygon and would reflect a lower probability of randomly selecting a case with a value within the specified range. Wider intervals (encompassing more cases) would correspond to larger areas and would reflect a higher probability of randomly selecting a case with a value within the specified range.

Probability theory is an integral component of inferential statistical analyses. No matter which inferential statistical test we choose, probability plays a role. It is used to determine the probability that sampling error may have produced an apparent relationship between variables within a sample. In this way it helps us know how safe it is to generalize, that is, to assume that a relationship between variables found within a sample also exists within the sample's population.

REFUTING SAMPLING ERROR

There are two general methods for demonstrating that an apparent relationship between variables within a sample was not the result of sampling error. They are (1) replication and (2) statistical analyses.

Replication

Suppose that we work in an extremely large state hospital system that employs 1000 medical social workers. We observe among the 18 medical social workers in our particular unit that female workers have higher levels of job satisfaction than male workers. Is our observation conclusive evidence of a relationship between the two variables (i.e., gender, job satisfaction) among all the other medical social workers in the system? Certainly not.

But how can we demonstrate that the apparent relationship between the two variables does not exist only within our small nonrandom sample? After all, we have no reason to believe that the 18 social workers in our unit (what might be regarded as no more than an "availability" or "convenience" sample) are typical of the other medical social workers elsewhere in the system.

In an ideal world with unlimited research resources, we could use replication to determine if the relationship is more than just a fluke. *Replication* entails repeating a research study one or more times using the same methods but different research samples to see if the same findings are produced. To use replication, we could simply use another group (sample) of medical social workers (the staff of another unit) and see if the same relationship between job satisfaction and gender is present.

But even if it were, that might not be enough evidence to dismiss sampling error as the reason for the apparent relationship. Perhaps we could draw a sample of 18 social workers 100 times and each time determine if the same relationship exists. Then if, for example, the relationship occurred at least 95 times out of 100, we might conclude that the relationship probably is a real one.

Of course, in the real world, repeated replication is impractical. Obtaining resources and access to data even once is often difficult, so how could we ever be able to conduct our research study 100 times? Some replication occurs in social work research, however. Replication usually is used to see if a relationship between variables that was identified in a previous research study will be found to still exist at a different time or with a different sample of research participants. It is used far less to demonstrate initial support for the existence of a relationship between variables.

While the cost of repeated replication makes it impractical, other methods for determining whether an apparent relationship exists between variables employ some of the principles of replication. Later in this chapter we shall discuss how the concept of "95 times out of 100" is applied in making decisions while using statistical analyses of data collected in a single research study.

Statistical Analyses

There is another, less expensive way, to gain logical support for the inference that there is a true relationship between job satisfaction and gender—statistical analyses of data drawn from a single study. Suppose we had made an educated guess (prediction) that we would find a relationship between job satisfaction and gender among our sample of 18 medical social workers.

Suppose that we had arrived at this prediction through the process of synthesizing existing qualitative and quantitative knowledge on gender differences and job satisfaction among medical social workers. We used our own observations and experiences in working with medical social workers as well as the writings of scholars in the profession and many other sources, such as unpublished documents and interviews with persons who "ought to know." We even learned enough about the characteristics of medical social workers as a group (their demographic characteristics) to conclude that the 18 social workers in our convenience sample do not appear to be unusual in any obvious or important way. Based on what we learned, we hypothesized the following:

> Female medical social workers will have higher levels of job satisfaction than male medical social workers.

The fact that the two variables appeared to be related within our sample, exactly as we predicted they would be, would not be enough evidence to claim support for our prediction. It would help, but we would need to do more. First we would have to rule out the alternative explanations for an apparent relationship (rival hypotheses and design bias). Even if we were satisfied that they did not produce the apparent relationship between job satisfaction and gender that existed in our sample, the relationship still might have been produced by sampling error (the null hypothesis).

Our small sample of 18 medical social workers may have differed from the population of all medical social workers within the system in some important ways just because of the phenomenon of sampling error. We would have to demonstrate that the data we examined are so impressive, so clearly and strongly in support of our research hypothesis, that the apparent relationship is unlikely to have been the work of sampling error, that it is most likely a real relationship that exists within the system's population of medical social workers.

RESEARCH HYPOTHESES

There are many different definitions of hypotheses, but they all suggest the same idea: A hypothesis is a tentative answer to a research question. In its simplest form, it is a statement of a proposed relationship between or among variables.

As suggested in the previous example, hypotheses are generated in many different ways. They may evolve as the product of someone else's research study. This occurs most frequently when a qualitative research study inductively identifies and labels variables and then suggests possible relationships between them for subsequent studies to examine.

Hypotheses may also evolve from our own observations and reviews of the professional literature. Among other things, we use the literature to narrow or refine a general research question. Frequently, as the evidence in the literature starts to accumulate, we think we may have an answer to that question. We then try to express our tentative impressions, or our conclusions, in the form of a hypothesis.

A *research hypothesis,* also called a substantive hypothesis or experimental hypothesis, is a statement that expresses what we believe to be the relationship between or among variables. A research hypothesis can take on three different forms:

1. It can state that variables are related and predict the direction of their relationship (a directional, or one-tailed, research hypothesis).
2. It can state that variables are related but not predict the direction of their relationship (a nondirectional, or two-tailed, research hypothesis).
3. It can state that two variables are unrelated (a null research hypothesis).

This third (null) form of a research hypothesis should not be confused with the null hypothesis. It is unfortunate that these terms are so similar. But as we will explain in more detail on page 85, the null hypothesis is the belief that sampling error caused unrelated variables to appear to be related in a research sample.

The One-Tailed Research Hypothesis

A *one-tailed research hypothesis* states that there is a specific relationship between variables. It also predicts which values of one variable are to be found with, or are associated with, which values of another variable. Continuing with our previous example, a one-tailed research hypothesis might be as follows:

One-Tailed Research Hypothesis:

Female medical social workers will have higher levels of job satisfaction than male medical social workers.

It is important to note that a one-tailed research hypothesis predicts the direction of a relationship between variables, which is why it is sometimes called a directional hypothesis.

The Two-Tailed Research Hypothesis

A *two-tailed research hypothesis* (also referred to as a nondirectional hypothesis) states only that there is a relationship between variables. Unlike the one-tailed research hypothesis, it does not predict which values of one variable will be associated with which values of another variable. The following is a two-tailed research hypothesis for our example:

Two-Tailed Research Hypothesis:

Gender is related to job satisfaction levels.

This two-tailed research hypothesis does not predict whether males or females will be found to have higher levels of job satisfaction, as the one-tailed research hypothesis did.

The Null Research Hypothesis

The third form of research hypotheses states the belief that that there is no relationship between variables. In our example it would be this:

The Null Research Hypothesis:

There is no relationship between gender and job satisfaction.

It is important to note that a null research hypothesis is, in a sense, the opposite of either a one-tailed or a two-tailed research hypothesis. Null research hypotheses are rare. They are used to try to dispel false beliefs when we wish to gain support for our own belief that two variables that are generally believed to be related really are unrelated. In the past, for example, we sought to disprove the stereotype that people of one nationality are intellectually superior to people of another nationality. We did so by finding statistical support for the null research hypothesis that nationality and intelligence are not related. Similarly, we sought to demonstrate that people from certain backgrounds are no more likely than others to commit certain crimes. We set out to find support for the null research hypothesis that there is no relationship between those backgrounds and crime rates.

TESTING THE NULL HYPOTHESIS

We never refer to a one-tailed or two-tailed research hypothesis as proven or not proven; we state only that we found support for it or that we did not. This conclusion is based on whether, using our knowledge of research design and statistical analyses, we feel that all other explanations for an apparent relationship between variables (besides a true one) can be discounted.

One-tailed and two-tailed research hypothesis testing is a process of elimination. To gain support for a one-tailed or two-tailed research hypothesis that two variables are related, we must first be reasonably certain that nothing else caused the variables to be related within our sample.

As suggested earlier, we usually try to eliminate rival hypotheses and design bias as possible explanations by utilizing good research designs. But that still leaves us with sampling error, the null hypothesis. Before we can claim support for a one-tailed or two-tailed research hypothesis, we also have to demonstrate, using statistical analyses, that the null hypothesis is a highly unlikely explanation for a relationship between the two variables within the research sample. If we can do this, we would be reasonably safe in rejecting the null hypothesis. Only then would we be able to claim support for our one-tailed or two-tailed research hypothesis since we now would be left with only one possible explanation—a true relationship probably exists between the two variables within the population from which the sample was drawn.

What if we wanted to demonstrate support for a null research hypothesis of no relationship between variables? Let us assume that rival hypotheses and design bias have been adequately controlled for. There might still appear to be a weak relationship between the two variables in the sample. Does that mean the null research hypothesis was incorrect and that the variables really are related in the population from which the sample was drawn?

Not necessarily. We could still gain support for the null research hypothesis through statistical analyses. We could attempt to demonstrate that the relationship between the two variables in the sample is really so small or weak that it is fairly likely to have been produced by sampling error. In other words, we would hope to show that there is not strong enough evidence to reject sampling error (the null hypothesis) as the explanation for the apparent relationship between the two variables. If we could do this, we would then have demonstrated support for our null research hypothesis.

In the previous example, after a thorough literature review, we decided that we had justification for stating the following one-tailed research hypothesis:

One-Tailed Research Hypothesis:

Female medical social workers will have higher levels of job satisfaction than male medical social workers.

In performing a statistical analysis, the null hypothesis is actually tested—that is, there is no real relationship between or among the variables, and what appears to be one is really the work of sampling error. Thus, it is helpful to restate our one-tailed research hypothesis in its null form:

Null Hypothesis:

There is no relationship between the gender of medical social workers and their levels of job satisfaction.

If we were really seeking support for the one-tailed research hypothesis, we might draw a simple random sample (rather than a convenience sample) of 18 social workers from all 1,000 employees, thus reducing the likelihood of sampling bias. We also probably would not just trust our impressions of the job satisfaction levels of the 18 medical social workers in our sample. In addition to noting each social worker's gender, we would administer a standardized measuring instrument to him or her that provides a reliable and valid measurement of their job satisfaction (the dependent variable). As we analyzed the data, the scores of males and females might seem to provide a reason to reject (or not to reject) the null hypothesis, particularly since the number of social workers is small, and it would be easy to identify any differences in the distribution of job satisfaction scores between the two genders. If, for example, the female group and the male group each had a mean job satisfaction level of 60, we would not reject the null hypothesis since, even within the sample, there is no difference between the mean job satisfaction levels for males and females.

On the other hand, if the females were found to have a mean job satisfaction level of 90 and the males had a mean job satisfaction level of 10, we would feel that we had pretty strong support for the rejection of the null hypothesis. Such a clear pattern of a relationship between variables is rare. If it exists, we probably already know about it. But what if (as often occurs) there is a difference in the mean job satisfaction levels of the two groups, but it was not so dramatic? What if the mean job satisfaction level was, say, 70 for females and 50 for males? How likely is it that our observed relationship is a real one that represents a relationship between the two variables within the larger population?

Could we infer, based on these central tendency data alone, that as a group, female medical social workers (including those not in our sample) possess a higher mean level of job satisfaction than males? Such a conclusion would seem a little premature, even if we had carefully designed and implemented the research study so that we were fairly certain that rival hypotheses and design bias could be ruled out as alternative explanations for the apparent relationship. But what about sampling error? Any relationship between the two variables found in our small sample could still be the work of sampling error (the null hypothesis). After all, a sample of 18 research participants is relatively small.

Inferential statistical analyses could tell us the likelihood that sampling error might have produced the difference in the mean job satisfaction levels between the female and male social workers. It could determine the mathematical probability that a relationship between the independent and dependent variables within our sample data could have occurred as a result of sampling error. Thus, it can help us determine if an apparent relationship between variables within our sample data is a real one— that is, one that exists in the population from which our sample was drawn.

In attempting to gain support for a research hypothesis, we can never totally eliminate sampling error (the null hypothesis) as the explanation of an apparent relationship between variables. After all, even if females did have a mean job satisfaction level of 90 and males had a mean job satisfaction level of 10 in our sample, we theoretically could have drawn a highly unusual sample of 18 in which females might differ by that much from males, even if the two variables really are unrelated within the population from which our sample was drawn. While we never can be 100 percent certain that what we found was not the work of sampling error, we generally are convinced if we can be reasonably certain that what we observed was not a fluke occurrence caused by sampling error.

We do not want to report a relationship between variables that appears to be real when it is not. At the same time, we do not want to be so rigid or so unreasonable that we will not claim support for a relationship between variables just because there is a very remote possibility that sampling error may have produced it. If we did that, few, if any, research findings would ever see the light of day. Thus, we need guidelines to help us to know when to reject the null hypothesis and conclude that there is enough statistical evidence that variables really are related, and when not to reject it. Fortunately, they are available. We will discuss them later in this chapter.

STATISTICAL SIGNIFICANCE

Continuing with our example, it would be nice if it had been possible to repeat the research study with 100 different samples of 18 medical social workers within the hospital system (replication). We could then have seen if females showed somewhat higher levels of job satisfaction than males in most of the samples (say, in at least 95 percent of them). Usually, however, we get only one shot at doing a research study. Within a single research study and with only one research sample, we need some evidence that a relationship between variables is a real one. Statistical analyses can provide it.

At what point can we be sufficiently certain that the relationship between variables we find in our sample cannot simply be dismissed as the work of sampling error? When using statistics, we rely on mathematics, the laws of probability, common sense, and convention. We also use two very important and related concepts: *p*-values and rejection levels.

p-Values

All statistical tests of inference that we will discuss later in this book (and many more that we will not be discussing) have something in common. They produce a *p*-value. A *p-value* is the mathematical probability that a relationship between variables found within a sample may have been produced by sampling error. (It is important to note that the *p*-value tells us nothing about the likelihood that rival hypotheses or design bias might have produced it.) In theory, a *p*-value can range from 0.00 (would never occur because of sampling error) to 1.00 (definitely the work of sampling error). All *p*-values fall somewhere in between these two theoretical extremes, just like the mathematical probability of any event occurring.

In a sense, a *p*-value is the bottom line in a statistical analysis. (In fact, it often is found on the last line in the printout that is the product of computerized data analyses.) Different statistical analyses use different formulas, but the *p*-value that each produces is interpreted exactly the same way. Thus, it is possible to know the exact mathematical probability that sampling error produced a relationship between variables within a sample (the *p*-value) even if we do not fully understand the statistical analysis that produced the *p*-value. However, this can be dangerous. Unless we have a good understanding of the way in which a *p*-value was produced (and that it was produced using the appropriate statistical analysis), it is possible to misread the importance of it.

Rejection Levels

As noted earlier, the decision to reject the null hypothesis does not totally rule out sampling error as the explanation of an apparent relationship between variables. (It also does not address the possibility that some other variable or variables or unidentified research design problems may have caused the variables to be related.) It simply means that we have been able to demonstrate that there is a small likelihood that sampling error caused the relationship between the variables in a sample.

How small is small? Over the years, we have settled on the 95 percent certainty level as the point at which we are sufficiently confident to be able to reject the null hypothesis. Expressed another way, we feel safe in rejecting the null hypothesis if a statistical analysis demonstrates that there is less than a 5 percent probability that sampling error may have produced an apparent relationship between the variables (the *p*-value produced by a statistical analysis is less than .05). That much risk of mistakenly concluding that sampling error did not cause an apparent relationship between variables (when it really did) is considered acceptable in most research situations. This is referred to as the *.05 rejection level.* Rejection levels also are called *alpha levels,* or *significance levels.*

There is nothing sacred about the .05 rejection level. While it is the most widely used cutoff point for rejecting null hypotheses, other rejection levels also can be used. The decision to use rejection levels other than .05 is based on our assessment of the possible consequences of either mistakenly rejecting the null hypothesis or failing to reject it. A more demanding proof of a relationship between variables, such as a .01 rejection level, might be used when we wish to allow only a very small possibility that we might erroneously reject the null hypothesis and conclude that a relationship exists between variables. These more stringent rejection levels allow for even less likelihood that sampling error is the reason for an apparent relationship between the two variables than does the conventional .05 level. The .01 rejection level means that the probability of erroneously rejecting the null hypothesis is less than 1 out of 100.

In research studies in which the consequences of mistakenly rejecting the null hypothesis might be less problematic than mistakenly concluding that a relationship between variables was probably the work of sampling error (when it was not), we occasionally consider a higher rejection level such as .10 as acceptable. A .10 rejection level allows for twice the possibility of mistakenly concluding that variables are related in the population when they are related in the sample only because of sampling error as does a .05 level. Sometimes a less demanding rejection level, such as a .10, is used as evidence of a relationship between variables if the research design includes at least one replication. While achieving one .10 rejection level may be viewed as inconclusive support for a relationship between variables, achieving it two or more times in succession may lead to the conclusion that the null hypothesis can be rejected. Why? Because achieving two or more successive .10 levels starts to defy the laws of probability.

While some flexibility is allowed in selecting the threshold at which sampling error is reasonably eliminated as the explanation for an apparent relationship between variables, the choice of a rejection level should not be viewed as casual. Convention states that the .05 rejection level should be used unless we develop and state a compelling rationale for the use of another rejection level. The selection of a rejection level must always be made before data are collected. It would be unethical to change the level afterward. The decision could be construed as an effort to manipulate the study's findings, generally to gain support for the study's one-tailed or two-tailed research hypothesis.

When reporting the findings of a statistical analysis of data, the rejection level that was used as a cutoff to reject the null hypothesis is always reported. Usually, this is done using wording like: "The mean annual salary for females was $29,000, and for males it was $31,000. This difference is statistically significant at the .05 level." This can also be reported as "$p < .05$." The p is in lowercase italics and stands for probability. It usually is followed by a less than sign ($<$); however, if statistical significance is not achieved (the probability that sampling error might have produced the salary differences was, for example, .06 or .07), the greater than sign ($>$) can be substituted in front of the rejection level that was used: "$p > .05$".

ERRORS IN DRAWING CONCLUSIONS ABOUT RELATIONSHIPS

Of course, as we have already indicated, whenever we reject (or do not reject) the null hypothesis, we run the risk of being wrong. The two possible errors that we can make are referred to as Type I and Type II errors.

A Type I error occurs when we reject the null hypothesis and conclude that a relationship between variables in a sample exists in the population from which it was drawn, when in fact it really does not. Conversely, a Type II error occurs when we fail to reject the null hypothesis and conclude that a relationship between variables does not exist in the population from which it was drawn, when in fact it really exists. Neither type of error is inherently better than the other. Either one can mislead and misinform social work practitioners and researchers. Table 5.1 summarizes the difference between Type I and Type II errors.

Type I and Type II errors can result from many causes. Even though the probability of doing so was very low, we may have simply drawn a very nonrepresentative sample, one in which the relationship (or nonrelationship) between variables that we observed in the sample is atypical of the population. Type I and Type II errors also can result from the use of inappropriate analyses of data. If, for example, we incorrectly use a statistical test that requires certain conditions that are not present, an error of one type or the other can occur. If the appropriate statistical test is not used within the conditions for which it was designed, we can either falsely conclude that a true relationship between variables exists (Type I error) or a true relationship may remain unidentified (Type II error). Chapter 7 discusses the factors to be considered in selecting the most appropriate statistical test for any given data set.

We must ultimately decide which error, Type I or Type II, is more acceptable to us, should it occur. This is largely an ethical decision that requires a knowledge of social

TABLE 5.1   Type I and Type II Errors

	Our Decision	
Real World	*Reject Null Hypothesis*	*Do Not Reject Null Hypothesis*
Null hypothesis false	No error	Type II error
Null hypothesis true	Type I error	No error

work practice and the consequences of committing one error over the other. Usually, the consequences of making an error in deciding whether to reject the null hypothesis in social work research are not grave. The possibility of committing either a Type I or a Type II error should not preclude us from taking reasonable risks in interpreting research findings and drawing conclusions and implications from them. This is how we make progress in becoming knowledge-based social work practitioners.

Avoiding Type I Errors

No matter what we ultimately decide about whether to reject the null hypothesis, we can never totally eliminate the possibility of committing an error of one type or the other. Traditionally, researchers have been most fearful of committing a Type I error, that is, concluding that sampling error did not produce a relationship between variables when it actually did produce it. The .05 *p*-value that is most commonly used as the cutoff point in a statistical analysis can be thought of as the probability of committing a Type I error. In one sense, that is the whole business of a statistical analysis—determining the mathematical probability that we will commit a Type I error if we reject the null hypothesis.

How can we at least decrease the likelihood of making a Type I error? We might select a smaller *p*-value than the traditional .05, such as .01 or even .001, so that we can be even more confident (if that level is achieved) that sampling error did not produce the relationship between variables within the research sample. But, that may not be desirable because, while it would result in less likelihood of a Type I error, it would increase the likelihood of committing a Type II error, that is, mistakenly failing to reject the null hypothesis. (Conversely, if we try to avoid committing a Type II error by selecting a larger *p*-value such as .10 or .25 instead of .05, we increase the likelihood of committing a Type I error.)

There are two ways to reduce the possibility of making a Type I error while simultaneously reducing the likelihood of making a Type II error. First, we can use larger sample sizes. As samples get larger, there is less sampling error. (We will discuss this more in the next chapter.) When larger samples are used, the laws of probability take over, and the samples tend to look very similar to their populations—any relationships between variables within the samples are probably real ones that also exist within the population.

We can also decrease the likelihood of making a Type I error and a Type II error at the same time by replicating a research study. If the findings of the second study agree with those of the first study (that is, both suggest that the variables really are related), the relationship is likely to be a real one. A fluke sample may have been selected the first time, but one is unlikely to have been drawn two times in a row.

However, replication and the use of larger samples are not always feasible. In agency-based research, there may not be administrative support for repeating a study a second time. Or, the only sample available may be a small one that cannot be made larger. Both methods also can add considerable cost to a research study. Sometimes they cannot be considered because of funding realities.

While a concern with committing a Type I error has been the primary focus of analysis of research data in the past, Type II errors also can cause problems for researchers and practitioners. We will discuss ways to reduce the probability of their occurrence in Chapter 7.

STATISTICALLY SIGNIFICANT RELATIONSHIPS AND MEANINGFUL FINDINGS

The word *significant* is widely and loosely used in our profession and elsewhere to emphasize the importance of something, such as when we refer to a social worker's significant contribution to the passage of social legislation or the role of a significant other in the decision of a client to return to school. As with many other words that we use daily (e.g., value, relationship), it is best to set aside the everyday meaning of the word in order to understand its specific meaning in the field of statistics.

Statistical significance is the demonstration, through the use of mathematics and the laws of probability, that the relationship between variables in a sample is unlikely to have been produced by sampling error. A relationship that is declared to be statistically significant is one in which the *p*-value (the mathematical probability that sampling error produced the relationship) is less than the selected rejection level—usually, $p < .05$. For us, this is the only relevant meaning of the words *statistically significant* or *significant;* we must be careful to use the terms in this sense, and only in this sense.

The presence of a statistically significant relationship between variables may be dismissed as the result of rival hypotheses and/or design bias (which includes measurement bias and sampling bias). The results of inferential statistics, as suggested earlier, are useful only if the effects of other variables were controlled in some way, if the data that produced them are valid and reliable, and if those data were obtained from a representative sample correctly drawn from a population.

What if the alternative explanations for the existence of a real relationship between variables can be successfully dismissed? In that case, does the presence of a statistically significant relationship demonstrate that sampling error is a very unlikely explanation for the apparent relationship between the two variables? Yes. The relationship probably is real; the variables probably really are related in the population from which the sample was drawn.

But is the relationship between them a strong one? Is it necessarily a surprising one? Is it meaningful, or as some books describe it, substantive—that is, is it of practical value to the social worker? We must be careful to evaluate every statistically significant relationship between variables in the context of the question, "So what?" In social work practice, every statistically significant relationship is not a meaningful finding that cries out for immediate implementation.

Assessing Strength (Effect Size)

All that statistical significance means is the researcher has been able to demonstrate that sampling error is unlikely to have produced a relationship between variables in a research sample. It says nothing about the strength of the relationship between them. For example, suppose we find that there is a statistically significant relationship between type of treatment and treatment success at the .05 rejection level and that the relationship between gender and treatment success is statistically significant at the .01 rejection level. Can we then state that the relationship between gender and treatment success is five times as strong as the relationship between type of treatment and treatment success? No. All we can say is that, with type of treatment and treatment success, we have demonstrated that sampling error would produce the relationship less than 5 percent of the time; with gender and treatment success, we have demonstrated that sampling error would produce the relationship less than 1 percent of the time.

In fact, in an absolute sense, some statistically significant relationships are so weak as to be meaningless. Virtually all variables to some degree, are related to all other variables to a greater or lesser degree. Some types of statistical analyses can and do identify relationships that are so weak (especially when overly large samples are used) that they are worthless in a practical sense, even though the relationship is statistically significant (probably not the work of sampling error).

There are certain types of statistical analyses that (among other things) determine the strength of relationships between variables. Some of them are discussed later in this book. They are what statisticians refer to generically as *measures of association,* and they produce an indicator of the strength of a relationship between variables, usually referred to as the *effect size.* (One example is Pearson's product moment correlation, discussed in Chapter 8.) Their statistical formulas produce a positive or negative number between 0 and 1.0 (a *correlation coefficient*) that can simply be squared to produce the effect size. How is this then interpreted? The squared number is the amount of variation in the dependent variable that can be explained by the independent variable. For example, if .5 is the number produced by the formula, we can square it so that the squared number (.25) is the amount of variation (25 percent) in the dependent variable that can be explained by the independent variable.

One other simple statistical procedure, which actually is called effect size (or simply ES), is especially helpful in clinical experiments in which the effectiveness of an intervention is examined by offering it to research participants in an experimental group but not to those in a control group. It uses a simple formula:

$$ES = \frac{\text{experimental group mean} - \text{control group mean}}{\text{control group's standard deviation}}$$

The formula may look familiar. It is similar to the formula for the z score introduced in Chapter 4. In fact, ES can be interpreted using the table that we used to convert raw scores to z scores and then into percentiles (Table 4.3).

Suppose that a social worker, Kelly, wishes to examine the effectiveness of a new type of assertiveness training. She randomly assigns 30 clients to an experimental group (that receives the treatment) and another 30 to a control group (that does not receive it). After the treatment, all 60 research participants take a standardized assertiveness test. The mean score in the experimental group is 82, and the mean score in the control group is 78, with a control group standard deviation of 4. Using the appropriate test of statistical significance, the difference is found to be statistically significant ($p < .05$). But this still does not tell Kelly much about the strength of the relationship between treatment and assertiveness level. Perhaps the relationship between the independent and dependent variables was real, but relatively weak. How much effect did the intervention really have on assertiveness? Most importantly, the presence of statistical significance does not allow Kelly to compare the treatment's effectiveness with that of other, established methods of assertiveness training. So she computes the ES as:

$$ES = \frac{\text{experimental group mean} - \text{control group mean}}{\text{control groups standard deviation}}$$

$$ES = \frac{82 - 78}{4}$$

$$= \frac{4}{4}$$

The mean assertiveness score in the experimental group was 1.0 standard deviation (the ES) higher than the mean assertiveness score of the control group. Using Table 4.3, we can now put this into perspective. The average (mean) assertiveness score of those people in the experimental group was higher than 84.13 (50.00 + 34.13) percent of those people in the control group. This finding can now be used to help Kelly to understand something about the strength of the association between her variables (presence or absence of treatment and assertiveness scores). She can compute effect sizes for other similar studies of the effectiveness of traditional assertiveness training in her agency or elsewhere and then compare the results with her finding to determine if her treatment was more or less effective than the other treatments. This can be accomplished even if the other studies used another measure of association to compute effect size than the one Kelly used. Thus, like a z score, an effect size is a kind of common denominator that, among its other benefits, helps in the comparison of different data sets. Of course, we must always be careful in comparing research studies that may have used different instruments for measuring variables or research designs that may reflect different levels of rigor. We might still end up comparing apples and oranges.

Is the Relationship Surprising?

Other relationships, while fairly strong as indicated by measures of association, are already so well known, that the "discovery" of them within a research study is of little or no value. How valuable would it be to learn at this time, for example, that among people there is a statistically significant relationship between the presence or absence of prenatal care and infant health, or between alcoholism and spouse abuse? Previous research has adequately demonstrated both of these relationships. We would be surprised (and the finding might be valuable) only if it were found to be otherwise.

Still other relationships between variables that could be found to be statistically significant would not be surprising. They are just logical to assume. For example, the "finding" that students who do not study at all do less well on a statistics exam than students who study at least 10 hours would be pretty much worthless. It is so logical that it would be totally expected.

Complex Interpretations of Statistically Significant Relationships

Attempting to decide whether a statistically significant relationship between variables is a meaningful finding (one that promises to improve the effectiveness of social work intervention) often is a complicated process. It may entail both an examination of effect size and an assessment of how surprising the finding is. It may involve other considerations as well. For example, it may require an administrator to make a judgment about whether she or he can justify the cost of retraining staff to use an intervention that has proven to be more effective than one currently being used in light of service delivery time lost during training or the need for the money elsewhere in the agency. Or it may require a social worker working in the community to assess the political effect of using an intervention that research has demonstrated to be effective but that may antagonize key supporters of the agency.

The existence of a statistically significant relationship between variables can be determined by statistical testing, which is based on the laws of probability. The determination of whether a finding is meaningful or not, however, requires judgment; it entails the use of insight into many different aspects of the social work practice milieu. Researchers now often report indicators of the actual strength of the relationship between variables (effect size) as well as other relevant information (such as the size of the research sample on which a statistical analysis was based). This additional information allows the reader to begin to make a more informed decision about the meaningfulness of a finding of statistical significance.

CONCLUDING THOUGHTS

This chapter examined the underlying logic of statistical testing for relationships between variables. It stressed that research designs are the primary means of eliminating two possible explanations of apparent relationships between variables within a research sample, rival hypotheses, and design bias. Statistical analyses tells us the probability that an apparent relationship between variables may have been produced by sampling error, the natural tendency of a sample to differ from the population from which it was drawn. Statistical testing really tests the null hypothesis and only indirectly tests a one-tailed or two-tailed research hypothesis.

We have emphasized what statistical significance means—that sampling error is unlikely to have produced a relationship between variables found in a research sample. We also emphasized what it does not mean. When we reject the null hypothesis and conclude that the relationship between variables is statistically significant, we run the risk of a Type I error. If we fail to reject the null hypothesis, the relationship may in fact be a real one (a Type II error). In deciding whether to reject the null form of a research hypothesis, we must consider the ethical implications of making an error of one type or the other.

If we correctly reject the null hypothesis and conclude that the two variables probably are related in the population from which a sample was drawn, we still must address the issue of the value of such a finding. Even if we have statistical support for the likelihood of a true relationship between variables (in the form of statistical significance), the relationship may be very weak, well-known, or otherwise meaningless. We examined some ways to begin to evaluate these possibilities. Decisions about the value of a relationship between variables should always be made with reference to their potential to benefit or to harm those served, our clients.

STUDY QUESTIONS

1. Before we can claim a true relationship between variables, what alternative explanations for an apparent relationship must be eliminated?
2. Which one of the alternative explanations does statistical testing examine?
3. What alternative explanations are controlled primarily by the design of a research study?
4. What are some other terms for sampling error that are sometimes used?
5. What is the difference between a Type I and a Type II error? How does reducing the likelihood of committing one affect the likelihood of committing the other when the rejection level is adjusted either up or down from 0.05?
6. What is the null form of a statement (the null hypothesis) for a directional hypothesis about the relationship between the variables *age* and *political party preference?*
7. What is the relationship between the null hypothesis and sampling error in hypothesis testing?
8. Does a statistically significant relationship between variables mean that there is no possibility that the variables are unrelated? Explain.
9. When might we use a rejection level other than the conventional 0.05 to conclude whether statistical support exists for a research hypothesis? Provide examples from potential social work research studies.
10. Which rejection level, 0.01 or 0.10, suggests a greater likelihood of a true relationship between variables? Explain.
11. Discuss the advantages and disadvantages of implementing the results of a study that found a statistically significant 10 percent mean difference in job performance level between the female and male social workers who work for an employee assistance program. Discuss what additional information you would want before taking action on the study's results. Justify any assumptions or recommendations.
12. Discuss what you would do with a research study's finding that there was a significant difference ($p < .05$) between the mean client hospital readmission rate for those workers who used treatment A and those who used treatment B. How would you use the fact that treatment A had a mean client readmission rate of 15 percent and treatment B had a mean client readmission rate of 17 percent? Or the fact that treatment B requires 25 percent more staff than treatment A? Justify your answer. Does statistical analysis help us make an ethical decision in this situation? Why?
13. As an administrator of a local United Way agency, your job is to allocate funds for agencies that request them. Two agencies (A and B) require money from you so that they can

stay in operation next year. Both offer the same services, but you have enough money to fund only one. Agency A states that its clients had a mean treatment success score of 42 on a standardized measuring instrument that measures client functioning ($N = 1,000$). Agency B, using the same measuring instrument, states that its mean treatment success score was 44 for the same period. Agency B also had 1,000 clients. You take these data and calculate the appropriate statistic to determine whether sampling error played any role in the difference in scores. Your statistical analysis produces a finding of $p < .25$. Will you be able to use your statistical analysis to decide which agency to fund? Why? Discuss what additional information you would want before taking action on the study's results. Justify your answer.

14. You are an administrator in a very large family service agency. There are two treatment techniques (A and B) that your workers use to help parents whose children have school truancy problems. Half your workers use treatment A, and the other half use treatment B. You conduct a research study to determine which treatment is more effective in reducing truancy. When they first applied for services, all children in the study were truant a mean of 5 times per month. After treatment, the parents who received treatment A reported a mean of 2 instances of truancy per month, while the parents who received treatment B reported a mean of 3 instances of truancy per month. The difference of 1 is statistically significant at the 0.05 rejection level. How could you use these findings?

6

Sampling Distributions and Hypothesis Testing

Inference is dependent on a sample's representativeness. In order to infer that a relationship between variables found in a sample is also present in the population from which the sample was drawn, we need to know that the sample is sufficiently representative of its population. A sample is, however, at best, an *estimate* of what a population looks like. As observed in the previous chapter, simply drawing a random sample from a population in no way guarantees that it is truly representative of its population, since samples tend to differ from their respective populations because of sampling error. The difference between a sample's measure of central tendency (e.g., mean, median, mode) and its measures of variability (e.g., standard deviation, interquartile range, range) and those same measurements within its population can be thought of as its sampling error. For example, for any given interval-level or ratio-level variable, the difference between a sample's mean and standard deviation and its population's mean and standard deviation is sampling error.

SAMPLE SIZE AND SAMPLING ERROR

In Chapter 5, we noted that smaller samples tend to differ more from their populations than larger samples and thus are more likely to contain more sampling error than larger samples. The way that sample size relates to sampling error can easily be demonstrated. Imagine a research class of 30 students. We could collect data on each student's overall grade point average (GPA) and compute an overall mean GPA for the entire population of students ($N = 30$). Let us say that the mean GPA for the entire class of 30 students is 3.0, with a standard deviation of .5. The population's mean and its standard deviation (which would not contain sampling error) would be known respectively as its true mean and its true standard deviation.

If we were to draw a single random sample of three students ($n = 3$) from the entire class of 30 students and determine this sample's mean GPA and standard deviation, we would not expect them to be exactly the same as the population's mean and standard deviation. In fact, we probably would expect the mean and standard deviation to be different, perhaps quite different, and we would be surprised if they were exactly the same as the true mean and true standard deviation. The sample's mean GPA and standard deviation would almost certainly differ from the population's mean GPA and standard deviation—that is, it would contain a considerable amount of sampling error.

With the above in mind, now suppose that we draw a single random sample of 10 students from the same class of 30 students. We still would not expect the sample's mean GPA and standard deviation to be exactly 3.0 and .5 respectively. We would predict, however, that the sample's mean and standard deviation are likely to be closer to the population's mean and standard deviation than was the case with the 3-student sample because sample sizes of 10 are closer to "the long run" (see Chapter 5) than sample sizes of 3. Thus, the law of averages is more likely to take over with the larger samples than with smaller ones. What do we mean by this? Suppose that the first 3 cases drawn for a sample of 10 are among the lowest GPAs in the class. This pattern is unlikely to continue as the sample size approaches 10. Why? Because 3 of the lowest cases have already been selected, there are now a disproportionate number of higher GPAs left from which to draw. Thus, later selections are quite likely to be those with higher GPAs. The higher GPAs will help balance out the lower ones, and the mean for the sample of 10 will look closer to the true mean than it did with the smaller sample of only 3. With a sample of only 3, if the 3 cases drawn have very low GPAs, there would be no opportunity to balance them out with subsequent selections. A very low sample mean will result. Because of the same phenomenon (really a matter of probability), a sample of 10 is also theoretically more likely to have a standard deviation that is closer to the true standard deviation (.5) than a sample of 3. Of course, as we know, what is theoretically more likely to happen does not always happen, especially if only one sample is drawn. While unlikely, a sample of 3 *could be* more representative than a sample of 10!

Let us now take this example to its extreme. If we were to draw a random sample of 29 students, we still might expect the sample's mean GPA and standard deviation to differ a little from the population's mean GPA of 3.0 and standard deviation of .5, but the difference would probably be very small, much less than with a sample size of 3 or even 10. There would be very little room for sampling error, since only 1 case in the population would not be included in a sample of 29. (Of course, we would be highly unlikely to study a sample of 29 students out of 30. At that point, we might as well study the entire population of 30 students so that there would be no opportunity for sampling error.)

When a sample is selected, we want it to be representative of the population from which it was drawn. That makes it possible to generalize a finding from a sample to its population. To summarize, could a sample of 3 cases be perfectly representative of a population of 30, that is, have the same mean and standard deviation? Theoretically, yes, but this would happen very rarely in drawing many samples of 3 and replacing cases each time before drawing the next sample. Most samples would look quite different from the population and from each other.

If many samples of 10 are drawn from the same population, there might be a few more of these samples that would be perfectly representative of the population—the samples as a group would look more like the population than the samples of 3 cases. They would also be more similar to each other than the samples of 3 cases.

With samples of 29, even more might be perfectly representative and, among those that were not, their means and standard deviations would still be very close to the true mean and standard deviation. The samples also would be very similar to each other.

It should be clear by now that smaller samples are more likely to contain more sampling error and thus to be less representative than larger samples. While it is theoretically possible to draw a small representative sample, it will happen much less frequently in many repetitions than if larger samples are drawn.

SAMPLING DISTRIBUTIONS AND INFERENCE

Because of sampling error, samples are almost always a less than perfect estimate of the characteristics of the populations from which they are drawn. Since samples tend to vary from their populations, we can never assume that a sample's characteristics (statistics) are the same as those of its population (parameters). We can assume, however, that there is some degree of similarity between a sample and its population. (If this were not the case, why would we study a sample in the first place?)

A good estimate of the amount of sampling error within a sample would help us know to what degree we might be safe in inferring that a characteristic of a sample is also true of its population. Let us say, for example, that we observe a relationship between political conservatism and some other variable, such as gender, within a sample of cases. It would be helpful to know how accurate an estimate the mean conservatism score of the people in our sample is of the mean conservatism score of people in the population before we infer that the relationship within the sample really exists within the population. Or, how closely its mode, median, interquartile range, or standard deviation approximate their counterparts within the population. They take into consideration the size of a sample and how much sampling error it theoretically may contain. This is why we need to know *sampling distributions* (estimates of sample statistics) and how much they may differ from their counterparts (population parameters). Sampling distributions are a third hypothetical distribution (along with the distribution of a variable in a sample and the true distribution of that variable in its population). They are the necessary link between the other two that makes inference possible.

Comparing an Experimental Sample with Its Population

An estimate of the similarity of a sample to its population helps us gauge to what degree a drawn sample is sufficiently representative of its population in relation to one or more variables—usually dependent variables. If we can determine that a sample is sufficiently representative of its population, for example, we can then use this sample to introduce an independent variable and observe its effect on the dependent variable. Because the sample was assumed to be representative of its population, we can then infer (within limits, that is) that the effect on the dependent variable for the sample would also have occurred on that dependent variable if we had introduced the independent variable to the entire population.

Let us use another example of how an estimate of sampling error might be helpful in analyzing research findings. Suppose we wanted to evaluate the effectiveness of a new intervention designed to improve self-esteem among clients. We could draw a random sample of 25 clients ($n = 25$) previously identified as having low self-esteem and offer them our intervention. The intervention would not be offered to the rest of the population. (Our sample could thus be considered an experimental group.) We could then compare the people in the sample with the population from which they were drawn in relation to the dependent variable *self-esteem.* We could attempt to find support for a one-tailed research hypothesis:

> The experimental group will have a higher mean self-esteem level than the population's mean self-esteem level.

We can find support (or nonsupport) for a one-tailed research hypothesis by testing its null form. The null form of the above hypothesis would be:

> There will be *no difference* between the experimental group's mean self-esteem level and the population's mean self-esteem level.

Let us say that the mean self-esteem score for the people in the experimental group (after receiving the intervention) was 69, and the mean score for the population was 64 (higher scores = higher self-esteem). The null hypothesis contends that any difference between the two means is due to sampling error. Specifically, in our example, it would suggest that the 5 point average difference in self-esteem between the experimental group and the rest of the population is explained by the fact that they were not comparable in self-esteem levels to begin with—the experimental group may have been higher in self-esteem before receiving the intervention just because of sampling error. In determining how safe it would be to reject the null hypothesis, we would have to know what percentage of the time, in drawing an infinite number of samples of 25 cases each, a sample would have a mean that is 5 points higher than the population based only on sampling error.

Comparing a Nonexperimental Sample with Its Population

For either ethical or practical reasons, we may not be able to introduce or manipulate an independent variable within a specific research sample to study its effect on a dependent variable. Or we may simply wish to study a specific category of people contained within a population (a sample) to see if they differ from the general population in some way. For example, we might be able to identify a sample of 35 people ($n = 35$) who know they are HIV-positive and ask them to complete a standardized self-report measuring instrument that measures the variable *self-esteem*. We could then compare the self-esteem level of the people in our sample with the general population's mean self-esteem level, using a data collection instrument (such as a scale) that has been standardized on the general population. We could then test the following one-tailed research hypothesis:

> People who know that they are HIV-positive have a lower mean self-esteem level than the general population's self-esteem level.

We would seek support for the above one-tailed research hypothesis by testing its null form:

> People who know that they are HIV-positive have the same self-esteem level as the general population.

Let us say that the mean self-esteem score for the people in the sample was 61, and the mean score for the population was 64 (higher scores = higher self-esteem). The null hypothesis contends that any difference between the two means is due to sampling error. In determining how safe it would be to reject the null hypothesis, we would have to know what percentage of the time, in drawing an infinite number of samples of 35 cases each, would a sample have a mean that is 3 points lower than the population, based only on sampling error. That would help us determine whether we should reject the null hypothesis by telling us that the difference did or did not occur because of sampling error.

At this point it might be a good idea to reiterate that the null hypothesis is only a statistical hypothesis related to the laws of probability. Rejecting it does not in itself provide adequate support for a research hypothesis. Since the sample was not randomly drawn to begin with (it was, of necessity, more of a convenience sample), we may still want to try to determine whether the sample was biased in some way before concluding that we have support for the research hypothesis that people who are HIV-positive have lower self-esteem levels than the general population. Perhaps, for example, our 35 sample members were identified from files of people actively seeking counseling and thus are not representative of all HIV-positive people. That may make them atypical—they may have lower self-esteem than those who feel no need to seek counseling or who seek other forms of help.

SAMPLING DISTRIBUTION OF MEANS

A sampling distribution is a social construct. As such, it does not exist and is only theoretical—that is, it is based on the theoretical results of drawing an infinite number of samples of a certain size from a population. We could, for example, theoretically construct a sampling distribution of the means for samples of 25 students for the variable *SAT scores* (combined verbal and math) among BSW students enrolled in accredited departments and schools of social work in North America in the current year (a specific population at a specific time). Let us assume that these scores form a normal distribution within the population with a mean of 1,000 and a standard deviation of 200. To create a sampling distribution of the means for samples of 25 students, we would (theoretically) have to randomly draw an infinite number of samples of 25 students from this population, replacing cases each time before the next sample is drawn. We would then compute the mean SAT score for each sample. If it were possible to construct a frequency polygon for the means of all of these samples, it would have three interesting characteristics:

1. It would be a normal distribution.
2. Its mean would be the same as the population mean (1,000).
3. Its standard deviation would be called the *standard error of the mean*. It would not be the same as the standard deviation of the population, but would be computed as:

the standard deviation (population)
_____
    square root of the sample size

It should not be surprising that the mean of a sampling distribution would be the same as the mean of the population from which it was constructed. Means of individual samples vary from the population's mean and from each other. But since any sampling distribution (of any size sample) is based on an infinite number of samples of SAT scores, the law of averages (the long run) eventually would prevail. Samples with lower means and those with higher means would cancel each other out when they were averaged together. Thus this mean of the means would be exactly the same as the true mean (the mean of the population), no matter what sample size produced the sampling distribution.

Similarly, we would expect the frequency distribution to be a normal distribution. In sampling distributions of samples of any size, most sample means would be relatively close to the true mean, and increasingly fewer would occur as we move farther below or above the true mean.

The third characteristic of a sampling distribution of means may be a little more surprising, at least until we think about it. The standard error of the mean is not simply the standard deviation of the population. Why not? Sample size (and thus sampling error) must be factored in. Recall that we demonstrated earlier that smaller samples are more likely to have more sampling error than larger samples. Remember also that as larger samples are drawn, the probability of drawing either all small values or all large ones decreases. The formula for the standard error of the mean (whose origins are beyond the scope of this text) takes this into account—it adjusts for sample size.

In our example above, the standard error of the mean would be:

$$\text{standard deviation (population)} = \frac{200}{\text{square root of the sample size (5)}}$$

$$= 40$$

We could now add the standard deviation of the standard error of the mean to the frequency polygon. We could then determine that any given sample's mean was a certain distance—that is, units of standard error or *z*-scores—above or below its true (population) mean. Finally we could take the *z*-score of that sample mean and go to a table of the normal curve (i.e., Table 4.3) to determine the percentile that corresponds to that *z*-score (as we did in Chapter 4). This percentile would tell us what percent of all samples would have a mean at or below the mean of our sample. We will see how valuable this can be for testing hypotheses in the next section of this chapter.

When drawing samples from a given population, there are as many different sampling distributions of means as there are different sample sizes. The size of their standard deviations (their standard error of the mean) will vary based on the size of the samples on which they are based. Sampling distributions constructed from smaller samples will always have larger standard deviations than sampling distributions constructed from larger samples since the square root of their sample size (the divisor in the formula) will be smaller than the square root of a larger sample size.

Returning to our example, if we draw an infinite number of samples of only 4 students and compute the mean SAT score for each individual sample, the means of all samples will vary widely from one another. Some samples might (theoretically) consist of the four highest scores; they will thus have very high means. Other samples might consist of the four lowest scores, which will produce very low means. It would be impossible to produce a sample with a mean at either extreme with our earlier sample of 25 students. Even if we somehow selected the top 25 scores or the bottom 25 scores, the mean of the sample would be closer to the true mean. So there would be less variation overall (standard error of the mean) in the larger samples than in the smaller ones. Let us confirm this logical conclusion mathematically. For samples of 4, the standard error of the mean would be:

$$\text{standard deviation (population)} = \frac{200}{\text{square root of the sample size (2)}}$$

$$= 100$$

Figure 6.1 is a sampling distribution for samples of 4. Note how its shape differs from the sampling distribution for samples of 25 in Figure 6.2.

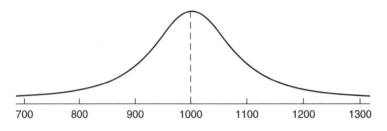

FIGURE 6.1   Sampling Distribution of Mean SAT Scores: *n* = 4.

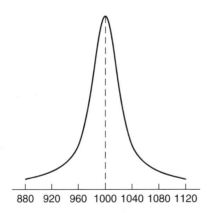

880	920	960	1000	1040	1080	1120

FIGURE 6.2   Sampling Distribution of Mean SAT Scores: *n = 25.*

There are two other factors that determine what a theoretical sampling distribution for a given variable might look like—the shape of the distribution of the population and whether its true mean and distribution are known. However, these factors are not as important as it might be logical to assume.

Samples Drawn from Normal Distributions

If our variable of interest, usually the dependent variable, is normally distributed within a given population, it is possible to combine our knowledge of normal distributions with the contents of this chapter to test one-tailed and two-tailed research hypotheses. Frequently, we wish to conduct a research study to see if a treatment intervention makes a difference. We may wish to know, for example, if a particular type of group experience seems to improve clients' appreciation of diversity.

Let us say that client appreciation of diversity scores on a particular standardized measuring instrument have been found to be normally distributed among 1,000 clients in an agency with a known mean of 50 (standard deviation = 5). Higher scores (values) indicate greater appreciation of diversity than lower scores. We then randomly select a sample of 16 clients from the population of 1,000, provide a group treatment intervention to this sample (an experimental group), and calculate the experimental group's mean appreciation of diversity score (e.g., 60) to see if it is significantly higher than its population's mean appreciation of diversity score of 50 (standard deviation = 5). We could write this assumption as a one-tailed research hypothesis:

> The mean appreciation of diversity score of the experimental group will be higher than the mean appreciation of diversity score of the population.

To test our one-tailed research hypothesis, we need to compare data drawn from the 16-member sample with a standard normal sampling distribution table (i.e., Table 4.3). We thus compare our sample's mean appreciation of diversity score with the score that we might expect to get from simply drawing a random sample (of a given size) from a population and doing nothing with those clients.

By using the concepts of *rejection regions* and the standard error of the mean, we can determine just how typical or atypical our experimental group (or sample) is in relation to how appreciation of diversity scores are distributed within the population. The term *rejection region* refers to a specific region(s) of a normal curve. When it contains a measurement from a sample, this suggests that it is safe to reject the null hypothesis. In order to understand the concept of rejection regions, we rely heavily on the use of normal distributions and z scores as presented in Chapter 4.

Rejection Regions for Two-Tailed Research Hypotheses.   The rejection region for statistical tests that test research hypotheses depends on (1) the rejection level selected and (2) whether the research hypothesis is one-tailed or two-tailed.

In the above example, we hypothesized that our group experience intervention would increase the appreciation of diversity of experimental group members (a one-tailed research hypothesis). In a two-tailed research hypothesis, however, we just say that our group intervention will affect the appreciation of diversity of our experimental group, but not whether it would raise or lower it:

> The experimental group's mean appreciation of diversity score will be different than the population's mean appreciation of diversity score.

For two-tailed research hypotheses, the z scores of the two rejection regions (the point where they begin) are located using procedures similar to those discussed in Chapter 4 (and Table 4.3) that are used to locate a raw score's corresponding z score. The steps for locating the two rejection regions for two-tailed research hypotheses are:

1. Divide the selected rejection level by 2.
2. Subtract the derived value from .50, and multiply by 100.
3. Locate the derived proportion in the body of a normal distribution table (i.e., Table 4.3).
4. Determine the z score that corresponds to that proportion.

If we are using the conventional .05 rejection level, for example, the calculations for the preceding four steps would look like this:

1. $.05/2 = .025$.
2. $(.50 - .025) \times 100 = 47.50$ (1/2 of 95.00).
3. Find 47.50 in the body of a normal distribution table (i.e., Table 4.3).
4. The z score corresponding to 47.50 is $+1.96$ or -1.96.

How do we interpret the results of these calculations? When a rejection level of .05 is used, the rejection regions for a two-tailed research hypothesis are the areas at or above $z = +1.96$ and at or below $z = -1.96$. Such a result must be achieved in order to reject the null hypothesis for a two-tailed research hypothesis. Figure 6.3 provides a graphical illustration of this concept.

In our two-tailed research hypothesis, the experimental group's mean appreciation of diversity score would have to be at least 1.96 standard deviations higher than

(+1.96) or at least 1.96 standard deviations lower than (−1.96) the population's mean appreciation of diversity score of 50. As we know, the standard deviation of the sampling distribution of the means (more correctly referred to as the standard error of the mean or just standard error) that we use to test this two-tailed research hypothesis is not simply the standard deviation for the population. The standard deviation that we use must be specific to the size of the sample, in our example 16. It is the standard deviation of the parent population (in this case 5) divided by the square root of the sample size (in this case 4). In our example, 5 divided by 4 equals 1.25.

Thus, to feel reasonably safe in rejecting the null hypothesis for our two-tailed research hypothesis, our experimental group's mean appreciation of diversity score would have to be

at least 1.96 × 1.25, or 2.45 points, *higher* than 50, or at least 52.45

or

at least 1.96 × 1.25, or 2.45 points, *lower* than 50, or less than 47.55

It should be noted that +1.96 or −1.96 is the required z score for all two-tailed research hypotheses that use the .05 rejection level, not just the one in our example. Only the standard deviation for the sample (the standard error of the mean) will vary within the equation, based on the sample's size and its square root.

Rejection Regions for One-Tailed Research Hypotheses. What if we had hypothesized that our intervention with the experimental group would produce a higher mean appreciation of diversity score than the level found in the general population (i.e., mean = 50, standard deviation = 5)? A one-tailed research hypothesis could be written as follows:

The experimental group will have a higher mean appreciation of diversity score than the mean appreciation of diversity score found within the population.

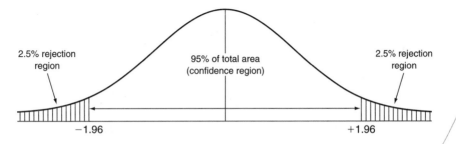

FIGURE 6.3   The Normal Distribution Showing the 95% Confidence Region and Two 2.5% Rejection Regions for Two-Tailed Research Hypotheses

Now where would the rejection region lie? Since a one-tailed research hypothesis predicts the direction of a relationship between variables, there is a variation in the above procedure for obtaining its appropriate rejection region—the selected rejection level is not divided by 2. Thus, the .05 rejection region for a one-tailed research hypothesis is derived as follows:

1. $.50 - .05 = .45 \times 100 = 45.00$
2. Find 45.00 in the body of a normal distribution table (i.e., Table 4.3).
3. The z score corresponding to 45.00 is +1.65 or −1.65.

How do we interpret the results of this calculation? When using a one-tailed research hypothesis and a rejection level of .05, the calculated z must be at least +1.65 or −1.65 in order to reject the null hypothesis. We would use only one or the other, since a directional hypothesis, by definition, would predict not only the existence of a relationship between variables but its direction as well. Which cutoff point would we use in our example—the +1.65 or the −1.65? In order to claim support for our one-tailed research hypothesis, the experimental group's mean appreciation of diversity score would have to be at least +1.65 standard deviations higher than the population's mean score of 50. That is because we hypothesized that our experimental group would have a higher mean appreciation of diversity score than is found within the population from which it was drawn. If, instead, we had hypothesized that our experimental group's mean appreciation of diversity score would be lower that of the population, we would have used the $z = -1.65$ cutoff point.

Since our sample size is still 16, the standard error of the mean for our sampling distribution would be the same as when we had a two-tailed research hypothesis—1.25. With a one-tailed research hypothesis, however, the experimental group's mean appreciation of diversity score would now have to be at least $1.65 \times 1.25 = 2.0625$, rounded off to 2 points, higher than 50 for us to reject the null hypothesis.

Thus, the experimental group's mean appreciation of diversity score would have to be at least 52 for us to be reasonably certain (95 percent) that there really is a predicted association between the treatment intervention and the experimental group's relatively higher levels of appreciation of diversity when compared to the population.

Figure 6.4 graphically portrays the rejection region (z = at least +1.65) for a one-tailed research hypothesis where the upper tail is specified as the rejection region. Likewise, Figure 6.5 provides an illustration of the rejection region (z = at least −1.65) for a one-tailed research hypothesis where the lower tail is specified. Unlike Figure 6.3, Figures 6.4, and 6.5 contain only one rejection region, the one that reflects the direction of the one-tailed research hypothesis.

When using a normal distribution to test a one-tailed research hypothesis, only z scores that fall within the specified rejection region allow us to reject the null hypothesis. A sample statistic (in this instance, the mean) in the region suggests that the probability that sampling error produced the relationship between the two variables in our sample is less than .05. We could conclude that by selecting an infinite number of samples of 16 and offering no intervention, we could expect to draw a sample with a mean

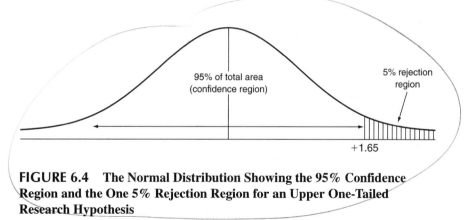

FIGURE 6.4   The Normal Distribution Showing the 95% Confidence Region and the One 5% Rejection Region for an Upper One-Tailed Research Hypothesis

appreciation of diversity score that differs from the mean of its population by at least 1.65 standard deviations in the predicted direction less than 5 times out of 100. So, we would be able to claim that sampling error is unlikely to explain the relationship between the intervention and the appreciation of diversity scores. We could state that the relationship between the variables was found to be statistically significant.

By glancing at Figures 6.3, 6.4, and 6.5, it can be observed that a one-tailed research hypothesis has certain advantages. As can be seen, it moves the critical rejection regions closer to the mean of the sampling distribution, thus improving the probability of rejecting the null hypothesis. This is only logical; when we predict the direction of a relationship using a one-tailed research hypothesis, we should get extra credit if support for the relationship between variables and the predicted direction of the relationship is found. As noted in the previous chapter, using a one-tailed hypothesis (if it can be justified) can decrease the likelihood of making a Type II error (missing a true relationship between variables). A relationship in which the direction of the re-

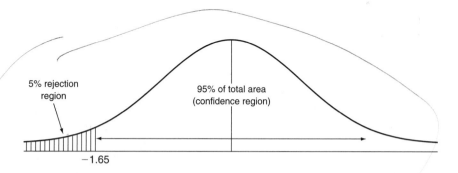

FIGURE 6.5   The Normal Distribution Showing the 95% Confidence Region and the One 5% Rejection Region for a Lower One-Tailed Research Hypothesis

lationship was predicted and then found to exist is less likely to be the work of sampling error than one in which the direction was not predicted in advance.

Note, however, that if the wrong direction has been specified in a one-tailed research hypothesis—that is, if we incorrectly predicted the direction of the relationship—the probability of the rejection of the null hypothesis is zero. There simply is no rejection region on the other side of the distribution. We are given no prediction credit for results that were the exact opposite of what we predicted. Thus one-tailed research hypotheses should not be used unless the direction of a relationship can be confidently predicted or we are interested only in those sample outcomes that fall in one tail (direction) of a sampling distribution of a variable.

Samples Drawn from Skewed Distributions

While many variables are normally distributed within a population, the distribution of other variables is skewed, as illustrated in Figure 4.5 in Chapter 4. What would the sampling distribution of the means look like for a variable when a sampling distribution is skewed? In other words, what would be the shape of a frequency polygon of means from an infinite number of samples randomly drawn from a population in which the variable is not normally distributed? Actually, it will approximate a normal distribution if the size of the sample is fairly large. This fact is based on what is called the *central limit theorem,* which states that if the size of the sample is large, the sampling distribution of means created from a variable that is skewed within its population will be approximately normal. It will be more normal (bell-shaped) for very large samples than for samples that are somewhat smaller. The standard deviation (standard error) of large samples is computed the same way as with normally distributed variables.

How large is large enough to produce a sampling distribution that is normally distributed? It depends on the shape of the distribution within the population—that is, its amount of skewness. In most skewed distributions, a sample of 30 is usually large enough to produce a sampling distribution that is essentially a normal one, as portrayed in Figures 4.3, 4.4, and 4.6. Sometimes, if the distribution within the population is only slightly skewed, even smaller sample sizes will produce normal sampling distributions.

To indicate the importance of the central limit theorem, we will use an example to which we all can relate. The scores on a standardized statistics test administered to all MSW students in North America generally would not form a normal distribution. They tend to be negatively skewed within the student population, with most students getting fairly high grades and a small number (outliers) getting quite low grades. What does the central limit theorem tell us about a sampling distribution of this variable? We should be able to take the scores of all MSW students and randomly draw an infinite number of samples of 30 students, replacing each student's score before each subsequent sample is drawn. We could then compute the mean for each sample. We could take all of the sample means and create a histogram and a frequency polygon, as described in Chapter 2. According to the central limit theorem, the frequency polygon created from these samples would approximate a normal curve, even though the scores within the population are negatively skewed.

ESTIMATING PARAMETERS FROM STATISTICS

With what we have learned so far, we can now produce a reasonably accurate estimate of a variable's parameter (a characteristic of a population) from the variable's statistic (a measurement of a variable taken from a sample). This procedure is called *parameter estimation.*

To understand parameter estimation, we need to introduce two related terms— confidence interval and confidence level. A *confidence interval* is a range into which we would estimate a population parameter to fall based on a sample statistic. *A confidence level* is an estimate of the probability that the true population parameter lies within the confidence interval. Together, a confidence level and its confidence interval form an estimate of the true parameter based on a statistic. Thus, in conducting a parameter estimation, we seek to fill in the three blanks in the following statement:

> Based on measurement of variable *x* within our sample (a statistic), there is a ____ percent probability that the true mean of variable *x* within the population from which it was drawn (a parameter) is between ____ and ____.

In the above statement, the first blank is the confidence level. The second and third blanks are the lower and upper limits of the confidence interval. How would we arrive at the correct numbers to fill in these blanks? We set the first blank's number to reflect how confident we wish to be that the true population mean falls within our confidence interval (second and third blanks). If we want to be 95 percent confident that it will (the conventional level comparable to .05), we use the 95 percent confidence level; if we want to be 99 percent confident, we use the 99 percent confidence level; and so on.

What about the two remaining blanks, which deal with the confidence interval? How do we arrive at the correct numbers to place in them? By applying logic, we can see that finding the lower and upper limits of a confidence interval is easier than we might think. Suppose we want to estimate the client satisfaction scores of all 2,000 active clients in a large public social service agency. It might be impractical to administer the standardized client satisfaction measuring instrument to all of them. We can estimate the population's mean client satisfaction score, however, by simply asking 100 randomly selected clients to complete the measuring instrument and then computing this sample's mean client satisfaction score.

Let us say that our sample's mean client satisfaction score is 40. Perhaps we believe that the variable *client satisfaction* is normally distributed in the population from which it was drawn. But whether it is or is not is not important since our sample is considered sufficiently large (well over 30). Thus, the standard error of the mean will be the same either way (a conclusion based on the central limit theorem). This fact is important to an understanding of how we arrive at a confidence interval.

The true parameter (the population mean) can be thought of as the mean of the sample, plus or minus some amount of sampling error. We can never exactly determine how large this error is, but there are some things that we can determine. First, we can determine the probability distribution of all possible errors in an infinite number of samples of 100 cases—the sampling distribution of these errors. Because the sample is fairly large, we already know that the distribution will be normally distributed.

Second, we can determine the standard error of the mean. Remember that the standardized client satisfaction measuring instrument has a known mean of 50 and a standard deviation of 5. Using the formula presented earlier, the standard error of the mean (standard deviation of the sampling distribution) is the standard deviation of the population (5) divided by the square root of the sample size ($n = 100$). So the calculation would be $5/10 = .5$ (the standard error). We know that a probability distribution of the sample means in an infinite number of random samples of 100 drawn from a population would form a normal distribution with a standard error of .5 or one-half point.

Constructing a 95 Percent Confidence Interval

Suppose we want to be 95 percent confident that the true client satisfaction score of all active clients falls between two scores (the confidence interval) of our sample's mean of 40. Remember that 95 percent of a normal distribution lies between the points $z = -1.96$ and $z = +1.96$. This can be verified using Table 4.3; it is also illustrated earlier in this chapter (see Figure 6.3). We now can arrive at our confidence interval as presented below:

Lower limit (n = 100):

$$\begin{array}{rl}
\text{sample mean} & = 40.00 \\
-1.96 \times .5 \text{ (standard error)} & = \underline{-\ .98} \\
& = 39.02
\end{array}$$

Upper limit (n = 100):

$$\begin{array}{rl}
\text{sample mean} & = 40.00 \\
+1.96 \times .5 \text{ (standard error)} & = \underline{+\ .98} \\
& = 40.98
\end{array}$$

Now we can fill in the blanks and state the following:

Based on measurement of client satisfaction within our sample ($n = 100$), there is a 95 percent probability that the true mean of client satisfaction among clients in the agency is between 39.02 and 40.98.

Constructing a 99 Percent Confidence Interval

Using the same data, we also could have produced a confidence interval reflecting a 99 percent confidence level. Using Table 4.3, we could learn that over 99 percent of the distribution would fall between the z scores -2.58 and $+2.58$ more than 49.50 percent of a normal distribution falls between a z-score of ± 2.58 and the mean). Instead of using $z = +1.96$ or -1.96 this time, as we did to find the confidence interval for a 95 percent confidence level, we would now use $z = +2.58$ or -2.58 instead:

Lower limit (n = 100):

$$\begin{array}{rl} \text{sample mean} & = 40.00 \\ -2.58 \times .5 \,(\text{standard error}) & = \underline{-1.29} \\ & = 38.71 \end{array}$$

Upper limit (n = 100):

$$\begin{array}{rl} \text{sample mean} & = 40.00 \\ +2.58 \times .5 \,(\text{standard error}) & = \underline{+1.29} \\ & = 41.29 \end{array}$$

Now we can state the following:

Based on measurement of client satisfaction within the sample ($n = 100$), there is a 99 percent probability that the true mean of client satisfaction among clients in the agency is between 38.71 and 41.29.

Note that whether we use the 95 or 99 percent confidence levels, the confidence interval each one contains may seem quite small—it encompasses just a few points. This is because a sample of 100 cases is quite large in the absolute sense. We would expect that any sample of 100 would have relatively little sampling error, since a sample of 100 would begin to approximate "the long run."

Let us take the same example to illustrate how decreasing the size of a sample affects the upper and lower limits of a 95 percent confidence interval. This time we will use a sample size of 25 instead of 100. Remember, the square root of 25 is 5 so the standard error for a sampling distribution of samples of 25 is now 5/5 = 1.

Lower limit (n = 25):

$$\begin{array}{rl} \text{sample mean} & = 40.00 \\ -1.96 \times 1 \,(\text{standard error}) & = \underline{-1.96} \\ & = 38.04 \end{array}$$

Upper limit (n = 25):

$$\begin{array}{rl} \text{sample mean} & = 40.00 \\ +1.96 \times 1 \,(\text{standard error}) & = \underline{+1.96} \\ & = 41.96 \end{array}$$

Now we can state the following:

Based on measurement of client satisfaction within our sample ($n = 25$), there is a 95 percent probability that the true mean of client satisfaction among clients in the agency is between 38.04 and 41.96.

The 95 percent confidence interval using a sample size of 100 ranges from 39.02 to 40.98 (a range of 1.96 points). The sampling interval for a sample size of 25 ranges from 38.04 to 41.96 (a range of 3.92 points). Thus, the smaller the sample, the larger the range of the confidence interval, and the larger the sample, the smaller the range of the confidence interval. This should not be surprising since we know now that a sample of 100 should contain less sampling error than a sample of 25.

OTHER DISTRIBUTIONS

As the central limit theorem suggests, when sample sizes are small (i.e., < 30), and distributions of variables are badly skewed, sampling distributions may not be very accurate as estimates of the population. The mean of a sampling distribution may not be a good estimate of the mean of the population.

With some variables, even if we believe the variable to be normally distributed within the population, we may not be able to construct a sampling distribution because we do not know a key element of the equation for its standard error—the standard deviation of the variable within the population. Fortunately, there is still another group of distributions, *t* distributions, that allow us to compute exact confidence intervals when a variable is normally distributed, but we do not know its population standard deviation. The *t* distributions are central to many statistical significance tests, such as those presented in Chapter 11, and are discussed there.

CONCLUDING THOUGHTS

This chapter expanded on Chapter 5 by presenting the theoretical underpinning of sampling distributions and how they relate to inference. The chapter examined how our knowledge of normal distribution, when integrated with the concept of sampling distributions, is used to answer two related questions that are integral to inference: (1) How well does the sample serve as an estimate of the population? and (2) How confident can we be that the true mean of the population falls within a certain range of values? The first question is answered through the use of rejection regions. The latter question is answered through the use of confidence levels and confidence intervals.

The methods of statistical analyses presented in Chapters 8 through 11 rely heavily on the concepts and ideas presented in Chapters 5 and 6. An understanding of sampling distributions is critical to understanding how researchers use statistical tests to determine whether it is safe to conclude that they have support for their research hypotheses.

STUDY QUESTIONS

1. Discuss how sample size is directly related to sampling error. Use an original example to demonstrate your understanding.
2. Discuss how sampling distributions are used for inference.
3. What exactly is a sampling distribution of means? Explain in detail how a sampling distribution of means is used in constructing the rejection regions for one-tailed and two-tailed research hypotheses.
4. Discuss how a sampling distribution of means derived from numerous large samples drawn from a skewed population will form a normal distribution.
5. Discuss the concept of parameter estimation. How is it useful for social workers?
6. What is a rejection region? What is a confidence level? What is a confidence interval? Discuss how the three concepts are related to each other. Provide original examples throughout your discussion.
7. Discuss how the standard error of the mean is calculated. Is the standard error of the mean smaller or larger in samples of 12 than in samples of 24? Why?

CHAPTER

7

Selecting a Statistical Test

The two previous chapters presented a general discussion of how to test one-tailed and two-tailed research hypotheses. They described how, using the laws of probability, it is possible to determine the likelihood that sampling error may have produced a relationship between variables within a sample that was drawn from a population. Assuming that rival hypotheses and design bias (i.e., measurement bias, sampling bias) have been adequately controlled for, we are now in a position to estimate how safe it would be to conclude that the relationship between variables contained in our sample is a real one—that is, that it exists in the population from which the sample was drawn.

There are many different tests that can be used to see how safe it is to claim support for a one-tailed or two-tailed research hypothesis. All of theses tests rely on the principles presented in Chapters 5 and 6. This chapter completes our discussion of hypothesis testing and presents basic issues that need to be addressed before selecting the most appropriate statistical test to use.

THE IMPORTANCE OF SELECTING THE CORRECT STATISTICAL TEST

The manner in which a research study is conducted has the potential to enhance—or to harm—the credibility of the study's findings and, thus, its recommendations. Relying on literature that presents only one side of an issue, for example, or choosing to use a measuring instrument that may not be reliable with the population, or using a sampling method that may not produce a representative sample, or using a data collection method that may influence the data themselves can introduce biases into the study's findings and may cause the reader to doubt the study's credibility.

Even if all the research tasks have been completed well, that is, the study was well designed and implemented, the credibility of the findings still can be jeopardized by an additional error—the researcher may have used an inappropriate statistical test of inference. A critical reader of a research report always asks, "Was the appropriate data analysis method used to test the study's research hypothesis?" If not, the study's findings may produce only skepticism on the reader's part.

Why are inappropriate statistical tests sometimes chosen when appropriate ones are available for almost any type of data analysis? Frequently, it is because of the principle referred to as the rule of the instrument. This means that people often see the solution to any problem as requiring what they know and/or do best—that is, that with which they are most comfortable and familiar. There are many examples of this principle. Take, for example, the responses of different groups of people to fatal shootings within American schools. Many social workers suggest hiring more school social workers to identify and counsel young people who may feel alienated from their peers. Corrections professionals may think the money might better be spent on metal detectors or placement of armed guards within the schools. Politicians may believe the problem can best be addressed by passing tighter gun control laws. Religious leaders may see the solution as better moral education, and so forth. In short, both the problem and its solution can easily be defined from one's own perspective or vantage point.

How might the rule of the instrument affect the selection of a statistical test? Many of us, particularly those of us who received our social work education quite some time ago, did not receive extensive training in data analyses. Our knowledge is often confined to familiarity with only one or two forms. Facing the necessity of choosing a statistical test to analyze the relationship between variables, we may have a tendency to turn to the test with which we are most familiar, rather than explore the possibility of using a lesser-known or more recently developed one.

There also is a widely held misconception that because statistical tests have so much in common, it makes little difference which one is used. After all, they all rely on the same principles and the same laws of probability. So, why not just use a test that is widely used and understood by both the researcher and the potential consumers of a study's findings? Why bother to seek out one that may be more appropriate but is less widely known or would require additional study?

There are two responses to these questions. First, as suggested earlier, using an inappropriate statistical test will result in a loss of credibility for a study's findings among those who are knowledgeable about data analyses. Second, and perhaps more importantly, those who are not knowledgeable may just assume that the statistical test that was used was the correct one. Thus, they may fail to question a study's findings when the findings should have been challenged or disregarded. Assuming that a study's findings represent new knowledge, social workers may apply them in a manner that has the potential to harm their clients.

There are literally hundreds of statistical tests available. How do we determine which one(s) to use? This decision is relatively complicated, and several factors need to be considered. This chapter examines some of the factors and presents a basic model to help in the selection process.

FACTORS TO CONSIDER WHEN SELECTING A STATISTICAL TEST

Ideally, planning for the analysis of a data set begins early in the research process, at about the same time that decisions are made about what data collection instrument(s) will be used to measure variables of interest—that is, when the variables are operationalized and sampling issues addressed. Questions about how variables are to be measured and the size and methods of acquiring research samples are closely related to how data are analyzed. They help determine which statistical test(s) should and should not be used.

Are such decisions final? Generally, yes—it is customary to select the statistical test(s) prior to data collection. Sometimes, no—it is not especially unusual to encounter problems in a research study that may change either the way data are collected, from whom, and/or the level of precision with which variables realistically can be measured. For example, after data are collected and examined, the distribution of values of a variable may necessitate grouping the values of an interval-level variable, such as age, into ranges, so that they must now be regarded as being at the ordinal level of measurement. When something like this occurs, it is considered both ethical and absolutely essential to select statistical tests different from those that were specified in the original research design.

Whenever the final choice of a statistical test(s) is made, five considerations most directly influence that choice:

1. The sampling method(s) used
2. The distribution of the variables within the population
3. The level of measurement of the independent and dependent variables
4. The amount of statistical power that is desirable
5. The robustness of the tests being considered

We will examine each of these factors in some detail.

There may also be other issues to consider in the decision-making process that may determine which test is (or is not) used to test a research hypothesis. For example, if one of the variables is at the nominal or ordinal level of measurement, we may need to determine the number of value categories (different measurements) of the variable. If the variable is dichotomous (e.g., yes/no, older/younger), some tests are appropriate. But if there are three or more value categories for the variable (e.g., yes/no/undecided, young/middle-aged/older), other tests must be used.

Sampling Method(s) Used

The characteristics of a sample and the way that it is drawn from a population influence the choice of a statistical test. Certain statistical tests require the use of certain sampling methods. The topic of sampling is covered in detail in most social work research methods texts. We must be fully aware of the kind of sampling method used in a research study in order to select the most appropriate statistical test. Below are some of the questions that need to be addressed:

1. Did the sampling method use a single sample or more than one sample? If so, how many?

2. How large a sample or samples were drawn?

3. If more than one sample was used, were the samples independent of each other, or were they related in any way? For example, were they matched in regard to certain variables to assure that they were comparable?

4. Were the cases within each sample drawn independently? Did the selection of one case in any way, for example, increase or decrease the likelihood that any other case within the population would also be selected?

5. Was a probability sampling method used (one in which the exact probability of any one case being selected could be calculated)? If so, was the probability of being selected the same for every case, or were cases selected disproportionately from one or more subsamples?

Answering these five questions allows us to begin to narrow the search for an appropriate statistical test. It eliminates a majority of the existing tests because of their inappropriateness for the particular sampling method that was employed. It is only one step, however, in the process of elimination that is used in selecting a test.

Distribution of the Variables within the Population

A second major consideration in selecting a statistical test is the way in which the primary variables of interest (usually the dependent variables) are distributed within the population from which the sample was drawn. Are they normally distributed? Some of the most common statistical tests require them to be normally distributed.

As seen in Chapter 3, a seriously skewed distribution of an interval-level or ratio-level variable usually precludes the use of the mean as a measure of central tendency or the standard deviation as a measure of variability. Unless the dependent variable is normally distributed, many potentially useful tests that contain the mean and/or standard deviation in their formulas must be eliminated from consideration for research hypothesis testing.

As noted in Chapter 4, normal distributions are rarely perfect in their symmetry; their data may only approximate bell-shaped curves. Many times, full descriptive data for a dependent variable in a population do not exist. So, how do we know if the distribution is a normal one?

The decision about whether the distribution of a dependent variable in a population is normal enough to be considered normally distributed is often a judgment call. It requires, among other things, a knowledge of the robustness of the test being considered, a concept discussed later in this chapter. Generally, a dependent variable whose values at least approximate a bell-shaped curve in the population justifies the use of certain statistical tests that require a normal distribution of the variable.

Judgments of this type are common and necessary in research. We make a similar judgment, for example, when we decide (1) when enough literature has been reviewed, (2) that our sample is sufficiently large and/or representative of the population from which it was drawn, (3) that we can or cannot justify the use of a one-tailed research hypothesis, or (4) when we determine the most appropriate rejection level for rejecting the null hypothesis.

Level of Measurement of the Independent and Dependent Variables

A third factor to consider in selecting a statistical test is the level of measurement of the variables of interest. Were they measured in a way that they can be considered nominal, ordinal, interval, or ratio? Well-planned construction and use of measuring instruments help generate the highest possible level of measurement of a variable (given ethical and practical constraints). If we are not careful, however, we can end up settling for less measurement precision than might have been available. For example, we may permit a variable that could have been measured at the interval or ratio level of measurement to be measured at only the nominal or ordinal level. We might, for example, ask supervisors to rate a staff member's job performance as outstanding, average, or below average when using an existing standardized measuring instrument instead would have produced interval-level data. As noted in Chapter 1, once measurements have been made in such a way that they produce lower-level measurement, it is usually impossible to achieve the higher level of measurement precision that was initially possible.

Why is loss of measurement precision important? After all, there are different statistical tests designed for use with different levels of measurement. So what difference does the level of measurement make? In fact, the distinction between interval-level and ratio-level measurement is relatively unimportant in the selection of a statistical test. Many books on data analyses use the term *interval/ratio* to note the presence of either level of measurement, or they use the term *interval* to denote either. But measuring a variable in a way that produces only nominal-level or ordinal-level data when interval-level or ratio-level data were possible can result in a real loss. It can fail to generate sufficient evidence to support a one-tailed or two-tailed research hypothesis, even though the relationship between the variables may be a real one. The resulting data analyses may result in a Type II error. Had interval- or ratio-level measurement been produced (and thus a different test used), that same relationship might have been statistically significant and the null hypothesis rejected.

The use of a measuring instrument that yields lower-level data (i.e., nominal, ordinal) automatically precludes the use of all statistical tests that require interval- or ratio-level data. This would not be problematic except, as we shall see, those statistical tests that require interval- or ratio-level data for one or more variables are some of the best statistical tests for identifying true relationships between variables (avoiding Type II errors). They are some of the most powerful tests.

Amount of Statistical Power That Is Desirable

Statistical power is the ability of the statistical analysis of data to correctly reject the null hypothesis—that is, its ability to correctly detect a true relationship between variables. Another way to think of the power of statistical analysis is its ability to avoid committing a Type II error.

Based on their mathematical computations, some statistical tests are inherently more powerful than others; that is, all other conditions being equal, some tests are better than others at detecting a true relationship between variables. Some may allow us to justify the rejection of the null hypothesis, while less powerful tests applied to the same data set under the same conditions would not allow us to reject the null hypothesis. The powerful tests have more demanding conditions for their use than the less powerful ones. These conditions must be met in order for the tests to be used correctly.

As presented in Chapter 3, where appropriate, the standard deviation is preferable to the range as an indicator of variability, and the mean is a more precise indicator of central tendency than is the median or mode. Why? Both the mean and the standard deviation require computations using every case value within the variable's distribution and are therefore more precise. Less precise measures such as the trimmed mean, interquartile range, or range do not use every case value in their computation. Thus, they offer less precise descriptions of the distribution of a variable.

The same principle applies in understanding the concept of statistical power as it relates to the respective power of different statistical tests. All other factors being equal, more powerful tests tend to be those that use all the values for all cases in their computations (directly or indirectly) rather than, for example, the ranks assigned to cases or the frequencies for different nominal-level value categories of a variable. Thus, they take full advantage of the greater precision in measurement that is available. Not surprisingly, the more powerful a statistical test, the more complex its formula.

Avoiding Type II Errors.   Chapter 5 examined ways to reduce the likelihood of committing a Type I error. But Type II errors also need to be avoided. All tests possess a certain inherent power based on their mathematical formulas. But any test can be made more or less powerful by the conditions related to its use. There are five conditions that relate to the power of a statistical test and how it affects the likelihood of making a Type II error.

1. The actual strength of the relationship between variables that exists within the population.   This is the issue of effect size—the amount of influence that the independent variable exerts on the dependent variable (Chapter 5). If two variables are strongly related, we are almost certain not to miss their relationship in our statistical analysis (commit a Type II error), no matter what statistical test we use. If the relationship is very weak (and some weak relationships between variables may still be of interest), the likelihood of making a Type II error is much greater, no matter what statistical test we use. Unfortunately, we cannot influence the actual strength of the relationship between variables; it generally is regarded as a given. All we can hope to do is to get a good estimate of it. That is why we often compute effect size.

2. The likely amount of sampling error in sample data, which is a function of the amount of variability of a variable in a population. In examining the relationship between variables with larger standard deviations (more variability) among their values, we are more likely to commit a Type II error than when examining relationships between variables with smaller variability. Statistical testing will be less powerful. This is because with larger variability in a population, sampling error is likely to be greater; it is easier for samples to vary more from their populations than in populations where case values are relatively similar to each other. With a greater likelihood of sampling error, we are less likely to reject the null hypothesis, even when variables really are related, and thus run a higher risk of committing a Type II error.

3. The predetermined statistical rejection level (e.g., .05, .01, .10) that is used with the test. At the beginning of a study, we could select a higher rejection level than the conventional .05. As noted in Chapter 5, however, there must be justification for doing this (usually within the literature). If, for example, we decide to use the rejection level of .10 as the cutoff point at which we will reject the null hypothesis, we can increase the likelihood of not missing a true relationship between variables in our sample that also exists in the population and, thus, we reduce the likelihood of committing a Type II error. As also noted in Chapter 5, however, this will increase the likelihood of committing a Type I error.

4. Whether a one-tailed or two-tailed research hypothesis was used. The use of a one-tailed research hypothesis will produce a larger rejection region than when a two-tailed research hypothesis is used and will thus also decrease the likelihood of committing a Type II error. The rejection region (see Figures 6.4 and 6.5) will be twice as large as either of the two rejection regions when a two-tailed research hypothesis is used (see Figure 6.3). But, as we will recall from Chapter 6, there is no rejection region (critical value) at all if the relationship is found to be in the direction opposite to that expressed in a one-tailed research hypothesis. If that is the case, we can only conclude that we failed to find support for the one-tailed research hypothesis.

5. The likely amount of sampling error in sample data, which is a function of the size of the research sample used. Selecting larger samples makes statistical tests more powerful. Conversely, selecting smaller samples makes statistical tests less powerful. When larger samples are used, the long run is approximated. The law of averages states that larger samples contain less sampling error than smaller samples. Thus, larger samples are more likely to be able to dismiss sampling error as the cause for a relationship between variables in them, and thus we are able to reject the null hypothesis. With larger samples we are unlikely to miss a true relationship (commit a Type II error).

To summarize the conditions that affect statistical power: A statistical test is less likely to produce a Type II error (it is more powerful) if:

1. The true relationship between variables is strong rather than weak
2. The variability of the variables is small rather than large
3. A higher (e.g., .10 rather than .05) rejection level is used

4. A one-tailed research hypothesis is used, and the direction of the relationship between the two variables is correctly predicted

5. The sample used is large rather than small

What We Can and Cannot Control.   We cannot adjust the actual strength of a relationship between variables—it is a given. For the same reason, we cannot affect the amount of variation that exists among the values of a variable in its population.

In relation to the third factor, while we have the capacity to adjust the rejection level used (e.g., to use .10 instead of .05 as the cutoff point), that would come at a cost. By reducing the likelihood of committing a Type II error, we increase the likelihood of committing a Type I error.

We could also decrease the likelihood of making a Type II error by using a one-tailed rather than a two-tailed research hypothesis, but this may not be an option. The literature usually dictates whether it is justifiable to predict the direction of a relationship between variables.

That brings us to the fifth factor in statistical power—sample size. It is the factor affecting power, over which we generally have the greatest control. Selection of a sample size, although sometimes constrained by various ethical and practice considerations, allows us to conduct a statistical analysis using a test that will generate the optimal amount of statistical power.

Statistical Power Analysis.   In data analyses, more powerful is not always better, since a statistical test that is too powerful can identify relationships between variables that may be statistically significant but very weak or otherwise meaningless. But a statistical test that is not powerful enough to detect a true relationship between variables also can be problematic. Using such a test can cause us to fail to identify a potentially valuable relationship between variables. Especially if the true relationship is relatively weak (but still of interest), it may be that a more powerful test should be used or that the conditions under which it is used should be changed, usually by increasing sample size.

What we need is the optimum amount of statistical power. We want it to provide an acceptably low probability of risk for committing both Type I and Type II errors. We need a reasonable balance between the two. There is a mathematical process called *statistical power analysis* that allows us to determine what sample size would constitute the right amount of power for our data analysis or, if a statistical test has already been conducted, to draw conclusions about whether it was not powerful enough or too powerful for what we were hoping to learn from it.

Tests of statistical inference (such as those discussed in subsequent chapters) allow us to determine the *p*-value or the probability of mistakenly rejecting a true null hypothesis (committing a Type I error). In contrast, a statistical power analysis allows us to determine the probability of committing a Type II error, given the statistical test used and the conditions under which it is used. Statistical power analyses are very complicated mathematical procedures that are beyond the scope of this text. The authority on them is Jacob Cohen whose book, *Statistical Power Analysis for the Behavioral Sciences,* not only explains how they are performed but also provides handy tables that allow the reader to determine the likelihood of committing a Type II error based on the rejection level used, the effect size (the estimated strength of the relationship between the variables in the population), and the sample size. These are three of the five factors that affect statistical power that were discussed in the previous section of this chapter.

A statistical power analysis is especially useful in selecting a research design. It allows researchers to identify the optimal size research sample(s) to use. It is possible to use Cohen's tables to select a sample that will generate just enough statistical power to reduce the likelihood of making a Type II error to an acceptably low level, while not adding unnecessary cost to the research study. Conducting a statistical power analysis to select the optimal size research sample helps avoid (1) selecting a sample that is larger than needed, thereby unnecessarily increasing the cost of the study, and (2) inadvertently conducting a study with a sample that is so small that there is virtually no probability that statistical significance will be achieved, even though the variables really are related.

If we have no choice in the matter of sample size, if the only available sample is relatively small, the tables can be used to tell us if it is worthwhile to conduct the study. They may suggest that, given the estimated strength of the relationship between the variables (effect size), there would be a very high probability of committing a Type II error with the small available sample. Perhaps the statistical power generated by the analysis would not be enough to provide support for the existence of the relationship, even though it may exist. We might attempt to generate more power by increasing the usual .05 rejection level to .10 or even .20. But that might make the probability of committing a Type I error unacceptably high.

Even after data have been analyzed, statistical power analysis can perform a second valuable function. Let us assume that we find insufficient statistical support to be able to reject the null hypothesis—the relationship between variables is not statistically significant. So we fail to reject the null hypothesis. But, as always, an error might have occurred, in this case a Type II error. If statistical power analysis is used, the probability of committing a Type II error can be reported along with the finding of nonsignificance. For example, the research report might read, "There was a lack of statistical support for the research hypothesis ($p > .05$)." However, a statistical power analysis revealed that there was a .35 probability of committing a Type II error. This is useful information. It admits that the statistical testing used had relatively low statistical power. It better puts the finding of nonsignificance in perspective. It may suggest the advisability of replicating the research study to further explore whether a Type II error might have occurred and whether the relationship between variables might not exist after all.

Robustness of Tests Being Considered

In everyday English, power and robustness mean something very similar. They do, however, have very different meanings when used in statistical analyses. As we have just discussed, the power of a statistical analysis is its ability to detect a true relationship between variables. *Robustness* is the degree to which a specific statistical test produces accurate findings when one or more of its assumptions is not met. Robustness of a test is relative; every test is more or less robust. A relatively robust test is one that produces reasonably accurate results even if one or more of the assumptions for its use cannot be fully met.

As noted earlier, all statistical tests require certain conditions for their use, usually called *assumptions*. Assumptions most often relate to the sampling methods used, the shape of the distribution of one or more variables in the population, the amount of variability in one or more variables, and/or the level of measurement of one or more variables.

The *t* tests described in Chapter 11 are good examples of robust tests. Two of their assumptions are that, in examining the relationship between variables, any dependent variables should be at the interval or ratio level of measurement and should be normally distributed within the population. When used with variables that are somewhat skewed, however, the results are still quite accurate. A certain amount of flexibility about the usual assumption of a normal distribution is common among many other tests that are regarded as relatively robust.

PARAMETRIC AND NONPARAMETRIC TESTS

There are two general categories of statistical tests—parametric and nonparametric. *Parametric tests* require that:

1. At least one variable (usually the dependent variable) should be at the interval or ratio level of measurement

2. The dependent variable should be normally distributed (in the population); if samples are drawn from different populations and then compared, the distributions of the variable in these different populations are required to have equal or near equal variances

3. Cases should been selected independently—that is, they are randomly selected and, if an experimental design was used, also randomly assigned to experimental and control groups

Some additional requirements apply to specific parametric tests. Some tests allow us to waive one or more of the above three requirements. A test's special requirements are listed in more advanced statistics books, often along with a statement about its robustness, that is, what assumption(s) of the test, if any, can be waived (and to what degree). Generally, if the mean and the standard deviation are appropriate descriptive statistics for summarizing a study's findings, parametric statistics may be appropriate for examining the relationships between variables.

Nonparametric tests have fewer assumptions. They are designed for research situations in which one or more conditions for the use of parametric tests cannot be met. They do not require a normal distribution of the dependent variable in the population from which the sample was drawn. Some nonparametric tests are intended for independently drawn samples; others are not. The number of samples, the number of cases in each sample, and the presence or absence of "ties" (cases with the same value of a variable) also are important factors in selecting the most appropriate nonparametric test from the many that exist.

Most nonparametric tests require only nominal- or ordinal-level data, but some are more demanding, requiring greater measurement precision. As a group, nonparametric tests are less powerful than parametric tests. That is, they would be more likely to result in Type II errors than parametric tests if used with the same data set under the same conditions.

Because nonparametric tests generally are designed to be used with nominal- or ordinal-level data (or interval- and ratio-level data that are not normally distributed), they are often ideally suited to social work research. As noted earlier, many dependent variables cannot be assumed to be at the interval or ratio levels of measurement. Many also are dichotomous (e.g., success/failure; rehospitalization/nonre-hospitalization; passage/nonpassage of legislation; employment/unemployment of clients).

Nonparametric tests should not be regarded as a second-best choice designed for situations in which criteria for parametric statistics cannot be met, however. They have some distinct advantages over parametric tests and often are the best tests for addressing some statistical needs. A nonparametric statistic, for example, is especially useful when one or more of the following three conditions exist:

1. Samples have been compiled from different populations, and we wish to compare the distribution of a single variable within each of them
2. Variables are at the nominal level of measurement, or value categories of the variables allow for only the rank ordering of responses
3. Very small samples (e.g., as small as 6 or 7) are all that are available for study

Fortunately, the relative lack of power of nonparametric tests can be compensated for, at least in part. As noted above, increasing sample size increases the power of any statistical test. Many nonparametric tests can be made just about as powerful as their parametric counterparts with the use of sufficiently large samples.

In many situations where nonparametric tests are appropriate, two or more tests could potentially be used, but they are likely to require different size samples. As a general rule, the test that uses the larger sample is likely to be the more powerful one. If we anticipate the need for more power in testing (such as when we anticipate that a relationship between variables may be weak but still worth trying to document), we should consider the possibility of drawing a larger sample and using a test that is designed for use with larger samples.

MULTIVARIATE STATISTICAL TESTS

A research hypothesis may indicate that we need to examine more than just the relationship between two variables (bivariate analysis). We may need to examine the complex relationship among three or more variables in order to attempt to sort out how they are interrelated. In that case, a selection must be made from among the more mathematically complicated tests that are collectively referred to as *multivariate analyses.*

There are dangers in using a series of bivariate statistical analyses to test the relationships between a number of independent variables and a single dependent variable.

Examining so many possible combinations of variables can easily result in a Type I error by causing us to stumble onto a spurious (not real) relationship. The laws of probability would tell us that if we examine 100 pairs of variables that are not related, the sampling error will be great enough in 5 of them to allow us to reject the null hypothesis and erroneously conclude that they probably are related (using .05 as the rejection level). That is one reason why we need to understand the principles behind multivariate analyses and to have a familiarity with them. They can reduce the likelihood of Type I errors.

There are situations where a multivariate analysis is the logical choice. Multivariate analyses are consistent with the multiple causation and systems theories of human behavior that dominate much social work literature. Like these theories, they allow us to attempt to sort out the complex interaction of variables that exist within practice and research milieus. For example, they allow us to sort out the complex relationship among rates of alcoholism, illegal drug usage, unemployment, and family violence, where the relationships are not simple cause-and-effect ones.

Multivariate analyses differ from bivariate analyses in two important ways. First, as already stated, they examine the relationship among three or more variables. Second, and more importantly, they examine the relationship among the variables simultaneously.

Suppose we wish to examine the relationship among the independent variables *per capita income* and *rates of child abuse* and the dependent variable *incidence of violence in schools* within various cities. Two bivariate analyses might look at (1) the relationship between income and incidence of violence in schools, and (2) the relationship between rates of child abuse and incidence of violence in schools. By contrast, a single multivariate analysis, using a single procedure, would look at the total picture, including how income and rates of child abuse might be related and how all three variables might be related as a group.

With the availability of computer-assisted data analyses software packages, multivariate analyses are used much more commonly in social work research than in the past. The mathematics of multivariate analyses is far more difficult to understand than that of bivariate analyses—it is a subject better suited to advanced courses in data analysis. The brief descriptions of several multivariate tests in the chapters that follow will give some insight into their theoretical underpinnings and in what data analysis situations they are especially helpful.

GENERAL GUIDELINES FOR TEST SELECTION

Generally, we should select a statistical test that promises to provide the amount of statistical power we require, given the conditions (e.g., sample size, estimated strength of a relationship) that exist. A statistical test should also only be used under the conditions for which it was intended.

How can we begin the process of elimination involved in selecting the correct test? A good first step is to identify the level of measurement of the variables of interest. While this will not answer many of the questions involved in the selection process (for example, the need for bivariate or multivariate analyses, sampling method used, or the shape of a variable's distribution), it will go a long way toward shortening the list of possible tests.

Figure 7.1 presents a general guide for selecting the most appropriate statistical test when the relationship between one independent variable and one dependent variable is examined (bivariate analysis). More specifically, Figure 7.1 displays the names of several commonly used parametric tests and their corresponding nonparametric alternatives. We discuss all of these tests in later chapters of this book.

Even the question of which test can be used with which level of measurement is answered the same way by all researchers and statisticians. For example, although parametric tests traditionally are believed to require interval- or ratio-level data for the dependent variable, some people argue that parametric tests can be used with ordinal-level data when the intervals within the ordinal data are approximately equal. Thus, the decision about whether it is acceptable to use ordinal-level data with parametric

Parametric Statistical Tests			**Nonparametric Statistical Tests**		
Test	Dependent (Criterion) Variable	Independent (Predictor) Variable	Test	Dependent (Criterion) Variable	Independent (Predictor) Variable
—	—	—	Chi-square	Nominal	Nominal
—	—	—	Fisher's exact	Nominal	Nominal (2 categories)
—	—	—	McNemar's	Nominal (before)	Nominal (after)
One sample *t*	Interval/ratio	Interval/ratio	Goodness-of-fit	Nominal	Nominal
Independent *t*	Interval/ratio	Nominal	Mann-Whitney *U*	Ordinal/skewed interval	Nominal
			Kolmogorov-Smirnov	Ordinal/skewed interval	—
Dependent *t*	Interval/ratio	Nominal	Wilcoxon Sign	Ordinal "plus"	(2 repeated measures)
One-way *ANOVA*	Interval/ratio	Nominal	Kruskal-Wallis	Ordinal/skewed interval	Nominal
Pearson's *r*	Interval/ratio	Interval/ratio	Spearman rho	Ordinal/skewed interval	Ordinal/skewed interval
			Kendall's tau	Ordinal/skewed interval	Ordinal/skewed interval
Simple linear regression	Interval/ratio	Interval/ratio	Logistic regression	Nominal	Nominal

FIGURE 7.1   **Using Level of Measurement to Begin to Select the Appropriate Statistical Test**

statistical tests requires a close review of the data and of others' opinions about the robustness of a specific parametric test.

There is consensus that the relationship between nominal-level variables can be examined using nonparametric statistical tests only. That is why there are no parametric counterparts for Chi-square, Fisher's exact test, and McNemar's tests.

There are a number of comprehensive books on statistical test selection, many of which are available in college and university libraries. Some books present highly detailed flowcharts for use in selecting statistical tests given various assumptions about a study's research design and the level of measurement of variables.

To use such reference books, it always is necessary to know:

- The level of measurement of the dependent variable(s)
- The level of measurement of the independent variable(s)
- Exactly how the research sample was obtained and its size
- How the dependent variable(s) (and independent variable[s], if appropriate) is (are) distributed in the population from which it was (they were) drawn

GETTING HELP WITH DATA ANALYSES

This chapter has focused on the process involved in selecting a statistical test to analyze the relationship between or among variables. It has introduced the complicated task of selecting the most appropriate statistical test or tests for hypothesis testing and noted some of the issues that need to be considered when selecting a test from the many that exist. It has not provided the answer to the question, "What statistical test should I use given my specific research situation?"

While Figure 7.1 and the books listed in the References and Further Readings section at the end of this book can be helpful in test selection, recent advances in computer technology have made it even easier to select a test and to address other related issues, such as the best sample size to use. Statistical software programs use the information provided by the researcher—for example, the level of measurement of the independent and dependent variables, the shape of their distributions, the statistical power desired, and the sampling method used—to suggest which statistical test(s) is (are) most appropriate. As these programs become more widely available, decision-making charts such as Figure 7.1 will no longer be necessary. (In fact, the authors of one of the most comprehensive test selection reference books now offer a computer version of their book.)

Computers cannot tell us what meaningful research problems to pursue or what hypotheses to test (not yet, anyway). They cannot tell us how to conceptualize, operationalize, design, implement, and gather data to test our research hypotheses. For now, these tasks are left to us. Computers can, however, quickly and effortlessly produce frequency distributions and attractive graphs that accurately describe our sample or population. They can calculate measures of central tendency and variability in a matter of seconds. They can also tell us the likelihood that sampling error produced a relationship between two or more variables in the data set (the likelihood of a Type I error if the null hypothesis were to be rejected). But even with computer-assisted statistical test selection and high-speed number crunching, we still need to know how to interpret the findings and decide if they are truly meaningful. If we conclude that they are meaningful, we still need to decide how to apply them to social work practice.

For those who lack access to software packages for computer-assisted statistical test selection and data analyses and/or to the most up-to-date reference books, consultation with experts can assist in the task of research design and statistical analysis. In schools and departments of social work and in many social service organizations throughout the world, there are people who know a lot about statistical analyses. They can help us if we know what questions to ask and how to ask them, and if we can comprehend and respond appropriately to the questions they ask.

Because so many statistical tests are available, even the experts cannot be knowledgeable about all of them. In fact, probably only a few dozen tests are commonly used in social work research; another group is seen occasionally in the literature; and a third group consists of a large number of relatively obscure tests designed for use in unique situations. Widespread access to computerized data analyses has resulted in some changes in this mix. Some tests (especially multivariate ones) that were avoided because of their long, complicated formulas have become more popular and widely used. Other tests that were very popular primarily because of their ease of calculation (e.g., some nonparametric tests) are now less popular, since computers have made the use of better alternatives feasible. Of course, new tests are also continuing to be developed.

CONCLUDING THOUGHTS

This chapter, along with Chapters 5 and 6, discussed various aspects of two related activities that are a central focus of most social work research—inference and hypothesis testing. Chapter 7 focused on the process of selecting the most appropriate statistical test to determine if there is support for a research hypothesis. In a nutshell, the process of hypothesis testing is a series of seven steps:

1. *State the research hypothesis(es).* Label the independent and dependent variables. State how each variable is conceptualized and operationalized.

Remember: The research hypothesis guides the entire conceptualization and operationalization process. In addition, it helps determine the best research design to use in an effort to rule out alternative explanations that could explain an apparent relationship between variables. Research hypotheses, if appropriate, should be supported by theoretical assumptions derived from a literature review.

A research hypothesis can be one-tailed or two-tailed (and, less frequently, in the null form, expressing the belief that variables are really unrelated). The research hypothesis is not statistically tested; it is either indirectly supported or not supported by directly testing the null hypothesis.

2. *For any research hypothesis, state the corresponding null hypothesis.* Conceptualize how the data would look if the null hypothesis were, in fact, correct.

Remember: The null hypothesis states that there is no relationship between the variables in the research hypothesis. It covers all outcome possibilities that are not explicit in the research hypothesis. Thus, if a one-tailed research hypothesis states that the level of job satisfaction for medical social workers has increased significantly over the last 4 years, the null hypothesis includes the possibilities that job satisfaction has not changed and also that it has decreased.

If the null hypothesis can be rejected, support is present for the one-tailed or two-tailed research hypothesis. Hypothesis testing is a process of indirect proof. We never directly prove that the research hypothesis is correct; rather, if the null hypothesis can be rejected, the one-tailed or two-tailed research hypothesis (the alternative hypothesis) is supported only indirectly. In those rare instances where there is a null research hypothesis (predicting no relationship between variables), support for the research hypothesis is achieved if the statistical analysis does not allow the researcher to reject the null hypothesis.

3. *Specify the statistical rejection level to be used.* If any level other than .05 is to be used, specify the justification for its use. Which type of error, Type I or Type II, are we more interested in seeking to avoid, and why?

Remember: This step entails determining the consequences of erroneously rejecting the null hypothesis or erroneously not rejecting it. The possibility of Type I errors can be reduced (among other ways) by setting a low rejection level (e.g., .01, .025, .05) rather than a higher one (e.g., .10, .15), which would reduce the likelihood Type II error. A statistical power analysis can help us estimate the latter.

4. *State all assumptions about the data and how they were collected.* What levels of measurement are assumed to exist? Which variables are assumed to be normally distributed? What specific sampling methods were employed? How large are the samples?

Remember: We must know the level of measurement for each of the variables to be analyzed. The method by which the sample is drawn, sample size, and the way our variables are distributed in the population also affect the choice of which statistical test to use.

5. *Describe the most relevant characteristics of the sample and/or population. Select and compute one or more inferential statistical test(s) to test the research hypothesis.* Is each test used appropriate for the conditions described in step 4? Is a consultant to be used in the selection of the tests? Is computation of the test to be computer-assisted? If so, what statistical software package will be used? Conceptually, how will each test generate a *p*-value?

Remember: The statistical test used does not determine the degree to which rival hypotheses or design bias (e.g., measurement bias and sampling bias) may have helped create an apparent relationship between variables in a research sample. It only determines the likelihood that sampling error played a role in the study's findings.

6. *Determine whether the relationship between variables is statistically significant.* Is the probability (*p*-value) smaller than the predetermined rejection level? If a one-tailed research hypothesis was used, is the direction of the relationship that was found the same as stated in the hypothesis? If so, are we reasonably certain that other factors (e.g., rival hypotheses, design bias) did not produce the relationship between the variables within the sample? If so, it probably is safe to reject the null hypothesis and to conclude that a true relationship between the variables exists within the population.

Remember: We can never be totally certain that sampling error did not produce an apparent relationship between variables. When we reject the null hypothesis, we are saying only that we are reasonably certain that the apparent relationship is a real one, but we might still be wrong—we may have drawn an atypical sample because of sampling error.

7. *Determine whether each statistically significant relationship is meaningful.* To what degree did sample size contribute to statistical significance? How strong is the absolute relationship between the variables (effect size)? How surprising are the study's findings? How useful are they for the social work practitioner, educator, or researcher? To what extent would we feel safe in generalizing the findings beyond our sample and the population from which it was drawn (the issue of external validity)?

Remember: These decisions require a thoughtful combination of ethics, common sense, convention, and practice expertise. They must be addressed before a study's findings are implemented in social work practice.

The chapters that follow present a description of statistical tests that have been widely used in social work research for many years and promise to remain popular. They are versatile and suitable for many types of data analysis situations. The emphasis will be on understanding what they do and what their results mean rather than on the mathematics of their computations. In today's professional environment, we usually can leave that job to computers.

STUDY QUESTIONS

1. How can the use of an inappropriate statistical test harm the credibility of a research study?
2. How might a researcher's use of an inappropriate test ultimately have a negative effect on services to clients? Discuss. Provide an original practice example in your discussion.
3. How does the rule of the instrument sometimes lead to the selection of an inappropriate statistical test?
4. What factors related to sampling methods help determine which statistical test is appropriate?
5. What two characteristics of a variable also affect which statistical test should be used?
6. How does the operationalization of a variable performed before data are even collected serve to limit (or expand) which statistical test or tests can be used? Provide original examples in your discussion.
7. What do we mean when we say that one statistical test is more powerful than another? What is statistical power analysis, and why is it a useful counterbalance to inferential statistical analysis? What do we mean when we say that one test is more robust than another?
8. What factors affect the statistical power of a test?
9. How is it possible for a test to be too powerful? What problems can a too-powerful test create?

10. How is it possible for a test to be not powerful enough? What problems can a test that is not powerful enough create?
11. What three general assumptions must be met for a parametric test to be used?
12. Why are nonparametric tests particularly useful in many social work research projects? How can we make them more powerful?
13. In what ways do multivariate analyses differ from bivariate analyses? Why are they less likely to cause a researcher to commit a Type I error?

CHAPTER

8

Correlation

In social work research, the term *correlation* is often used. It refers to the degree of association between or among variables. When we describe the correlation between two interval-level or ratio-level variables, for example, we are describing the degree to which certain values of one variable are associated with (that is, tend to be found with) certain values of the other variable.

The results of bivariate correlation analyses are extremely useful for interpreting research data. They can answer three questions:

1. What is the actual strength and direction of the relationship between variables within the sample studied?
2. How much of the variation in values of one variable are attributable to the variations in values of the other variable?
3. What is the probability that the relationship between variables within the sample is due to sampling error?

Frequently, two or more variables contained in a research study have neither been introduced nor manipulated in any way by the researcher. But the variables appear to be associated, or to co-vary. *Covariance* refers to the degree to which certain values of one variable to be found with certain values of some other variable.

As noted in Chapter 1, researchers generally use the labels *independent variable* and *dependent variable* to describe the relationship between variables in a research hypothesis. However, in this chapter and the next one, we will use their counterparts, *predictor variable* and *criterion variable* since, as we shall discuss, covariance is not in itself sufficient evidence that the values of one variable actually produced the values of the other variable.

USES OF CORRELATION

Correlation analyses are very versatile. For example, they are used for developing and refining some forms of data collection instruments, such as scales or indexes. They also are used to examine the reliability (consistency) of measurement instruments when, for example, the instruments are used with different populations, under different research situations, or at different times. In fact, the different methods for assessing reliability described in research methods books (e.g., inter-rater reliability, parallel forms reliability, test-retest reliability, coefficient alpha) depend on the concept of correlation.

Teachers use correlation analyses to evaluate the reliability of multiple-choice or true-false tests. They want to know the correlation between how individual students answered each question (who answered the question correctly and who did not) and how they performed overall on the test. A good question is one that students who had the highest overall grades on the test were less likely to miss than students who had the lowest overall grades on the same test. Correlation can thus help teachers conclude whether a test question is a good one and should be counted or discarded in determining final student grades on the test. As with all types of correlation analyses, however, such analyses only tell us about the reliability of a test question. And, as we know, reliability is not enough to guarantee a question's validity, that is, it does not assure that the question really measures what it purports to measure.

Correlation analyses are also widely used for description. Using data collected from a research sample or from an entire population, they provide a numerical summary of the relationship between or among variables. It might be useful for the reader of a report to know, for example, that within a sample of employees studied in a human service agency, there was a high negative correlation between the variables *employee's age* and *number of claims for disability insurance.* This knowledge might be valuable, even though such a correlation may not be typical or representative of human service agencies in general. It would help readers better understand the unique research sample and study setting and recognize any differences between the study's setting and their own.

Given the appropriate research design, correlation analyses can also be used for inference, that is, to determine the probability that a relationship between variables found within a sample may be a real one that exists within the population from which the sample was drawn. We have chosen to discuss correlation at this point in this book because correlation analyses can be used both for description and for inference. Thus, it forms a useful bridge between the discussion of descriptive statistical analyses in the early chapters and the discussion of inferential statistical tests that follow.

Scattergrams

When used for descriptive purposes, a correlation analysis between two variables (and not more than two) can be displayed in a scattergram. The graphs in Chapter 2 displayed how many times each value occurred for a given variable (frequencies) within a sample or population. But scattergrams simultaneously portray the values for *two* variables (for each case). They can thus begin to suggest the presence (or absence) of a relationship between the two variables.

If 23 clients, for example, completed a standardized self-administered measuring instrument that measures the variable *per capita income* and also completed a standardized self-administered instrument that measures the variable *client satisfaction with social work services,* a scattergram could easily portray each person's score on both variables (i.e., per capita income, satisfaction with social work services) with a single dot. The scattergram would have 23 dots—not 46—one to represent each of the 23 cases and their combination of measurements for the two variables.

Scattergrams can be used to:

1. Suggest a possible relationship between variables

2. Graphically report relationships that have already been demonstrated to exist through the use of other statistical analyses

3. Identify and present patterns of possible relationships between variables that may exist within certain subsamples of a larger data set, but that might have gotten lost or cancelled out when the entire data set was first analyzed. For example, when the data are first analyzed, the correlation between per capita income (first variable) and client satisfaction with services (second variable) may not be statistically significant among a large sample of clients with widely varying incomes. But when the same data are displayed using a scattergram, a fairly strong positive correlation (one that is likely to be statistically significant) may be apparent within, for example, the $12,000–$14,999 income range.

Like most of the other graphs presented in Chapter 2, scattergrams use two perpendicular lines (i.e., a horizontal *x* axis and a vertical *y* axis). Unlike the other graphs, however, scattergrams do not use the *y* axis to plot and display frequencies. As can be seen in Figure 8.1, the values of the first (predictor) variable are plotted along the *x*-axis and the values of the second (criterion) variable along the *y* axis.

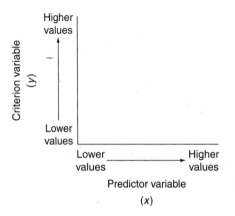

FIGURE 8.1   Basic Outline of a Graph for Depicting Values for Two Variables

The values for the predictor and criterion variables for a scattergram may or may not have identical intervals. For example, values for the predictor variable *number of siblings* can be marked off at equal intervals of one unit, while the values for the criterion variable *assertiveness score* can be marked off at equal intervals of five units. Most computer statistical software packages that produce scattergrams automatically draw them to scale based on the raw data.

How might a scattergram suggest a possible relationship between variables? Suppose that we are interested in studying the relationship between the two variables *number of treatment sessions a client attended* (predictor variable) and that client's *self-esteem level* (criterion variable). We might hypothesize that among clients being treated for problems related to low self-esteem, there will be a positive association between current self-esteem levels and number of treatment sessions they attend; that is, the more treatment sessions clients attended, the higher their self-esteem scores, and vice versa. We could randomly select 10 cases, for example, and could display the number of treatment sessions attended (the predictor variable) and the clients' self-esteem scores (the criterion variable) in a scattergram such as Figure 8.2.

Each dot in Figure 8.2 represents an individual client's number of treatment sessions attended (*x* axis) and self-esteem level (*y* axis). Ten dots on the graph represent the case sample (*n* = 10). Notice that, for example, Lydia attended 10 treatment sessions and had a self-esteem level of 30; William attended 18 sessions and had a self-esteem level of 40.

Correlation analyses are most often used to describe the degree to which a *linear* relationship exists between variables in a sample or population. The fact that the dots in Figure 8.2 are scattered somewhat randomly (rather than falling in a straight line sloping upward or downward from left to right) suggests that the correlation between

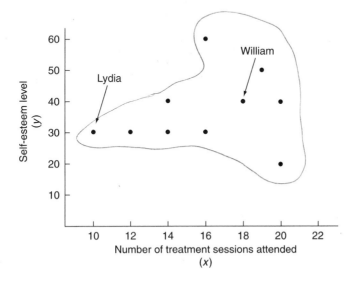

FIGURE 8.2   Scattergram: Number of Treatment Sessions Attended and Self-Esteem Level

the two variables was far from a perfect one (in which every dot would have fallen on the line).

The absence of a strong linear relationship between the variables suggests little support for the research hypothesis about the variables' relationship with one another in the population from which the sample was drawn. If the data in Figure 8.2 had suggested a stronger linear correlation between variables (and they had been collected in a carefully controlled explanatory research study), it might have been productive to use additional statistical analyses to actually test the research hypothesis about their true relationship in the population. The use of use of correlation analyses for inference is discussed in more detail later in this chapter.

PERFECT CORRELATIONS

As noted previously, the linear correlation in Figure 8.2 is far from perfect. In fact, the dots appear to be scattered almost randomly. An example of a perfect relationship between a predictor variable and a criterion variable can be seen in Table 8.1. The table displays the hypothetical measurements of two variables, *client's motivation for treatment* and *client's level of functioning*. For each client there is a pair of values—the value of the predictor variable (motivational level for treatment) and the corresponding client value of the criterion variable (functioning level). Note in Table 8.1 that if, prior to data collection, a one-tailed research hypothesis had been formulated (i.e., "Clients with higher motivational levels for treatment will have higher functioning levels than clients with lower motivational levels and vice versa"), the data would lend support to the hypothesis.

A relationship between the two variables in Table 8.1 is evident because, without exception, higher motivational levels for treatment are associated with higher levels of

TABLE 8.1   Motivation for Treatment and Level of Functioning ($N = 10$)

Name	Motivational Level (X)	Functioning Level (Y)
Floyd	1	2
Jane	2	3
Robert	3	4
Sue	4	5
Herb	5	6
Bill	6	7
Margareta	7	8
Ann	8	9
Dorothy	9	10
Lynne	10	11

functioning and vice versa. Floyd, for example, scored lowest on both motivational level for treatment (a value of 1) and functioning level (a value of 2). Jane scored second lowest on both levels (values of 2 and 3 respectively), and Lynne scored highest on both (values of 10 and 11 respectively). This perfect relationship also can be depicted in a scattergram, such as the one in Figure 8.3.

In Figure 8.3, the horizontal axis (*x* axis) represents the clients' individual scores (or measurements) of their motivational levels for treatment, while the vertical axis (*y* axis) represents the individual scores of their functioning levels. Each dot represents a pair of scores for one person. If connected, the dots would form a straight line—a perfect linear correlation. Such perfection is almost never seen in data drawn from social work research studies. It is used here to illustrate the concept of correlation in its most vivid form.

Figure 8.3 demonstrates two important characteristics of the perfect linear relationship between variables: *strength* and *direction*. With regard to strength, the overall relationship between the two variables contained in Figure 8.3 could not be stronger, as each one of the client's paired scores falls along a straight line. While Figure 8.3 is an example of a perfect positive correlation, Figure 8.4 is an example of a perfect negative correlation. In both figures, the dots fall in a straight line. In those more common situations where the relationship between variables is less than perfect, a line called a *regression line* (to be discussed in Chapter 9) can be drawn to represent the best fit among a scatter of dots.

In regard to the second characteristic of a correlation—direction—the relationship between the clients' motivation for treatment levels and their functioning levels, as dis-

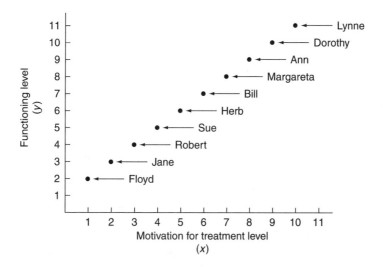

FIGURE 8.3   Scattergram of a Perfect Positive Correlation between Two Variables: Motivation for Treatment and Functioning Levels (from Table 8.1)

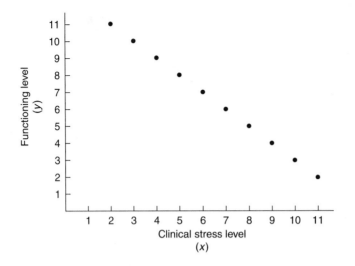

**FIGURE 8.4   Scattergram of a Perfect Negative
Correlation Between Two Variables: Clinical Stress
and Functioning Levels**

played in Figure 8.3, can be described as positive. In a positive correlation, high values
of *x* are associated with high values of *y*, and low values of *x* are associated with low
values of *y*. The line connecting the dots runs from lower left to upper right on the graph.

In a negative relationship, such as the one displayed in Figure 8.4, high values of
one variable are associated with low values of the second variable and vice versa. The
line connecting the dots runs from upper left to lower right on the graph. Figure 8.4
suggests that higher clinical stress levels (predictor variable) are associated with lower
functioning levels (criterion variable).

NONPERFECT CORRELATIONS

In social work research, some relationships between variables may have no discernable direction as well as no strength; there is no apparent relationship at all between
them. Figure 8.5 displays hypothetical data in which there is no perceivable relationship between the variables *self-esteem* and *aggression*. In other words, we could not
say that the more (or less) self-esteem that clients possess, the more (or less) aggres-
sive they are (at least in this sample anyway).

Virtually all relationships between variables reflect some degree of correlation,
usually ranging from barely discernable to nearly perfect. Any correlation within this
range is referred to as a *nonperfect correlation*. Figure 8.6 is a scattergram illustrating
a nonperfect positive correlation between the variables *number of treatment sessions
attended* and *clients' attitudes toward their peers*. The correlation is positive, but it is
not a perfect positive correlation, like the one reflected in Figure 8.3.

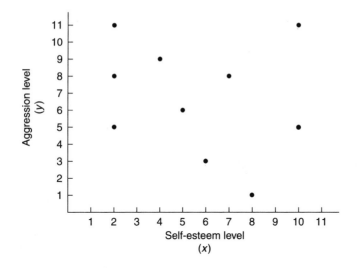

FIGURE 8.5   Scattergram of No Correlation between Two Variables: Self-Esteem and Aggression Levels

Figure 8.6 shows that three clients were seen only once by a social worker, but one client (Sue) scored a 2 on the Attitudes toward Peers Scale, another (Robert) scored a 4, and a third client scored a 6. So, the relationship between the two variables is far from perfect, even though the paired values represented by dots fall in an overall posi-

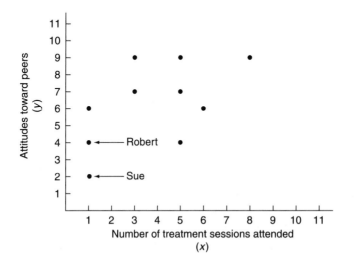

FIGURE 8.6   Scattergram of a Nonperfect Positive Correlation between Two Variables: Number of Treatment Sessions Attended and Attitudes toward Peers

tive direction (lower left to upper right). In contrast, Figure 8.7 reflects no relationship at all between the variables *depression level* and *motivation for treatment.*

INTERPRETING LINEAR CORRELATIONS

The dots in scattergrams (each reflecting one value for the predictor variable and one value for the criterion variable for each case) can fall in a variety of patterns, such as a straight line, a U shape, and a J shape. The dots in a scattergram might look like a series of waves (cyclical correlation), for example, or a line that is curved like either an arch or an upside-down arch (curvilinear correlation). A clear pattern in a distribution of dots and the fact that they form a straight or curved line indicate the presence of a relationship between variables.

Observing the pattern in which the dots in a scattergram fall is useful for understanding and drawing tentative conclusions about relationships between variables. It also tells us whether it is appropriate to use statistical tests that examine correlation but make assumptions about the overall pattern of a correlation between the two variables. The statistical tests in this chapter, for example, test only for the degree to which two variables are linearly correlated. They should not be used to examine relationships between variables that may be related, but not in a linear way.

Scattergrams are one way of displaying the paired values for two variables in any given data set. A more efficient way of displaying the relationship between two interval-level or ratio-level variables is to use a correlation coefficient. A *correlation coefficient,* expressed as the lowercase italicized letter *r,* provides a numerical indicator of both the strength and the direction of the relationship between variables.

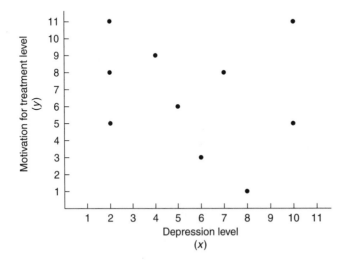

FIGURE 8.7   Scattergram of No Correlation between Two Variables: Motivation for Treatment and Depression Levels

The Range of Correlation Coefficients

As Figure 8.8 shows, correlation coefficients range between –1.0 (perfect negative) at one extreme to +1.0 (perfect positive) at the other extreme, with 0.0 (no linear correlation) at the midpoint. (If the correlation is positive, the + sign is generally not used, but is implied.) A correlation coefficient cannot be greater than 1.0 or less than –1.0. The closer the numerical value of the correlation coefficient is to either extreme, the stronger the linear relationship between the two variables. A coefficient of .72, for example, is closer to a perfect correlation than coefficients of either –.60 or .60 and therefore suggests a stronger correlation than either of the other two.

The closer the coefficient is to the middle of the range ($r = 0$), the weaker the relationship between the two variables. A correlation coefficient that is close to 0 suggests that the linear relationship is very weak.

Whether a correlation is positive or negative indicates the direction of a relationship between variables. The correlation coefficient (r) between a social worker's skill level and years of professional social work experience, for example, might be $r = .45$, a positive relationship. The correlation between skill level and level of apathy regarding one's work might be $r = -.35$, indicating a negative relationship; that is, persons who are most apathetic and uninvolved in their work are likely to be less skillful and vice versa.

The sign within a correlation coefficient (– or +) should be interpreted only as an indicator of the direction of a relationship between variables. Thus, if a correlation coefficient is negative (that is, preceded by a minus sign), this does not mean a negative value in the usual mathematical sense. It merely indicates that, to the extent suggested by the value of the correlation coefficient, lower values of one variable tend to be found with higher values of the other variable, and vice versa.

Interpreting Very Strong Correlations

Moderately strong correlation coefficients or even those that are relatively weak may have greater potential to contribute to our body of knowledge than very strong ones. Why? A very strong correlation probably describes a relationship between variables that is pretty obvious. In some human service agencies, for example, we probably could demonstrate a nearly perfect positive correlation between direct service workers' years of employment and the total number of clients they have seen. But such a correlation would not be either meaningful or surprising.

Often, a very strong correlation exists because the two variables are nothing more than two measurements of the same variable. For example, this might explain the finding

| –1.0 | 0.0 | +1.0 |
| (Perfect negative) | (No correlation) | (Perfect positive) |

FIGURE 8.8   The Range of Correlation Coefficients

of a near perfect correlation, say .93, between scores on an anger scale and scores on a hostility scale. The same interpretation might apply if a research study examined the relationship between assertiveness and timidity. Data analysis might produce a correlation coefficient of, say, −.95. Is this an important finding? Probably not. A logical interpretation might be that timidity and assertiveness are really opposite sides of the same variable.

A perfect correlation provides still another extreme example of this principle. If we performed a correlational analysis among a group of social work students for the variables *number of classes missed* and *number of classes attended* over the course of a semester, we would produce a perfect negative correlation coefficient (−1.0). This would not be surprising, since classes missed and classes attended are indicators of the same variable, *class attendance.*

What is the utility of very high correlation coefficients? It lies primarily in the area of research design. Very high correlation coefficients can demonstrate reliability (consistency) and thus are a necessary (but not sufficient) indicator of validity. A very high correlation between a college admissions test and subsequent grade point averages, for example, is an indication of the test's predictive validity—its ability to accurately predict academic success.

Other types of validity also can be indicated by the presence of very high correlation coefficients. For example, using a sample of clients, a very high positive correlation between their scores on a newly developed scale designed to measure antisocial attitudes and their number of arrests for antisocial behaviors is evidence of the new scale's *concurrent validity.*

Very high correlation coefficients also can be used in the construction of a scale. A very high correlation coefficient, for example, between responses to Item 16 on the first draft of a scale designed to measure homophobia and responses to Item 24 on the same scale suggests that the two items may be measuring the same indicator of the variable. In the future, one item could be deleted to make the scale shorter, or both can be left in, with one serving as a kind of reliability check on the other.

The Coefficient of Determination

As should be obvious by now, a correlation coefficient indicates both the strength and the direction of the relationship between two variables. But if the coefficient is squared (r^2), we can learn much more. The new number (r^2) is a measure of association. It indicates the proportion of the variation in one variable that can be accounted for or is related to the variation in values of the other variable. r^2 is called the *coefficient of determination.*

An *r* of .30, for example, describing the correlation between number of treatment interviews and self-esteem levels means that 9 percent ($.30^2 = .09$ or 9%) of the variation in self-esteem levels is related to the variations in number of treatment interviews. The other 91 percent (100% − 9% = 91%) of variation in self-esteem levels remains unaccounted for and is related to other variables.

In interpreting a correlation coefficient, it is important not to treat it as if it were equivalent to ratio-level data or to make statements that in any way give this impression. A correlation coefficient of –.80, for example, does not suggest a correlation that is twice as strong as a correlation coefficient of .40. At least in one sense—its ability to account for the amount of variation in the criterion variable that is related to the variation in the predictor variable—a correlation of –.80 describes an association *four times* as strong ($-.80^2 = .64$; $.40^2 = .16$; $.64/.16 = 4$).

It is also useful to remember that in the rare cases when correlation coefficients are as strong as +.80, there will be few exceptions to the pattern of relationships between values of one variable and values of the second variable, that is, virtually all high values of the first variable will be found in cases with high values of the second variable, and vice versa. A weaker correlation coefficient (such as +.40) will have a much higher percentage of cases that reflect a relationship between variables opposite to the overall direction of the association.

Correlation Is Not Causation

What a correlation coefficient cannot do is tell us whether the values of the criterion variable have been caused by the values of the predictor variable. As suggested earlier, correlation should not be used to make statements about causation.

Unlike a research experiment in which we introduce or manipulate the predictor variable, a correlational analysis generally is used to examine the pattern of a relationship between variables where the distribution of the predictor variable is beyond our control. Its natural variation was simply observed, often after the fact, along with that of the criterion variable. Thus, any interpretation of correlation that implies causation is incorrect.

Many pairs of variables tend to co-vary; they could thus be demonstrated to be correlated. Any statement suggesting causation, however, might be ludicrous. A few examples include (1) a positive correlation between ice-cream sales and drowning rates, (2) a positive correlation among geographical areas between Bible sales and whiskey sales, and (3) a positive correlation between highway speed limits and traffic fatalities. The correlation between the predictor variable and the criterion variable in each of these examples is easily explained (at least in part) by the presence of one or more other variables. For example, temperature, per capita income, and fuel costs (as well as the related miles driven), respectively, would help explain any linear correlations between the pairs of variables.

There are many different ways in which the presence of one or more other variables can affect the correlation of two variables. For example, other variables can precede and cause both to co-vary. They can even make two related variables appear to be more closely related than they really are, or they can make them appear to be less related.

To summarize, correlation is necessary but not sufficient for proof of causation. This means that where causation exists between variables, those same two variables always will be correlated. Just because two variables co-vary, however, is no reason to believe that the different values of one produce the different values of the other. There may be many other possible explanations for a correlation between them besides a cause-effect relationship.

Sometimes the ways in which other variables cause two variables to co-vary is less obvious. We all have heard media exhortations to young people to complete high school and, if possible, to go to college. The appeal usually includes correlation data about the relationship between the variables *educational level* (predictor variable) and *lifetime earnings* (criterion variable). A statement is made that the farther people go in school, the more money they will make over their lifetimes. A simple cause-effect interpretation of correlation data is implied. The correlation between educational level and lifetime earnings may be undeniable. Can it be interpreted to mean that staying in school will automatically increase one's earning potential? No!

The criterion variable *financial success in life* may be strongly correlated with other predictor variables, such as motivation, intelligence, personality, and socioeconomic status of parents. All these variables might reflect a stronger correlation with lifetime earnings than education level. They very likely contribute to both high levels of education and to lifetime earnings.

The complex interaction of variables that relate to lifetime earnings argues against any statement implying causation, despite the fact that a correlation with many different variables could be demonstrated to exist. All other things being equal (and when does this ever occur?), the high-school diploma or college degree might give a person an edge in being financially successful. However, this is not a conclusion that can be drawn from only a simple correlation between the variables *educational level* and *lifetime earnings*.

COMPUTATION AND PRESENTATION OF PEARSON'S *r*

A correlation can be computed using many different statistical formulas. The most commonly used one results in a *Pearson's product moment correlation coefficient,* or simply Pearson's *r.* Its assumptions require both the predictor and criterion variables to be at the interval or ratio levels of measurement and normally distributed within the population.

A Pearson's *r* can easily be calculated with the aid of a computer. Box 8.1 is provided for readers who wish to see the mathematical foundations of the *r* formula. It uses ratio-level data on the number of spouse abuse reports (the predictor variable) and the number of child abuse reports (the criterion variable). The raw data are listed in the *x* and *y* columns in Table 8.2. Notice how the predictor variable and criterion variable could easily be reversed. This would make the number of spouse abuse reports the criterion variable, and the number of child abuse reports would become the predictor variable.

If more than just a few bivariate correlation coefficients are reported as descriptive statistics within a research report, reporting them in tabular form may be helpful to the reader. A table designed for this purpose is called a *correlation matrix.* It lists all variables in a column on the left side and repeats them in a row along the top. Figure 8.9 is an example of a correlation matrix that displays the correlation between several interval-level and ratio-level variables. The reader can find the direction and strength of a correlation between any two variables by noting the correlation coefficient that appears in the matrix where the row in which the first variable appears intersects with the column headed by the second variable.

BOX 8.1
The Correlation Coefficient

Hypothesis: There is a positive association between the number of spouse abuse reports and the number of child abuse reports.

Null Hypothesis: There is no association ($r = 0$) between the number of spouse abuse reports and the number of child abuse reports.

Predictor Variable: Number of spouse abuse reports—ratio level.

Criterion Variable: Number of child abuse reports—ratio level.

Observed Frequencies: See Table 8.2.

Correlation Coefficient Formula:

$$r = \frac{N\Sigma XY - (\Sigma X)(\Sigma Y)}{\sqrt{[N\Sigma X^2 - (\Sigma X)^2][N\Sigma Y^2 - (\Sigma Y)^2]}}$$

where:
r = Correlation coefficient
N = Number of cases
ΣXY = Sum of xy column
ΣX = Sum of x column
ΣY = Sum of y column
ΣX^2 = Sum of x^2 column
ΣY^2 = Sum of y^2 column

Substituting values for letters:

$$r = \frac{(5)(985) - (76)(53)}{\sqrt{[(5)(1290) - (76)^2][(5)(919) - (53)^2]}}$$

$$= \frac{897}{\sqrt{(674)(1786)}}$$

$$= \frac{897}{\sqrt{1203764}}$$

$$= \frac{897}{1097.16}$$

$$= .82 \text{ (correlation coefficient)}$$

Presentation of Results:

$$r = .82, p < .05$$

Conclusions: The null hypothesis is rejected and the one-tailed research hypothesis is supported. In short, there is a statistically significant association between the number of spouse abuse reports and the number of child abuse reports. The coefficient of determination, r^2, is $(.82)^2$ or .67. This indicates that 67 percent of the variance in the number of child abuse reports can be explained by the number of spouse abuse reports.

TABLE 8.2   Number of Spouse Abuse and Child Abuse Reports in Five County Social Services Offices

Office Number	Spouse Abuse Reports (X)	Child Abuse Reports (Y)	X^2	Y^2	XY
Office 1	22	25	484	625	550
Office 2	20	13	400	169	260
Office 3	10	10	100	100	100
Office 4	15	5	25	25	75
Office 5	9	0	81	0	0
Totals	76	53	1290	919	985

When the results of hypothesis testing using a correlation analysis appear in a research report, a short narrative description is usually included to elaborate on its meaning. The text might read like this:

Among the 30 clients participating in the research study, the correlation between the number of treatment interviews they completed and their self-esteem scores was $r = .72$, $p < .01$ (one-tailed test). This means that their self-esteem was positively correlated with the number of times they were seen by the social worker.

Or the text may be:

The correlation between the predictor and criterion variables for the 30 clients was $r = .72$, $p < .01$, which indicates the presence of a statistically significant positive correlation between the two variables.

USING PEARSON'S *r* FOR INFERENCE

As noted earlier, correlation can be used for inference—testing the likelihood that an apparent relationship between variables in a sample may be the work of sampling error.

FIGURE 8.9   Correlation Matrix: Correlation between Selected Demographic Variables among Clients in XYZ Agency ($N = 109$)

	Age	Education	No. Siblings	Income	No. Children
Age	1.000				
Education	−.236	1.000			
No. Siblings	−.105	−.306	1.000		
Income	.391	.671	.069	1.000	
No. Children	.240	−.450	.388	−.253	1.000

How large an *r* do we need to conclude that we can safely reject the null hypothesis and be able to claim statistical support for the position that two variables may be related within a population? It should come as no surprise that it depends on the size of the sample.

It also should come as no surprise that for a relationship between variables to be considered statistically significant, a correlation coefficient must be larger than the corresponding correlation coefficient at some predetermined rejection level (referred to as a "critical value"). Unless previously stated and justified, the .05 rejection level is used as the reference point for determining whether we can claim statistical significance for a relationship between variables.

The table of critical values of *r* (Table 8.3) illustrates the minimum strength of the correlation coefficient required to achieve statistical significance at various rejection levels and with various samples sizes. With a sample of 11 individuals, for example, a correlation coefficient of +.6021 is required with a two-tailed research hypothesis to reach statistical significance at the .05 rejection level (+.7348 at the .01 level) and thereby to permit rejection of the null hypothesis. Of course other alternative explanations for a relationship between variables (besides sampling error) should have been adequately controlled too. With a sample size of 102 cases, however, rejection of the null hypothesis is possible with a relatively weak correlation (+.1946 at the .05 level and +.2540 at the .01 level). How can this be?

As noted in Chapter 7, increasing sample size increases statistical power. It is more likely that sampling error will cause two variables to appear to be related with a small sample than with a larger one. With larger samples, a relationship, even one that appears quite weak, is far less likely to be due to sampling error. If there were no true relationship between variables, the law of averages (the long run) should have taken effect with the use of a large sample—any early pattern of a relationship should have disappeared as new cases were added to it.

Example: Verbal Participation among Female Group Members

Leon is a social worker in a family service agency. He leads several treatment groups of female adolescents. He recently became aware of the wide variation in verbal participation among the group members. While virtually all members responded when spoken to, a few never made any unsolicited comments. Over a period of several weeks, Leon made it a point to ask some of the nonverbal members why they rarely spoke in the group sessions.

Of the seven members he asked, five had essentially the same answer—each was an only child in her family and had been taught by her parents that it was not her role to initiate communication. Leon then asked three of the most verbal adolescents, those who tended to dominate group discussions, how many siblings they had. Their responses were six, seven, and nine respectively.

Based on his limited inquiries, Leon began to speculate on a possible relationship between the predictor variable *number of siblings in the family* and the criterion variable *number of unsolicited comments* in group treatment. He conducted a quick literature review to learn about such phenomena as social traits of only children, communication patterns among siblings, and variations in verbal participation in adolescent treatment

TABLE 8.3   **Critical Values of r**

	Level of significance for a one-tailed test				
	.05	.025	.01	.005	.0005

	Level of significance for a two-tailed test				
N	.10	.05	.02	.01	.001
5	.8054	.8783	.9343	.9587	.9912
6	.7293	.8114	.8822	.9172	.9741
7	.6694	.7545	.8329	.8745	.9507
8	.6215	.7067	.7887	.8343	.9249
9	.5822	.6664	.7498	.7977	.8982
10	.5494	.6319	.7155	.7646	.8721
11	.5214	.6021	.6851	.7348	.8471
12	.4973	.5760	.6581	.7079	.8233
13	.4762	.5529	.6339	.6835	.8010
14	.4575	.5324	.6120	.6614	.7800
15	.4409	.5139	.5923	.6411	.7603
16	.4259	.4973	.5742	.6226	.7420
17	.4124	.4821	.5577	.6055	.7246
18	.4000	.4683	.5425	.5897	.7084
19	.3887	.4555	.5285	.5751	.6932
20	.3783	.4438	.5155	.5614	.6787
21	.3687	.4329	.5034	.5487	.6652
22	.3598	.4227	.4921	.5368	.6524
27	.3233	.3809	.4451	.4869	.5974
32	.2960	.3494	.4093	.4487	.5541
37	.2746	.3246	.3810	.4182	.5189
42	.2573	.3044	.3578	.3932	.4896
47	.2428	.2875	.3384	.3721	.4648
52	.2306	.2732	.3218	.3541	.4433
62	.2108	.2500	.2948	.3248	.4078
72	.1954	.2319	.2737	.3017	.3799
82	.1829	.2172	.2565	.2830	.3568
92	.1726	.2050	.2422	.2673	.3375
102	.1638	.1946	.2301	.2540	.3211

Source: From Table VII of R. A. Fisher and F. Yates, *Statistical Tables for Biological, Agricultural, and Medical Research,* published by Longman Group, Ltd., London (previously published by Oliver and Boyd, Ltd., Edinburgh) and by permission of the authors and publishers.

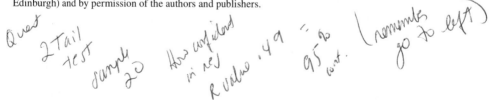

groups. Most of the literature seemed to confirm his rather unscientific observation that female adolescents with more siblings are more likely to volunteer comments than those with fewer siblings. He decided that he had sufficient justification for a one-tailed research hypothesis:

> Among female adolescents in treatment groups, there will be a positive correlation between the number of unsolicited comments and their number of siblings.

It was a policy in Leon's agency to videotape group treatment sessions for use in staff supervision. He received permission from the agency administrator and the adolescent clients to use the videotapes from all his group treatment sessions to test his hypothesis. He operationally defined a case as being a female adolescent who attended at least 75 percent of group sessions over a 4-month period. Thirty-seven clients met this criterion. Leon developed an operational definition for the variable *unsolicited comments.* An unsolicited comment was judged to have been made only if both Leon and a colleague (who viewed the tapes independently) agreed that it met that definition.

Leon totaled the number of unsolicited comments for each case and then divided by the number of sessions the client attended. This number provided the average number of unsolicited comments per session (the criterion variable) for each case. Case values for the predictor variable, *number of siblings* were acquired from agency records.

Leon used a statistical software package and a personal computer to analyze his data. He entered a pair of measurements (number of siblings and average number of unsolicited comments per session) for each case. Using Pearson's r, he achieved a correlation of .34 ($p < .025$). Leon knew that this meant that if he were to claim a relationship between the predictor and criterion variables, he would be on reasonably safe ground, assuming that something else (besides sampling error) had not produced the relationship between the two variables within his small sample. Another determination was required before support for his hypothesis could be claimed, however. Leon asked, "Was the correlation in the direction that he had hypothesized it would be—that is, was it a positive correlation?" If so, group members who had high values for the variable *average number of unsolicited comments per session* should also tend to have high values for the variable number of siblings, and vice versa. Yes, the data looked the way Leon had hypothesized that they would. He concluded that he had support for his one-tailed research hypothesis.

Leon was realistic about his findings. He had, for example, relied on a convenience sample and used only his own cases. Many potential design biases and other variables that might have affected his findings could have been present. Perhaps Leon had been a less effective facilitator with group members from small families who may have been less comfortable in group situations. Perhaps the nature of comments that clients had made in the groups may have been misperceived when the content of the tapes was analyzed because of the poor quality of the camcorder that was used. Leon also recognized that the .34 correlation coefficient between the two variables was really not that strong in an absolute sense. Less than 12 percent of the variation in number of comments was associated with the variable *number of siblings* ($.34^2 = .1156$). That left more than 88 percent of the variation unexplained.

Leon's findings, even though they were far from conclusive, were certainly not without value. He summarized them in a weekly staff meeting for other social workers. His colleagues provided a critique of his research methods and identified several other possible design biases and rival hypotheses that if methodologically controlled would improve the design if he chose to replicate his study.

Leon and the other social workers who ran adolescent groups decided to make some adjustments to their practice methods. They also agreed to evaluate the changes after 6 months. They decided to take three steps:

1. Staff would use the variable number of siblings (available on intake forms) to create more homogeneous groups among new clients. They felt that placing the most verbally assertive members (those with more siblings) in groups together would keep them from intimidating other group members who were less assertive. In turn, some of the members who the social workers believed to be less assertive (those with fewer siblings) might become more active and assertive when assigned to groups with persons more like themselves.

2. In other groups, new members from families with many siblings would be viewed as at risk to dominate discussions. Likewise, new members with no or few siblings would be viewed as at risk to be reticent to volunteer comments. This perception would affect the way in which the social worker would approach the role as facilitator with the more heterogeneous groups.

3. In all groups, leaders would facilitate discussion around such areas as attitudes toward the presence or absence of siblings, parental attitudes toward children's assertiveness, and so on.

Example: Worker Experience and Error Rates

Tanya is an administrator in a county department of social services. When she was hired, her agency's error rate for eligibility determinations for financial assistance applications was among the highest in the state. She assumed that the problem was related to the inadequate training of workers. She quickly took steps to increase training for all workers who had been employed by the agency for less than 6 months. She also required all senior workers who were not full-time supervisors to perform at least three eligibility determinations a week. To her surprise, one year after she implemented these decisions, the error rate had nearly doubled.

Tanya and her supervisor were very concerned about the new error rate figures. Tanya wondered if her efforts to address a problem might possibly have made it worse. Why was increased training of newer workers, combined with greater use of more experienced personnel, associated with a dramatic increase in erroneous eligibility determinations?

In discussing this paradox with a staff member, Tanya began to speculate on what may have gone wrong. There had been a series of major changes in federal eligibility requirements over the past few years. Tanya had asked her senior workers to do more eligibility determinations because she thought that they would make fewer errors. They were not given additional training, however, to update them on the newer eligibility requirements. In fact, the use of senior workers who had not been retrained may have been a major contributor to the increased error rate.

Tanya did not wish to make another administrative decision that might not help the problem—or might make it even worse. If she were to recommend future changes, she could not rely solely on a hunch. She intended to have data to back them up.

Tanya decided to examine the correlation between worker experience and error rate using data already available in the agency's management information system. Because she was interested in explaining differences in error rate, she labeled it her criterion variable; worker experience became her predictor variable. Based on a brief literature review and conversations with colleagues, she formulated a one-tailed research hypothesis:

> There will be a positive correlation between years of worker employment and error rate.

Tanya used her personal computer to analyze the data. For each of 42 workers currently doing eligibility determinations under her supervision, she entered a pair of values—number of years of experience and average number of identified errors per 100 cases (the last 100 reviewed).

The correlation coefficient reflecting the correlation between the variables *years of experience* and *error rate* was $-.21$ ($p > .05$). Even if the p-value had been less than .05, Tanya would not have been able to claim statistical support for her hypothesis. Why? The correlation within her data set was negative—the correlation was in the opposite direction to what she predicted in her one-tailed research hypothesis.

At first, Tanya was disappointed with her findings. The negative correlation suggested that the most senior workers in her sample had actually made fewer mistakes than those with less experience, not at all what she had expected. But she quickly reminded herself that the lack of support for her hypothesis did not mean that no new knowledge had been generated. In fact, her findings helped her to shift her focus away from past work experience and/or lack of recent training of senior workers as factors in the recent rise in error rates.

She then recalled that in her haste to reduce the error rate, she also had implemented another change—newer staff were given expanded training in making eligibility determinations. Perhaps the problem had been made worse by the introduction of the training for newer staff. Tanya knew that more training did not guarantee that workers would be better prepared to do their jobs. She began to question whether the training was accomplishing its goals. She decided that she would

1. Design and implement an evaluative study of the current training for new eligibility workers
2. Continue to give senior workers increased responsibility for eligibility determinations and encourage them to assist newer workers in learning their jobs
3. Report her research findings to her superiors, informing them of her approaches to the problem (steps 1 and 2) and making them aware of her concern about the high error rate and her attempts to correct it

NONPARAMETRIC ALTERNATIVES

Sometimes we cannot meet the assumptions of a parametric statistical test like Pearson's *r*, but we still wish to compute a correlation coefficient. This is possible using various nonparametric tests that require only ordinal-level data (or interval- or ratio-level data that are skewed). They are commonly used in situations where, if normally distributed interval or ratio level data were present, Pearson's *r* would be used. Two of the most commonly used such tests are so similar that they may be considered almost interchangeable. They are Spearman's rho and Kendall's tau.

Spearman's rho and Kendall's tau

Like Pearson's *r*, Spearman's rho and Kendall's tau produce a correlation coefficient that is either positive or negative and that has a numerical value between -1.0 and 1.0. But while Pearson's *r* uses the actual case values for each of two variables in its computation, rho and tau are calculated using only the ranks of research participants (or objects) for each of the two variables. For example, the two nonparametric tests could examine the association between the ordinal-level variable *motivation* and another ordinal-level variable, *socioeconomic class,* among all cases in a research sample or population. One case may rank first in motivation, but tie for third in socioeconomic class. Another may have ranked fifth on both variables, another second on the first and seventh on the second, and so on.

Like most statistical tests, rho and tau are available on many statistical software packages. They can, of course, be computed by hand as well. If this is done, however, two factors must be considered in determining which specific variation of their formulas should be used: (1) the size of the sample and (2) the number of ties (more than one case sharing a ranking for a variable) present within the raw data set.

While Pearson's *r* is most frequently used for inference, Spearman's rho and Kendall's tau can be used if the assumptions for Pearson's *r* cannot be met. The two nonparametric tests possess about the same statistical power; that is, they are about equal in their ability to detect the presence of a real correlation between variables. However, they are slightly less powerful than Pearson's *r*. When both Spearman's rho and Kendall's tau are computed using the same two variables within a data set, they generally produce slightly different correlation coefficients, but very similar *p*-values.

Example: Caregiver Attitudes and Longevity of Hospice Patients.   Meredith is a social worker in a hospice program that provides services to terminally ill people and their caregivers. After working with hundreds of cases, it seemed to her that people whose caregivers readily accepted hospice services were more likely to live beyond their projected date of death than those whose caregrivers were more reluctant to use the services. Meredith decided to test the following one-tailed research hypothesis:

> There is a positive correlation between caregivers' willingness to receive hospice services and the longevity of their patients.

Meredith tested the above one-tailed research hypothesis by conducting a small study using the nine patients and their caregivers who were referred for hospice services during the month of June. At the time of the initial interview, she and a social work student who observed the interview independently rated each caregiver and then categorized them as very reluctant, somewhat reluctant, or eager to receive services. Then, following the death of each patient, Meredith noted whether the patient died before, at about, or after the time of death the patient's doctor had projected when the patient was referred for services.

Meredith analyzed the data on the nine patients and examined the relationship between the predictor variable *caregiver's willingness to receive hospice services* and the criterion variable *longevity of the patient* using Spearman's rho. She noted that her sample was small and that there were several ties in the rankings she compiled for the two variables, so she used the appropriate formula for these conditions.

The formula produced a correlation coefficient (r) of .24 ($p > $ .05). By glancing at Table 8.3, it can be seen that, with only nine cases, she needed a minimum correlation coefficient of .5822 to achieve statistical significance at the .05 level.

Based on her statistical analysis, Meredith concluded that she could not reject the null hypothesis and claim statistical support for her research hypothesis. She decided that her hypothesis may have been wishful thinking. Just in case her hypothesis had been correct, however, she decided to test it again using a larger number of cases, all cases active in her agency over a one-year period.

USING CORRELATION WITH THREE OR MORE VARIABLES

Bivariate relationships frequently need further explication. They can also be misleading. We are unlikely to explain how long a hospice patient survives, for example, based solely on data on the variables *caregiver willingness to receive services, patient diagnosis, number of family members in the home,* or any other single variable. Both a systems perspective and other theories of multiple causation argue that many variables work together to affect a single variable such as longevity, a human behavior, or an attitude. A better understanding of how variables are related can often be improved by including more than two variables at one time in data analysis.

Partial *r*

In some situations, there is one variable that simply cannot be ignored if we are to understand the relationship between the predictor and criterion variables. For example, in order to assess a possible correlation between the variables *age* and *amount of charitable contributions to a family service agency,* it is only logical to also consider a third variable, *yearly income.* This third variable (often called an intervening or extraneous variable) cannot be physically controlled, but it can be controlled statistically.

A relatively simple statistical test, *partial r,* can be very helpful in this type of situation. Data on all three variables can be entered into the partial *r* formula or entered into a computer, and a correlation coefficient can be obtained between any two of the variables while the influence of the third is controlled by making mathematical adjustments in actual case values.

Using partial *r*, we would be able to determine how large (and statistically significant) a correlation between age and amount of charitable contributions to a family service agency would be if the variations in yearly income were not a factor (it was statistically equalized) in their relationship. A useful by-product of this analysis would be correlation coefficients reflecting the correlation between the yearly income and amount of charitable contributions to a family service agency (controlling for age) and between age and yearly income (controlling for amount of charitable contributions).

A variation of the nonparametric Kendall's tau also can be used when the assumptions of partial *r* cannot be met (normally distributed interval or ratio-level variables). It is called *Kendall's partial rank correlation coefficient.* Like partial *r*, it is most useful when there is one potentially intervening or extraneous variable that cannot be controlled for by the research design. It thus represents an obvious rival hypothesis for explaining the variations in values of the criterion variable—that is, it (rather than the predictor variable) may explain the variations or it may be causing the values to co-vary.

Multiple *R*

A more sophisticated type of correlation analysis is available for situations in which we are interested in knowing the amount of variation of the criterion variable that can be explained by several predictor variables working in combination with one another. Multiple correlation (multiple *R*) looks at a whole set of predictor variables together in order to determine the degree to which their combined variations correlate with different values of the criterion variable. It thus can be used to help identify the best set of predictor variables for explaining different values of the criterion variable.

It might tell us, for example, which interval-level or ratio-level demographic variables might collectively reflect the highest correlation with a variable such as rate of homelessness, incidence of spouse abuse, or sense of alienation. An at-risk population consisting of people with a certain combination of the right characteristics might thus be identified.

Multivariate correlation analyses such as multiple *R* often are superior to bivariate analyses both for describing the characteristics of a sample or subsample and for testing hypotheses. They can easily examine the complexity of the interaction of three or more variables in a way that bivariate analyses such as Pearson's *r* or even partial *r* cannot. They also help us avoid committing Type I errors by stumbling onto spurious (false) relationships that result simply from trying many combinations of bivariate analyses until, because of sampling error, one finally reflects a statistically significant correlation.

How does multiple *R* extend our understanding of the relationship among variables? What if, for example, two or more predictor variables reflect a high correlation with the same criterion variable? We would have a better chance of explaining the variation in the criterion variable if we could look simultaneously at those two (or more) predictor variables and their correlation with the criterion variable. Logic tells us that our ability to explain the variation of a criterion variable is improved if we can determine the combined explanation capacity of a group of predictor variables.

In short, multiple *R* determines the degree to which a group of predictor variables correlate with the criterion variable. Finding the best combination of predictor variables to do this is not a simple task.

Example: Social Work Students' Scores on a Statistics Exam.   Suppose that we want to find out how well several predictor variables might correlate with a social work student's score on a standardized statistics examination (the criterion variable). We might, for example, use four interval-level or ratio-level predictor variables: (1) number of statistics courses taken, (2) attitude toward mathematics, (3) undergraduate GPA, and (4) score on the mathematics section of the SAT. Let us assume that they all are normally distributed.

Let us also say that the bivariate correlation between these variables and the criterion variable are, respectively, .45, .26, .51, and .74. To find out which two of these variables might be the best pair to explain the different scores that occur on the statistics examination and how well they would, in combination, explain the variation, we could not simply add the various pairs of bivariate correlation coefficients together. Why not? For one thing, adding the correlation coefficients for some of the pairs (e.g., .51, .74) would produce a correlation coefficient greater than 1.00—and that is impossible. But more importantly, any two of the predictor variables (or three or all four of them) will share some of the same covariance with the criterion variable, so adding them together would be redundant. In other words, part of their bivariate correlation with the criterion variable will contribute nothing new to explaining the variation in values of the criterion variable; one predictor variable would account for some of the same variation as others. That is because the four predictor variables, in addition to having some correlation with the criterion variable, also have some degree of correlation with each other.

Continuing with our example, we would expect a fairly high correlation between the predictor variables *attitude toward mathematics, number of math courses taken, undergraduate GPA,* and *score on the SAT mathematics section.* Thus, the correlation between each of these variables and the criterion variable would not explain how much of the variation of the criterion variable is unique to that predictor variable. In fact, two predictor variables that are highly correlated with each other are unlikely to add much to our ability to explain variation in the criterion variable beyond what either one alone could have done. As noted earlier in this chapter, if they are nearly perfectly correlated (close to $r = +1.00$ or $r = -1.00$), they are probably just two measurements of the same variable, and the use of both would be of little value.

In short, Multiple *R* sorts out the degree to which any one predictor variable accounts for the variation in the criterion variable. It produces what is referred to as a beta weight for each predictor variable. *Beta weights* essentially are partial correlations and are based on (1) the correlation coefficient between each predictor variable and the criterion variable and (2) the correlation coefficients among the various predictor variables. By using both of these, Multiple *R* identifies what is unique within the correlation between a given predictor variable and a criterion variable—that is, the variation in the criterion variable associated with that predictor variable that is not already accounted for by some other predictor variable.

Even though a given predictor variable might have the highest bivariate correlation coefficient with the criterion variable (as in the case of the SAT mathematics score in our example), this is no guarantee that its beta weight will also be higher than that of the other predictor variables. If it is highly correlated with the other predictor variables, its beta weight actually may be relatively low.

Our example used only four predictor variables. But we probably could identify many more interval-level or ratio-level variables that might be expected to correlate fairly highly with scores on a standardized statistics examination. Multiple R can be used with a large number of predictor variables. Unless we have a considerably larger number of cases than we have predictor variables, however, we can be led into making too much of the correlation coefficient thus produced. It might be quite high just on the basis of sampling error. To avoid this problem, multiple R should be used only when the number of cases is substantially larger than the number of predictor variables to be included in the statistical analysis.

Variations of Multiple R

There are variations of multiple R, referred to as stepwise procedures, that can be very useful and are available in most statistical software packages. One of these, referred to as the step-up procedure, involves a kind of rank ordering of the predictor variables. First, the predictor variable that contains the most unique correlation with the criterion variable is identified. Then, the next predictor variable that accounts for the most additional unexplained (by other variables) variation of the criterion variable is added to see how much the multiple R correlation coefficient is affected.

The process can continue with other predictor variables added (in order of their contribution to the unexplained variance of the criterion variable) until a point of diminishing returns—that is, until those predictor variables are reached that are of little value in accounting for any sizable additional variance within the criterion variable. The process allows us to narrow the list to only those predictor variables that are most important in explaining the variation of the criterion variable.

Another procedure, referred to as the step-down procedure, works in a similar way, but in the opposite direction. It begins with all the predictor variables and eliminates them one by one, starting with the one that explains the smallest amount of variation of the criterion variable. Predictor variables previously omitted can be added back along the way to see how the multiple correlation coefficient is affected. Like the step-up procedure, the step-down procedure allows us to winnow down the list of predictor variables to a relatively small number that is most useful in explaining the variation in the values of the criterion variable.

As mentioned throughout this book, there is a form of statistical analysis for just about any situation. There is yet another situation when still another type of correlation analysis is appropriate. As we know, multiple R is used to obtain the correlation between one criterion variable and a group of predictor variables (sometimes called a *derived variable*). Another procedure, called *canonical correlation,* takes correlation even further. It is used to simultaneously examine the correlation between a weighted group of predictor variables (a derived predictor variable) and a weighted group of criterion variables (a derived criterion variable). The procedure is used when the criterion variable is somewhat abstract and cannot be adequately measured by using scores for any single variable.

For example, if we wanted to examine the relationship between a fairly abstract criterion variable such as interpersonal skills on the job and certain demographic characteristics, we might first ask workers to evaluate their coworkers on several different criterion variables that are believed to be indicators of the concept, such as cooperation, communication ability, friendliness, helpfulness, and so on. The weighted group of scores on these variables could then be correlated with another weighted group of scores on such predictor variables as education level, years of work experience, number of siblings, and so on, using canonical correlation to produce a multiple R.

We would then be able to evaluate the Multiple R thus produced (or any other one produced by the procedures described above) as to its strength and direction, using the same criteria that are used in evaluating the bivariate correlation coefficients produced by Pearson's r. All correlation coefficients, no matter what statistical procedure produced them, are interpreted the same way, as previously described.

OTHER MULTIVARIATE TESTS
THAT USE CORRELATION

As should be evident by now, correlation is a generic concept based on covariance. It relies on the assumption that when certain values of one variable are found together in consistent patterns with certain values of another variable, there may be a relationship between the variables—they share something in common. We now present an overview of two somewhat specialized multivariate techniques that have been widely used since computer analyses of data has become available in most academic and practice settings. They are factor analysis and cluster analysis. Both employ a form of correlation analysis to complete a task that is useful to researchers.

Factor Analysis

Researchers use factor analyses to perform several different tasks. One common use is to reduce the length of a measuring instrument such as a scale or index by eliminating items that are redundant, that is, that measure the same indicator of a variable more than once.

The first draft of a measurement scale or index often is quite long. It contains many items that are believed to be indicators of the variable being measured. After a newly developed scale or index has been administered to a group of people, a factor analysis on the completed instruments can be performed. The results would reveal to what degree peoples' responses to one item correlate with their responses to other items. Why would this be useful to know? How would it suggest which items are redundant? When two or more items consistently produce the same responses from the same individuals, they may be assumed to be measuring the same indicator (redundancy). Items that produce dissimilar responses from the same individuals may be assumed to be measuring different indicators of the variable (no redundancy).

For example, in a scale that measures the variable *attentiveness in class,* one item might ask how frequently a student has fallen asleep in class. Another item might ask how often the student yawns in class. If, in a large sample of students, there is a strong pattern (positive correlation) of responses wherein individual students almost without exception respond the same (frequently, sometimes, or never) to both items, it may be assumed that the two items measure the same indicator of attentiveness and are thus redundant. If, however, individual students tended to give different responses to the two items, we might conclude that they measure two different indicators of attentiveness.

By examining correlation among responses to items, a factor analysis groups the items into factors (which can be thought of loosely as indicators or derived variables). For example, it might list four different items in one factor because responses to them were similar among individuals. This would indicate that all four items probably are measurements of the same factor. We could then look at the four items themselves to determine what they have in common.

Returning to our previous example, a factor analysis might suggest that the four items that ask about falling asleep, yawning, head nodding, and resting one's head on one's hand constitute one factor. We might label it something like "physical manifestations of attentiveness." We may then decide that any one of the items is sufficient and the other three can be deleted, or we may wish to leave two, three, or all four of them in the next version of the scale as a kind of subscale. Similar options would also exist for the other factors that were identified by our factor analysis.

Factors derived from a factor analysis are independent of other factors—each measures a different indicator or derived variable. This does not mean, however, that an individual item will show up in only one group of items (a factor). The same item may be a part of two (or even more) factors.

The issue of how many items to retain can be complicated. Among other considerations, we may ask how long a measuring instrument can be before respondents refuse to complete it. Researchers sometimes elect to retain two or more items from the same factor as a reliability check, that is, to see if an individual is responding consistently and thus honestly. If so, responses to the items should be identical or nearly identical.

A factor analysis also assists in the creation of equivalent forms of the same instrument, a desirable characteristic of a scale or index. One item selected from an identified factor can be used in one form and another item from the same factor in another form of the scale or index. It should not matter which specific item or items is present in a form, so long as all the factors are represented in all forms of the instrument. Then, no matter which form of the instrument a person completes, the measurement of the variable should be the same.

There are a number of other features of factor analyses that allow us to construct the exact measuring instrument we require. For example, factors can be refined using a process called *factor rotation.* While the process is complicated and has many different variations, all of them are designed to help us develop more precise meanings of the factors within any given data set.

A second practical use of a factor analysis, in addition to instrument construction, is for the preliminary screening of large groups of variables prior to multiple regression or discriminant analysis (both discussed in the next chapter). Using a factor analysis, redundant predictor variables (those that emerge as part of the same factor as other variables) can be identified. It may then be possible to eliminate all but one, thus making the job of either type of analysis much easier.

A factor analysis has many practical uses in fields such as business and marketing. A restaurant owner may do a factor analysis of customers' food preferences to try to identify menu items that are redundant (i.e., may appeal to the same customers). Once identified, some of these items can be eliminated and replaced with others that have the potential to broaden the restaurant's clientele base without offering more menu alternatives.

Marketing managers sometimes perform factor analyses to determine what factors lead people to buy a certain product. Then they develop magazine advertisements based on the results of their analyses. The advertisements are written carefully to avoid redundancy (the same factors) while covering all identified factors.

How might a social worker use factor analyses for making everyday, practical decisions? Client follow-up study data could be analyzed and the results examined to determine which factors constitute the variable *client satisfaction*. Then staff development sessions could be used to build in all of these factors while not engaging in unnecessary redundancy (overkill). Or, annual performance evaluations of staff could be analyzed to identify factors that supervisors deem important to good performance. Then, these factors could be emphasized in orientation sessions for new staff or, if the criteria being used seem inappropriate, they could be discussed with supervisors and the need for changes emphasized.

Factor analyses can be helpful in improving many forms of evaluation in social work. For example, they can (and should) be used to refine measuring instruments used by students to evaluate their instructors. Their use might help limit a tendency to place disproportionate weight on such factors as niceness or the ability to entertain.

Cluster Analysis

While a factor analysis performs the task of clustering items into factors, a *cluster analysis* is used primarily to cluster the cases themselves. A cluster analysis often is performed prior to hypothesis testing. It makes hypothesis testing possible by creating the value categories of a variable when none previously existed. Cluster analyses create subsamples of cases based on the fact that cases in each subsample have similar measurements (values) of the various indicators of some variable. Thus, the cases are similar to each other , but different from cases in other subsamples.

We might use a cluster analysis, for example, to attempt to create groups of cases with similar religious beliefs based on their similar beliefs about a divine being, the existence of life after death, and so forth. After the cluster analysis, each group formed would probably contain some persons who belong to the same religious denomination, but also people who belong to different denominations as well as people with no formal religious affiliation. A member of a group may have the same religious affiliation as a member of another group, but their religious beliefs would be different. After the groups have been formed, we could then test a hypothesis about the relationship between religious beliefs and, for example, attitudes about some social issue.

Cluster analyses can be used in many ways by social workers. Often the similarity of people's attitudes, beliefs, values, or behaviors is more important to understanding them than their label or diagnostic category. It might be useful, for example, to use a cluster analysis to create subsamples of psychiatric patients based on their reports of self-defeating behaviors, rather than upon their DSM-IV diagnosis. Then we could test a hypothesis about the relationship between the type of self defeating behaviors exhibited and, for example, whether patients will attempt to avoid taking prescribed medications. We could also simply use the clusters or groups thus formed to constitute several homogeneous treatment groups that might have therapeutic goals quite different from each of the other groups.

CONCLUDING THOUGHTS

This chapter presented some of the many uses of correlation. As noted, correlation is used to design research studies, to refine data collection instruments, to describe the relationship between and among variables in a population or sample, for inference testing, and even to create value categories to facilitate subsequent hypothesis testing. All correlation analyses produces a correlation coefficient that describes the strength and direction of a relationship, the covariance that exists between and among variables. It can be squared to gain an estimate of the amount of variation in the criterion variable attributable to the variation in the predictor variable or, when using Multiple R, to two or more predictor variables in concert.

We pointed out the effect that sample size has on statistical significance when using correlation analyses and why a correlation coefficient may be statistically significant while really quite weak. Even when a statistically significant correlation coefficient is obtained, the correlation may not be strong enough to represent a meaningful finding. It should also be remembered that the value of a finding of correlation must be assessed using common sense and knowledge of social work practice. A statistically significant, relatively low correlation coefficient may represent a meaningful finding in one study, but a relatively high correlation coefficient in another study may be relatively unimportant. Identifying no association ($r = 0$) between variables that are believed to be related may represent the most important finding of a study.

Chapter 9 builds closely on the concepts contained within this chapter. It examines simple linear regression and another important product of statistical analyses that we have only briefly mentioned to up to this point, prediction.

STUDY QUESTIONS

1. What can a scattergram portray that other graphs cannot? What does each dot in a scattergram depict?
2. Construct hypothetical data on the variables *number of siblings* and *mother's highest school grade completed* for members of your class. Create a scattergram similar to

Figure 8.3 to portray your data. Does the scattergram suggest that the two variables are related? If so, in which direction?

3. Why do we use the terms *predictor variable* and *criterion variable* rather than the terms *dependent variable* and *independent variable* in discussing correlation analyses?

4. In a correlation coefficient, what do the sign and the number each reflect?

5. What do we mean by *linear correlation*? Provide examples of variables that might be correlated in a nonlinear way.

6. What does r^2 tell us about the relationship between variables? Provide examples in your discussion.

7. Interpret each of the following hypothetical values for r: $r = -.45$; $r = +.45$; $r = +1.0$; $r = -1.0$.

8. Fill in the blanks to complete the following sentences:

   Correlation coefficients range from _____ to _____. A correlation coefficient suggests the _____ and the _____ of the relationship between variables. A correlation coefficient of _____ indicates a perfect positive relationship; _____ indicates a perfect negative relationship; and _____ indicates that there is no linear correlation between variables.

9. What are two nonparametric tests that can be used to examine correlation when the assumptions of Pearson's r cannot be met?

10. What do we call a type of correlation analysis that examines the correlation between two normally distributed interval-level or ratio-level variables while controlling for the effects of a third variable?

11. What do we call the multivariate form of a correlation analysis discussed in this chapter?

12. What does it mean when we say that one predictor variable is redundant when we use this type of analysis? What do we call the procedures for adding or subtracting predictor variables based on their ability to help explain variations in values of the criterion variable?

13. Find an article in a professional social work journal that used multiple correlation as the method of data analysis. What were the predictor variables? What conclusions did the author generate from the study? Do you feel the study was relevant to your future practice? Why? What other predictor variables could the author have used?

14. When using multiple correlation, why can we not simply add together the individual bivariate correlation coefficients between two predictor variables and the criterion variable to find their combined correlation with the criterion variable? Explain.

15. Describe at least two ways social workers can use factor analysis.

16. Why would a cluster analysis sometimes be a better way of grouping cases than such commonly used value labels as liberal and conservative? Provide an example.

9

Regression Analyses

As presented in Chapter 8, a correlation coefficient (expressed as an *r* value) provides an overall picture of the relationship between two variables—its strength and direction. With sample data, we can then use the laws of probability to determine if this relationship is strong enough so that we can feel reasonably safe in concluding that it probably was not caused by sampling error.

Another, related procedure, *simple linear regression,* takes a correlation between variables a step farther. For any case within the population, simple linear regression can be used to predict (with some degree of accuracy) the value for the criterion variable based on the value for the predictor variable.

WHAT IS PREDICTION?

In statistical analyses, prediction has a meaning similar to that of everyday usage. Specifically, it refers to determining (without measuring) what the specific case value for a variable is most likely to be. When we refer to prediction, the different values of the criterion variable may occur in the future, or they may already have occurred. Thus, prediction might entail, for example, using the number of hours that Jolene studied for an exam on Sunday night (the predictor variable) to produce a best guess as to either (1) what her grade will be on an the exam on Monday (one criterion variable) or

(2) how many hours she spent in social activities on Sunday night (another criterion variable).

Understanding statistical prediction involves many of the statistical concepts discussed in the previous eight chapters. The mean and standard deviation (Chapter 3), the normal distribution (Chapter 4), and correlation (Chapter 8), for example, are all important to understanding prediction.

Suppose we want to predict the score of a new enrollee named Joe on a standardized life skills measuring instrument following a 12-week life skills training course for people with developmental disabilities. The instrument is administered in the program at 6 weeks (mid-program) and 12 weeks (termination). It produces scores that range from 0 (very poor life skills) to 100 (excellent life skills).

To predict Joe's most likely score following completion of the course, we would have to rely on some fact that we already know. If the only datum that we have is the mean life skills score at completion for all people who have completed the course, this mean (e.g., 82) would be our best estimate for predicting Joe's final life skills score at the end of 12 weeks.

A prediction based on only a group's mean would provide a rather crude estimate. But we can do better. To improve the prediction, we might look to other data for help. Suppose we also know Joe's individual score from his 6-week assessment and the group's mean score after 6 weeks. We could use these data to make a more informed prediction about what Joe's final score is likely to be at 12 weeks.

Let us say, for example, that Joe's life skills score at 6 weeks was 79 and that the group's mean score at 6 weeks was 75. The distribution in Figure 9.1*a* shows that Joe scored higher than the group's mean at the 6-week assessment period. Thus, it would be reasonable to suggest that Joe would also score higher than the group's mean at the 12-week assessment period (presented in the distribution in Figure 9.1*b*).

Without any additional information about Joe or the program, we can statistically improve the accuracy of the prediction by considering the correlation between the scores at the 6-week and 12-week assessment periods. As we know from Chapter 8, the correlation coefficient (r) between the two variables would help by telling us (roughly) how accurate our prediction will be. If the correlation is equal to 0.0, data from the 6-week assessment will not help us predict scores at the 12-week assessment. However, if our correlation is +1.0 or −1.0, then we could use the data from the 6-week assessments to make perfectly accurate predictions about the 12-week assessments.

Understanding how perfect predictions are made requires an understanding of standard deviations and the normal distribution. Suppose there is a perfect positive linear correlation ($r = +1.0$) between the scores at the 6-week assessment and the scores at the 12-week assessment. Thus, a person's position within the group at the 6-week assessment period would correspond perfectly to his or her position within the group at the 12-week assessment period. For example, if one person's score was 1.0 standard deviation above the group's mean score at the 6-week assessment period, then his score at the 12-week assessment period would also be 1.0 standard deviation above the group's mean score. If another person's score was 1.5 standard deviations below the group's mean score at the 6-week assessment period, then her score at the 12-week assessment period would also be 1.5 standard deviations below the group's

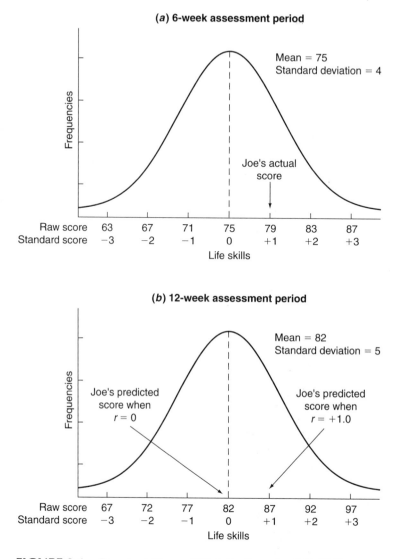

(a) 6-week assessment period

Mean = 75
Standard deviation = 4

Frequencies

Joe's actual
score

| Raw score | 63 | 67 | 71 | 75 | 79 | 83 | 87 |
| Standard score | −3 | −2 | −1 | 0 | +1 | +2 | +3 |

Life skills

(b) 12-week assessment period

Mean = 82
Standard deviation = 5

Frequencies

Joe's predicted
score when
$r = 0$

Joe's predicted
score when
$r = +1.0$

| Raw score | 67 | 72 | 77 | 82 | 87 | 92 | 97 |
| Standard score | −3 | −2 | −1 | 0 | +1 | +2 | +3 |

Life skills

FIGURE 9.1   Standard Normal Distributions for Life Skills at 6-Week and 12-Week Assessment Periods

mean score. By using the means and the standard deviations for the two distributions of the variable at the 6-week and 12-week assessment periods and the z score formula (Chapter 4), we could compute exactly what every individual's score should be.

Take a closer look at Figures 9.1*a* and 9.1*b*. They show both the raw scores and the standard scores for the 6-week and 12-week assessment periods. The standard deviation for the 6-week assessment period is 4, since the raw scores change by increments of 4 along the base of the 6-week distribution. This being the case, Joe would have scored 1.0 standard deviation above the mean for the 6-week assessment on the standard normal distribution (75 + 4 = 79). If the correlation between 6-week and 12-week assessment scores was 1.0, we would know that Joe should have the same relative position on both normal distributions.

Thus, to predict Joe's score at the 12-week assessment period, we would find the raw score that corresponds to one standard deviation. As can be seen from the distribution in Figure 9.1*b*, Joe's predicted 12-week assessment score would be 87. It is 1.0 standard deviation (5) above the mean (82) for the 12-week scores.

As noted previously, perfect predictions are rare in the real world. Comparing the normal distributions for two variables that have a less than perfect correlation is not as straightforward as when $r = +1.0$ or -1.0. When the correlation between two variables is less than perfect, we can use a simple linear regression analysis to help make predictions.

WHAT IS SIMPLE LINEAR REGRESSION?

Simple linear regression can be performed when two variables are correlated to some degree and the relationship is a linear one as reflected on a scattergram. As stated at the beginning of this chapter, simple linear regression makes it possible to predict (with varying degrees of accuracy) the value(s) of a criterion variable from a known value(s) of a predictor variable.

Simple linear regression is especially useful in experimental research designs in which we are able to manipulate or introduce the value of the predictor variable. When these designs are used, it may be possible to demonstrate that the predictor variable actually caused the value of the criterion variable. (The terms *independent variable* and *dependent variable* might be more appropriate if this were the case.)

Simple linear regression can also be used in the types of research situations we more commonly encounter in social work—where we can only select and measure (but not introduce or manipulate) the predictor variable. For example, once a simple linear regression has been performed on a data set, the equation that it generates can be used to compute the predicted value of a student's graduate grade point average (GPA), the criterion variable, from the student's GPA in undergraduate school (the predictor variable). Or, we could predict an individual's score on a standardized self-report measurement instrument that measures hostility toward authority (criterion variable) from that person's number of previous felony arrests (predictor variable). In either example, simple linear regression would be used to predict how well a person (or case) will perform on the criterion variable based on a measurement of the predictor variable. However, the relationship identified between two variables is not assumed to be one of cause and effect, only covariance.

Two important products of simple linear regression are a regression equation and a regression line that graphically reflects the equation. Before we discuss what they are and how they are used, however, we will first look at how to formulate a research question for a simple linear regression analysis and the limitations of simple linear regression.

Formulating a Research Question

A simple linear regression is an extension of a correlation analysis of the relationship between two normally distributed interval-level or ratio-level variables. It is meaningful only if the relationship between variables has been found to be statistically significant and the correlation between them is fairly strong. When performing a simple linear regression, it is not necessary to restate the research and null hypothesis since the null form of the research hypothesis—that there is no relationship between the criterion and predictor variables—will already have been tested and rejected using Pearson's *r*.

Instead of restating the research hypothesis, we typically formulate a research question to specify what we hope to learn from a simple linear regression. It asks how will knowing the value of the predictor variable improve our ability to predict the value of the criterion variable. The following are possible research questions that can be answered using a simple linear regression analysis:

Research Question:

How much does knowing a student's GPA in undergraduate school help to predict his or her GPA in graduate school?

Research Question:

How much does knowing the number of previous felony arrests help to predict an individual's degree of hostility toward authority as measured by a standardized self-report instrument?

Limitations of Simple Linear Regression

A simple linear regression analysis produces an equation, called a *regression equation*. Using the equation, we can predict (with some degree of accuracy) the value of a criterion variable (Y) for a particular case by knowing the value for the case's predictor variable (X). The major benefit is that we can predict the most likely measure for a criterion variable without actually measuring it, if we just know the measurement for a case's predictor variable.

There are limitations to what we can legitimately do using simple linear regression. We cannot make predictions about measurements of the criterion variable for cases whose values for the predictor variable are either larger than the largest X value or smaller than the smallest X value in the sample data that was the basis for the computation of the equation. Suppose, for example, that the predictor variable *number of hours of vigorous exercise per week* was used to predict the value of the variable *attitude toward parenthood*. If the sample on which the regression equation was computed included individuals who exercised between 2 and 15 hours per week, then no matter how strong the correlation, we could not use the equation to predict attitude toward parenthood for individuals with less than 2 or more than 15 hours of vigorous exercise per week.

Other statistical limitations of simple linear regression are the same as for Pearson's *r*. Both Pearson's *r* and simple linear regression require interval-level or ratio-level data, and both assume a normal distribution of the predictor and criterion variables (see Chapter 8).

COMPUTATION OF
THE REGRESSION EQUATION

Another example will show how to compute a simple linear regression equation. Suppose that, using a random sample of seven female clients, we have tested the research hypothesis that there is a positive correlation between educational level (predictor variable) and assertiveness (criterion variable). Educational level was measured by recording the last year of school completed, and assertiveness was measured by the completion of a self-report standardized measuring instrument that measures assertiveness. The correlation between the variables in our hypothetical study was +1.00, a perfect positive correlation. Even with our small sample, that strong a correlation is very unlikely to be the work of sampling error, so we have rejected the null hypothesis and concluded that we have statistical support for our research hypothesis.

The measurements of the two variables (i.e., educational level, assertiveness level) are presented in Table 9.1. If we study the data in Table 9.1, we can make a number of observations. For all cases, the measurement of *Y,* the criterion variable (assertiveness level), is greater than for *X,* the predictor variable (educational level). A closer look at Table 9.1 reveals that for each case, *Y* is more than twice the value of *X.* In fact, in all seven cases, *Y* is exactly 2(*X*) + 5. We can now express the relationship between the two variables as a regression equation:

$$Y' = 5 + 2(X)$$

This equation is just a variation of the usual equation for a straight line, which is written as $Y = a + b(X)$. However, in a regression equation, the notation Y' is used to denote a predicted value (not an actual one). If we plotted the data in Table 9.1 using a

TABLE 9.1 Educational and Assertiveness Levels (*n* = 7)

Name	Educational Level (*X*)	Assertiveness Level (*Y*)
Rochelle	9	23
Carny	12	29
Belinda	6	17
Amanda	8	21
Maria	11	27
Ky	15	35
Ruth	13	31

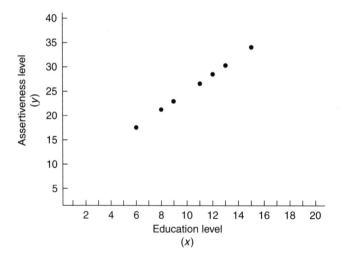

FIGURE 9.2   Scattergram of Educational and Assertiveness Levels

scattergram and connecting the dots as in Figure 9.2, we would have a perfect straight line reflecting the perfect positive correlation between the variables.

As Table 9.1 portrays, Rochelle has 9 years of education (X) and has an assertiveness level of 23 (Y). Thus, the regression equation reflects (exactly) the relationship between her education level and her assertiveness score: $Y' = 5 + 2(9) = 23$. Unlike what we would be likely to find in the real world (a less than perfect correlation), the equation $Y' = 5 + 2(X)$ holds true for the other six women as well.

The general equation produced by simple linear regression analysis is:

$$Y' = a + b(X)$$

where:

Y' = the predicted Y value from a particular X value

a = the point where the regression line would intersect the y axis, the constant

b = the slope of the line, where the amount of change in Y is directly related to the amount of change in X, the regression coefficient

X = a selected value of the predictor variable used to predict the value of the criterion variable

Hand computations of regression equations are lengthy processes, especially for large data sets. With the help of a computer and almost any statistical software package, however, simple linear regression analyses take very little time. Most software packages also are programmed to display the data within a scattergram showing dots

BOX 9.1
The Least-Squares Regression Equation

Problem: What is the least-squares regression equation ($Y' = a + b[X]$) for the data in Table 8.2?

Predictor Variable: Number of spouse abuse reports—ratio level.

Criterion Variable: Number of child abuse reports—ratio level.

Slope Formula:

$$b = \frac{N\Sigma XY - (\Sigma X)(\Sigma Y)}{N\Sigma X^2 - (\Sigma X)^2}$$

where:
b = Slope
N = Number of cases
ΣXY = Sum of xy column
ΣX = Sum of X column
ΣY = Sum of Y column
ΣX^2 = Sum of x^2 column
ΣY^2 = Sum of y^2 column

Substituting values for letters:

$$b = \frac{(5)(985) - (76)(53)}{(5)(1290) - (76)^2}$$

$$= \frac{897}{674}$$

$$= 1.33 \text{ (slope)}$$

y-intercept Formula:

$$a = \overline{Y} - b\overline{X}$$

where:
a = y-intercept
Y = Mean of Y column
bX = Slope times mean of X column

Substituting values for letters:

$$a = \left(\frac{53}{5}\right) - (1.33)\left(\frac{76}{5}\right)$$

$$= 10.6 - (1.33)(15.20)$$

$$= 10.6 - 20.2$$

$$= -9.62 \ (y\text{-intercept})$$

Presentation of Results: $Y' = -9.62 + 1.33(X)$

Conclusion: A slope of 1.33 means that for every unit change in X (for every increase of 1 unit in the number of spouse abuse reports), there was a change of 1.33 units in Y (the number of child abuse reports increased by 1.33). Note from Box 8.1, $r = .82$.

for all cases, the correlation coefficient (*r*), and the regression equation. For those who wish to see how a regression equation is calculated using a formula, Box 9.1 has been provided. It uses the data displayed in Table 8.2 in Chapter 8.

MORE ABOUT THE REGRESSION LINE

The regression line is a straight line of "best fit" for a given set of data and can be presented mathematically (the regression equation) or graphically using a scattergram. The values in Table 9.1 as illustrated in Figure 9.2 reflect a perfect positive correlation (*r* = +1.0), but it is far more likely that the actual data in our example would look more like those in Table 9.2 and Figure 9.3. They reflect a less than perfect linear correlation between the variables *educational level* and *assertiveness level.*

A single straight line cannot be drawn through the seven dots in Figure 9.3, since the correlation between the two variables displayed is not a perfect one (it is neither +1.0 nor –1.0). If we used a computer to compute Pearson's *r* for the data, we would learn that *r* = +.76 for the two variables in Figure 9.3. But to be able to predict the most likely assertiveness level for a woman not among the seven cases based on our knowledge of her educational level we would need to do more than just compute this correlation. We would need to find or produce the line with the best possible fit—one, and only one, line that would pass through "the center of the dots," hitting as many as possible while not missing the others by too much.

How would we find this line? What would its slope be—that is, how vertical (as opposed to horizontal) would it be? We could draw several lines through what appears to be the center of the distribution of dots, but it would be hard to determine from just visual examination which one would be the best fit. Some lines would hit some dots but miss others; some would be more vertical, others more horizontal.

The Least-Squares Criterion

The dots above and below the line represent actual values for each of two variables. The line that we would seek for the data in Figure 9.3, its regression line, is a line of predicted values (*Y'*). Notice how the actual values above the line are predicted by the line to be lower than they actually are and the values below the line are predicted by the line to be higher than they actually are. This is basic to understanding simple linear regression. Unless the correlation is perfect, it generally does not provide perfectly accurate predictions, only "best guesses."

A regression analysis obtains a regression line—that is, determines the equation reflecting its slope and where it would intercept the *y* axis—by using what is referred to as *the least-squares criterion.* No matter where we drew a straight line in Figure 9.3 we would miss some of the dots. The vertical distance between each of the respective dots and that line could be measured, however. Then each of these distances (referred to as deviations) could be squared and their squares added together (totaled). The sum of the squared deviations from the regression line would be different depending on where we drew the line—some would be larger; some would be smaller. The least-

TABLE 9.2   Educational and Assertiveness Levels (*n* = 7)

Name	Educational Level (X)	Assertiveness Level (Y)
Rochelle	9	20
Carny	12	21
Belinda	6	14
Amanda	8	25
Maria	11	21
Ky	15	28
Ruth	13	30

squares criterion asserts that the best line, the regression line that should be used, is the one that produces the smallest sum of squared deviations from that line.

Fortunately, there is a much easier and better way to arrive at a regression line for a data set than by trying an almost infinite number of lines, determining their sum of squared deviations, and then selecting the line with the least squares. It involves the computation of the regression equation. Box 9.1 presents a mathematical formula to calculate the slope and the point of the *y*-intercept for any pair of interval-level or ratio-level variables.

The formula generates the linear equation for the regression line that we are seeking, the least squares line. Both the *a* value (where the line intercepts the *y* axis) and the *b* value are likely to be fractions, not whole numbers, as in our first example, in

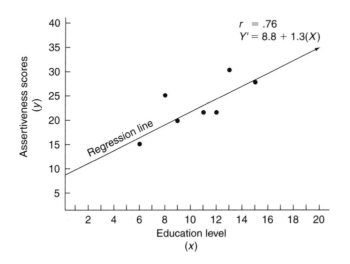

FIGURE 9.3   Scattergram of Educational and Assertiveness Levels

which a perfect correlation existed. For example, the computer-generated equation for the regression line shown in Figure 9.3 is $Y' = 8.8 + 1.3(X)$.

The Regression Coefficient (*b*)

In a regression equation, the regression coefficient (*b*) is the slope of the regression line. (Slope as used here has essentially the same meaning as it does when we refer to the slope of a hill—that is, the proportional relationship between vertical rise and horizontal distance.) In a regression equation, *b* can be thought of as the amount and direction of change in *Y* for each unit of change in *X*. If *b* is positive, as *X* increases, *Y* will increase at a specific constant rate. If *b* is negative, as *X* increases, *Y* will decrease at a specific constant rate. Likewise, as *X* decreases, *Y* will increase at a specific constant rate. The *b* value suggests the rate of change in the value of *Y* (the criterion variable) for each unit of change in the value of *X* (the predictor variable).

The slope of the regression line (*b*) indicates exactly where, between the vertical and horizontal axes, the line would fall. High *b* values reflect lines that are nearly vertical; low *b* values reflect lines that are nearly horizontal.

The regression coefficient (*b*) within a regression equation is closely related to the correlation coefficient (*r*) for the two variables. But, unlike the value of *r*, which always ranges between +1.0 and −1.0, the value of *b* may be any number. Also, as we have suggested, *r* and *b* will always correspond in terms of positive and negative values. If *r* is negative, *b* is negative; if *r* is positive, *b* is positive.

After the data are entered into a computer program and a regression analysis is completed, the computer output will usually display both the correlation coefficient and the regression equation. The *b* value for Figure 9.3 is 1.3; it is shown in the upper right-hand corner of the figure. Since it is a positive number, this means that for each unit increase in *X*, *Y* increases 1.3 points. Thus, for each 1-point increase in educational level, we can predict that assertiveness level will be 1.3 points higher. An actual assertiveness score can be predicted to be the education level times 1.3, plus the value of *a*.

The *y*-Intercept (*a*)

Most statistical software packages also display the starting point for the line. The starting point is the *y*-intercept, the point at which the regression line, if extended beyond the sample data as in Figure 9.3, would cross the *y* axis and become negative (if that is theoretically possible). This is the point that might represent the predicted value of *Y* when *X* equals 0. In our example, then, the predicted assertiveness score of a woman with 0 years of education would be 8.8. Of course, it would be theoretically impossible to have a negative number of years of education.

As noted earlier, however, we should not predict the assertiveness level of a woman with 0 years of education using simple linear regression since the sample data on which the regression equation was developed did not include anyone with less than 6 years of education. Since we did not actually study women with very little or no formal education, we have no way of guessing what the assertiveness level of such women might be. It might, in fact, be quite high. In other words, the relationship between the two variables may not be completely linear if women with all possible levels of education had been studied.

Statistical software packages draw the correct regression line in a scattergram and also show the place where it crosses the y axis. The value of *a* can be positive or negative. A positive *a* value tells us the regression line will meet the y axis at a value above 0; a negative *a* value indicates the regression line (extended, if necessary) would cross the y axis at a value below zero.

Predicted Y (Y')

Y' is the estimated score for the criterion variable for a given value of the predictor variable. We can predict the value of a criterion variable for a single case by computing Y' for any value of X that falls within the range of scores that were used to produce the regression equation. In the upper right-hand corner of Figure 9.3 we can see the regression equation $Y' = 8.8 + 1.3(X)$. The X component of the formula is any specific value of X for which we wish to predict a Y value. The following are two calculations for the predicted Y values of two different cases when we substitute specific values for X (13 and 6 respectively):

Calculation 1:

Let us determine Y' by substituting 13 for X:

$$Y' = a + b(X)$$
$$= 8.8 + 1.3(13)$$
$$= 8.8 + 16.9$$
$$= 25.7 \text{ (predicted value of } Y \text{ when } X = 13)$$

Calculation 2:

Let us determine Y' by substituting 6 for X:

$$Y' = a + b(X)$$
$$= 8.8 + 1.3(6)$$
$$= 8.8 + 7.8$$
$$= 16.6 \text{ (predicted value of } Y \text{ when } X = 6)$$

The X values of 13 and 6 were chosen at random. They could have been any numbers within the range of the distribution of X within the sample studied. What do the X and Y' values mean? When X is 13, the predicted value of Y is 25.7 (calculation 1); when X is 6, the predicted value of Y is 16.6 (calculation 2). Thus, a client who has an educational level of 13 is predicted to have an assertiveness score of 25.7, and a client with an educational level of 6 is predicted to have an assertiveness score of 16.6.

An alternative approach to predicting the value of *Y* involves using the actual regression line as presented in a scattergram. We could find, for example, the exact value (*X* = 13) along the *x* axis of the scattergram in Figure 9.3. Next we could run a vertical line straight up until we reach the regression line. Then we could draw a straight horizontal line to the left until we touch the *y* axis.

Note that we hit the same *Y′* as predicted in the equation above (Y' = about 25.7). This method of prediction is not nearly as precise as using a regression equation. It does provide a visual understanding of the data, however, and can be used as a quick check on a result obtained mathematically. We could use the same method to check the value for *Y′* when *X* = 6 to verify that our math was correct.

Interchanging *X* and *Y* Variables

The example conceptualized years of education as the predictor variable (*X*) and assertiveness level as the criterion variable (*Y*). We could have conceptualized the relationship between the two variables the other way around. Assertiveness could be thought of as the predictor variable and years of education as the criterion variable. As emphasized earlier, labeling variables as predictor and criterion variables needs to make theoretical and logical sense. In this instance, we could build a logical case for a relationship between the two variables in either direction.

In computing the correlation between two variables, the correlation coefficient would be the same regardless of which variable we label the predictor variable and which we label the criterion variable. The predictor and criterion variables are not interchangeable in a regression analysis, however. If we enter years of education into our computer as the predictor variable and assertiveness as the criterion variable, we get one result (the regression equation above). But if we enter assertiveness as the predictor variable and years of education as the criterion variable, we get a different regression equation. We must be clear which is intended as the predictor variable and which is intended as the criterion variable (as stated in the research question). We must then be careful to input our data so as to reflect this understanding if we hope to get the regression equation that we seek.

INTERPRETING RESULTS

How valuable is a prediction that can be made from a regression line? The answer depends on the strength of the correlation between the two variables. When the correlation is very weak (e.g., approaching 0.0), there is no point in even calculating the best-fitting straight line to make predictions about the value of the criterion variable. The predictions would be wrong much more often than they would be correct. When a correlation is strong, however, the line can be used for predictive purposes with reasonable accuracy. Thus, there is a direct relationship between the magnitude of *r* and the accuracy of predictions.

The formula in Box 9.1 clearly shows how correlation is directly related to simple linear regression. As *r* decreases (e.g., approaches 0.0), the accuracy of prediction using simple linear regression decreases; as *r* increases (e.g., approaches +1.0 or –1.0), the accuracy of prediction increases.

Presentation of *Y'*

The presentation of *Y'* is straightforward. The regression equation $Y' = 3.5 + 6.8 (X)$, for example, could be stated in words as "for every unit increase in *X*, there will be a 6.8 unit increase in *Y*." Using the variables *client's educational level* (*X*) and *assertiveness level* (*Y*), this would read, "for each 1-year increase in a female client's educational level, her assertiveness level will increase by 6.8 points."

The Standard Error

An indicator referred to as the *standard error* can provide an estimate of how well the regression equation can predict values of the criterion variable from known values of the predictor variable. When $r = +1.0$ or $–1.0$, all dots on a scattergram will fall exactly on the regression line. In this case, the standard error equals 0.0. The closer the standard error is to either +1.0 or –1.0, the more confident we can be that the regression equation will give us accurate predictions. The further *r* is from being perfect (as it approaches 0.0), the more errors will be made in making predictions of *Y* using the regression equation. When $r = 0.0$, the standard error would be at its maximum and the regression equation would be of no value whatsoever in predicting the value of a criterion value from the known value of the predictor variable.

USING REGRESSION ANALYSES IN SOCIAL WORK PRACTICE

While the primary function of regression is the prediction of a value of a criterion variable from knowing a value of a predictor variable, it is sometimes combined with the results of a correlation analysis to add additional information to hypothesis testing. We will examine two hypothetical examples to see how this can be done.

Example: Socializing with Family Members and Life Satisfaction

Shondra is a social worker in a family service agency. Over the last year, she saw 80 clients for counseling related to depression. During this time, she formed the impression that the clients who seemed most depressed had little time to spend socializing with family members. She also noticed that clients who had a considerable amount of time to spend socializing with family members did not seem as depressed as most other clients. Shondra decided to do a small-scale research study to see if she could find statistical support for her observations.

Shondra wanted to determine how well information about the amount of time a client spent socializing with family members would improve her ability to predict the client's life satisfaction level. Her predictor variable was *the amount of time the client spent socializing with family members during the previous week (X)*, and her criterion variable was the *client life satisfaction level (Y)*.

Over the next several months, Shondra had each of 50 new clients complete a standardized self-report measurement instrument that measures life satisfaction at the interval level. She also asked each how many hours he or she had spent socializing with family members during the previous week (ratio level). The life satisfaction instrument produces scores ranging from 0 (lowest level) to 200 (highest level).

Shondra entered the pairs of measurements for the two variables (one pair per case) into her personal computer and selected simple linear regression from the menu. The Pearson's *r*, and regression equation, and *p*-level produced for the data were as follows:

$$r = .70$$
$$Y' = 1.49 + 4.69(X)$$
$$p < .0005$$

Shondra studied the above findings. The relatively high correlation (*r* value) and the statistically significant *p*-value indicated that the regression analysis was justified and might produce fairly accurate predictions for values of the criterion variable. She computed r^2 and noted that the amount of time clients spent with family members was related to a fairly sizable amount of the variation of their life satisfaction levels ($.70^2 = .49$, or 49%).

Based on the regression equation generated, a slope (*b*) of 4.69 indicated that for each unit of increase in *X*, there is an increase of 4.69 units in *Y*. For each additional hour spent socializing with family members, for example, there was an average increase of 4.69 points on the life satisfaction instrument (a decrease in depression).

Shondra could use her findings to predict a future client's life satisfaction by knowing how many hours the client had spent socializing with family members during the week. She realized that her findings probably could not be generalized to other clients with different problems (i.e., those with a presenting complaint other than depression) and perhaps not even to other clients being treated for depression in other settings. She also knew that she could not predict life satisfaction level for clients who had spent more or less time with family members during the week than those people in her original 50-case sample.

After completing her study, Shondra saw her 51st client, David, who came to the agency to be counseled for depression. During their first interview, David told Shondra that he had spent 15 hours socializing with family members during the previous week. Shondra computed David's predicted life satisfaction score (*Y'*) as follows:

$$Y' = 1.49 + 4.69(15)$$
$$= 1.49 + (70.35)$$
$$= 71.84 \text{ (predicted value of } Y \text{ when } X \text{ equals 15)}$$

To test how accurate her prediction had been, Shondra had David complete the life satisfaction instrument and obtained his actual score. She compared his actual score (i.e., $Y = 73$) to his predicted score ($Y' = 71.84$) and was pleased to find that they were close.

Example: Worker's Case Load Size and Number of Sick Days Taken

Miriam is an administrator in a child protection agency. With recent cutbacks in funding, caseloads have increased for her staff. In the past, her child protection workers typically managed a caseload between 30 and 40 clients. More recently, workers were assigned to as many as 60 active cases. Miriam noticed that since caseload size had increased, there also seemed to be an increase in sick days taken by her workers.

Miriam wondered if the size of a worker's caseload might be a good predictor of the number of sick days that the worker would take. The predictor variable for her correlation and simple linear regression analysis was caseload size, and the criterion variable was number of sick days taken. Both variables were measured at the ratio level.

To shed some light on her research question, Miriam reviewed employee records over the past year. There were 22 front-line child protection workers on staff during the year. She reviewed their employee records and randomly selected a 1-month period for each worker. She noted the workers' average caseload size and the number of sick days taken during that month.

After entering the data into her personal computer, Miriam performed a simple linear regression analysis and printed the results. The printout contained the following:

$$r = .76$$

$$Y' = -6.8 + .25(X)$$

$$p < .0005$$

Miriam noted a statistically significant ($p < .0005$) strong correlation coefficient ($r = +.76$). Based on the strong correlation, Miriam was confident that her regression equation could generate reasonably accurate predictions. The direction of the relationship between the two variables was also positive, exactly what she had expected. She noted that the regression coefficient (b) of .25 meant that for every unit change in X, there is an increase of .25 in Y. In other words, for every additional case added to a worker's caseload, the number of sick days a worker is likely to take would increase by .25.

Miriam could use her findings to predict the number of sick days that a given worker might be expected to take in a month. She knew, however, that her study's findings might be useful for prediction only among those workers in her agency whose caseload was no smaller or larger than those contained in her sample of 22 cases.

Miriam used her regression equation to predict how many sick days a worker named Roberto, who had a caseload of 43, would be likely to take for the month:

$$Y' = -6.8 + .25(43)$$

$$= -6.8 + 10.75$$

$$= 3.95, \text{ rounded to 4 (predicted value of } Y \text{ when } X \text{ equals 43)}$$

Miriam's best guess was that Roberto would take 4 days of sick time during the month.

REGRESSION WITH THREE OR MORE VARIABLES

Not surprisingly, simple linear regression has its multivariate counterpart, *multiple linear regression.* Multiple correlation and multiple linear regression have many similarities and are closely related. They have both theoretical and actual differences, however.

In theory, all correlation analyses (including Multiple *R*) are designed to analyze data where we have no control over the distribution of the variables (random variables) in the population. We can only measure the predictor and criterion variables retroactively, after they have already been distributed among cases or objects. Consequently, a correlation coefficient is supposed to be no more than an indication of how these variables co-vary naturally—that is, without our interference. No matter how high the correlation coefficient produced, in theory it is presumptuous to imply that the predictor variable in any way caused the variations in the values in the criterion variable.

In contrast, linear regressions were designed for situations in which an experimental research design is in place—where we either introduced or directly manipulated the predictor variables. That is the way regression was designed to be used. In reality, regression analyses are now also used in many situations for which we have only random variables whose distributions are beyond our control, and correlation is sometimes used with experimental designs. This generally causes no major problems, so long as we are confident that the measurement of the predictor variables is accurate and other assumptions about their distributions are met.

In those relatively rare situations in which experimental research designs are employed and normally distributed interval-level or ratio-level predictor and criterion variables exist, regression analyses (simple or multiple) are the statistical procedures of choice. If the predictor variables are really randomly distributed (that is, their distribution is outside the control of the researcher), either correlation or regression analyses can be used, but correlation is really the more correct of the two.

As noted in Chapter 8, Multiple *R* produces a correlation coefficient that tells us the degree of correlation between a group of predictor variables and the criterion variable. When squared (R^2), it can tell us what percentage of the variation in values of the criterion variable can be explained by the group of predictor variables. Multiple linear regression does even more. The use of a multiple regression equation helps us estimate the actual value of a criterion variable, knowing the corresponding values for two or more predictor variables.

A regression equation produced by a multiple regression analysis is longer and more complicated than that produced by a simple linear regression. It must incorporate two or more predictor variables as well as the criterion variable. A regression equation produced by a multiple regression analysis that contained three predictor variables would use subscripts to denote the different predictor variables and might look like this:

$$Y' = 12.5 + 5.9x_1 + .89x_2 = 78.4x_3$$

In addition to producing an equation, a multiple linear regression analysis tells us three things:

1. Whether an apparent relationship between the predictor variables and the criterion variable in a research sample is likely to be the work of sampling error (the *p*-value)
2. The strength and direction of the relationship between variables (the correlation coefficient)
3. How accurate the regression equation is likely to be as a predictor of values of the criterion variable (the strength of the correlation)

A multiple linear regression also provides an assessment of the relative value (i.e., respective contributions) of different predictor variables for predicting values of the criterion variable. The formula for multiple linear regression is similar to that of simple linear regression, but not surprisingly, it is more complex. Like the formula for Multiple *R,* it takes into consideration the fact that the predictor variables are not only correlated with the criterion variable, they are also correlated to a greater or lesser degree with each other. We could not just add up their individual prediction powers, because some of the prediction power of one predictor variable duplicates the power within another predictor variable.

The regression counterpart of Multiple *R*'s beta weights are referred to as *beta co-efficients.* Like beta weights, they reflect the relative importance of a predictor variable in predicting the value of the criterion variable, given which other predictor variables were present in the equation.

There are other similarities between Multiple *R* and multiple linear regression. Stepwise procedures help us select the smallest possible number of predictor variables while not sacrificing too much in our ability to predict. Like Multiple *R,* this can be accomplished by using either a step-down or step-up procedure—that is, by systematically dropping or adding different predictor variables. Statistical software packages can quickly provide the best (in terms of prediction of the criterion variable) combination of predictor variables (whatever number we choose) that will produce the best multiple linear regression equation.

Multiple linear regression can even be used with nominal-level or ordinal-level predictor variables. We do this by creating dummy variables (see Chapter 1) from a single nominal-level or ordinal-level variable. The variable *marital status,* for example, is at the nominal level of measurement and often contains five different value categories (e.g., currently married, separated, divorced, widowed, never married).

By creating four dummy variables, this nominal level variable could become four ratio-level variables, with the value of 0 representing a state of no measurable quantity for each of its values. Thus, one dummy variable could be currently married (0 = no; 1 = yes); a second could be separated (0 = no; 1 = yes), a third could be divorced (0 = no; 1 = yes); and a fourth could be widowed (0 = no; 1 = yes).

In this way, a group of four dummy variables (one less than the number of value categories used for the nominal-level variable *marital status*) can be added to a multiple linear regression analysis as four predictor variables. Why not five? A person who has values of 0 for the first four dummy variables has never been married. To include "never marriedness" as another dummy variable would be redundant (the same data) and will produce misleading results when a multiple linear regression analysis is performed.

Like all types of statistical analyses, multiple linear regressions can produce results that, if we are not careful, can lead us into Type I or Type II errors. Several assumptions for their use must be met. An advanced statistics text can help explain and thus avoid such undesirable phenomena as collinearity (two highly correlated predictor variables that can distort the results of an analysis), self-fulfilling prophecies, and regression to the mean.

OTHER TYPES OF REGRESSION ANALYSES

There are many other types of regression analyses. We will briefly discuss two that appear fairly frequently in social work professional literature.

Discriminant Analysis

In social work research and practice, we often wish to learn how best to predict the value categories of a nominal-level (or ordinal-level) criterion variable such as recidivism (i.e., will abuse again, will not abuse again), rehospitalization (i.e., will be rehospitalized, will not be rehospitalized), or employment (i.e., will remain employed, will not remain employed) using several interval-level or ratio-level predictor variables. We may want to identify that group of interval-level or ratio-level predictor variables that will do the most accurate job of predicting the value category for the criterion value of a given individual, or we may simply wish to know how people in one value category differ from those in the other categories. Because the criterion variable is only at the nominal or ordinal level, multiple regression cannot be used. In such situations, discriminant analysis is appropriate.

In the previous chapter we described a statistical procedure (cluster analysis) to create homogeneous groups of cases. Discriminant analyses, in contrast, begin with groups that are believed to be essentially homogeneous. They comprise the value categories of the criterion variable. Discriminant analyses can be used, then, (1) to try to better predict what value category (of the criterion variable) a person will fall into based on his or her measurement of certain predictor variables, and (2) to identify how people who fall into the one value category differ from people in each of the other value categories.

When conducting discriminant analyses, the criterion variable can be dichotomous, as in the previous examples, or it can contain three or more value categories such as religious affiliation (e.g., Christian, Muslim, Jewish, Buddhist, Hindu, and so forth). If religious affiliation were our criterion variable, we could use a discriminant analysis either (1) to determine what group of interval-level or ratio-level predictor variables might be most helpful in predicting a person's religious affiliation, or (2) to try to identify those variables (e.g., income, education level, age, and so forth) that might distinguish the members of one religious affiliation from members of the others.

A discriminant analysis works in a way similar to other types of multivariate analyses. It creates a derived variable (in this case called the *discriminant function*) from the weighted values of several predictor variables. Stepwise variations of the procedure are available. Statistical software programs also can produce a useful table called a *confusion matrix*. Using the data that were analyzed, it displays the type and number of errors that a given group of predictor variables might have produced. It does this by displaying both the number of cases that actually were in a given value category of the nominal-level (or ordinal-level) criterion variable and the number that a discriminant analysis would have predicted to be there. It thus provides the likely number of prediction errors in any direction if a certain group of predictor variables were used and allows us to judge whether that number is acceptably low.

While discriminant analyses are closely related to multiple regressions, in a statistical sense they are less powerful than multiple regressions (there is more likelihood of a Type II error) because the criterion variable is only nominal or interval level. Discriminant analyses should not be used when both predictor and criterion variables are at the interval or ratio level. Why throw away measurement precision and statistical power unnecessarily?

Logistic Regression

Logistic regression is still another procedure (actually a group of statistical procedures) that is commonly used for prediction. It is used to predict the likelihood that a given value category of a dichotomous dependent variable will occur. The prediction is based upon the measurements of one or more independent variables.

Dichotomous dependent variables are common in social work research, particularly in outcome research or evaluation. For example, consider the many dichotomous outcome possibilities for research studies related to adolescents. Do adolescents commit crimes or not? Do they drop out of school or not? Do adolescents in foster care return home or not? Do adolescent females get pregnant or not? These dichotomous situations are best defined as an event and a nonevent, something we can also think of as simply a yes-or-no situation. In other words, the two value choices for the dependent variable are mutually exclusive choices.

Logistic regression is conceptually similar to other forms of statistical analyses described in this chapter. Its formula results in an equation that allows us to predict the likelihood of a given value category of the dependent variable—usually the category identified as the problem for a given case or person. Using it, we could, for example, compute a logistic regression equation that tells us the probability of pregnancy occurring (the problem) for a given adolescent. Since our dependent variable consists of only two choices (i.e., pregnant, not pregnant), we would also learn the probability of the nonevent by calculating the probability of the event. It will be 1.0 minus the probability of the event occurring. For example, if the probability of pregnancy occurring for a specific adolescent is .19, the probability of pregnancy not occurring will be .81 (1.0 − .19 = .81).

Logistic regression is similar to linear regression and to discriminant analysis in that they all attempt to predict the value or value label of the dependent variable from a knowledge of a number of predictor or independent variables. But there are fewer assumptions for its use. As noted earlier in this chapter, to use linear regressions and discriminant analysis, all variables must be at least at the interval level. For example, a multiple linear regression could predict the degree of risk for adolescent pregnancy, given predictor variables such as level of sexual activity, age, and family income, assuming all of these variables are normally distributed within the research population. When using logistic regression, however, the variables need only be at least at the nominal level. Thus, logistic regressions can estimate the probability that an adolescent will become pregnant based on her responses to questions about whether she is 15 years of age or younger, lives in an inner-city neighborhood, and is currently sexually active.

Another critical assumption of linear regression is that the dependent variable is continuous and is normally distributed. A linear relationship is characterized by a constant change. In describing the relationship between sex education and teen pregnancy, we would hypothesize a linear relationship between the two variables only if, for example, we believed that for every hour of sex education that adolescents receive, their risk of pregnancy reduces by a certain percent.

Of course, such a scenario of constant change is rare in the real world. In the real world, the probability of the event (i.e., pregnancy) may be affected very little (say, 1%) by 3 hours of sex education for teenagers who are not sexually active, but may change quite a bit (say, 5%) for adolescents who are sexually active. In this scenario then, the relationship between knowledge of sexuality and pregnancy is nonlinear. Logistic regression can be used in this situation and in others when we believe that two variables are related but we believe that their relationship is not linear.

When logistic regressions have been used, the results can be directly interpreted in terms of the odds of an event occurring or not occurring. For example, the results of a logistic regression could tell us that a female adolescent who over a certain age lives in an inner-city neighborhood, and is sexually active has, say, a 33 percent chance of getting pregnant. But what does this 33 percent figure mean? The results of logistic regressions are always interpreted by comparing the events to the nonevents, or in our case the probability of pregnancy to the probability of no pregnancy. Thus, we can calculate the ratio of the two events. The ratio of pregnancy to nonpregnancy would be roughly 1 to 3 when a female adolescent is over a certain age, lives in an inner-city neighborhood, and is currently sexually active.

CONCLUDING THOUGHTS

This chapter presented a brief overview of simple linear regression and several related procedures that are used for prediction, an extension of correlation. Based on the correlation between variables within a data set, they produce an equation that enables us to predict the value of a criterion variable if we know the value of one or more predictor variables for a given case.

Simple linear regression is a useful techniques when a reasonably strong linear correlation exists between two normally distributed interval-level or ratio-level variables. When there is only a weak correlation between the two variables, or the correlation is strong but not linear, creation of a simple linear regression equation is an exercise in futility. It does little to enhance our ability to predict a value of the criterion variable by knowing the value of a predictor variable.

Chapter 9 also presented a brief overview of three related multivariate procedures, multiple regression, discriminant analysis, and logistic regression. Unlike multiple regression, which requires all variables to be interval or ratio level, the criterion variable can be only nominal or ordinal level when discriminant analysis is performed, and both the dependent and independent variables need be only nominal level to perform logistic regression.

STUDY QUESTIONS

1. What can simple linear regression do that correlation cannot do? Provide examples in your discussion.
2. What statistical insights discussed in earlier chapters are critical to an understanding of simple linear regression? Describe how they relate to it.
3. Explain why it is not necessary to state a research or null hypothesis when using simple linear regression. What alternative to restating a hypothesis do researchers commonly use when performing simple linear regression analysis?
4. Using examples drawn from social work practice, discuss why it is not a productive use of time to use regression when the correlation coefficient between two variables is low. Draw two scattergrams to illustrate your point, with one scattergram showing a low correlation and the other showing a high correlation. Discuss the two scattergrams in relation to simple linear regression.
5. What do we mean when we say that the predictor and criterion variables are not interchangeable for statistical purposes when we perform a simple linear regression? What implications does this have when we program a computer to conduct a simple linear regression analysis?
6. In your own words, explain why you think we should not predict *Y* when an *X* value is below the minimum or above the maximum value used in generating *Y*.
7. Describe two situations in which you believe that it would be appropriate to perform a regression analysis in a social service agency with which you are familiar. How would the results have the potential to help the agency?
8. For each of the two major examples of the use of simple linear regression in this chapter, discuss additional methodological limitations (in addition to those mentioned) that might serve to depreciate the statistical findings. You may wish to consult a book on social work research methods and review the section on threats to internal and external validity.
9. What type of research situations would be especially suited to the use of multiple linear regression? Give an example of how a social work practitioner might use it to predict the amount of some client behavior.
10. Describe how a social worker in your answer to the previous question might use dummy variables to include a nominal-level variable such as gender as a predictor variable in the analysis.
11. Which form of multivariate analysis is designed to help predict the value of an interval-level or ratio-level criterion variable from the measurements of two or more interval-level or ratio-level predictor variables that have been introduced or manipulated by the researcher?
12. Describe how dummy variables can be used to perform a multiple linear regression using a nominal-level predictor variable. Provide an example.

13. How do step-up and step-down regression differ from each other? Describe how each works.

14. What are two different ways in which social workers can use discriminant analysis to learn more about people who participate in hate crimes against minority groups?

15. Why is logistical regression especially useful for social workers who wish to know the probability that a problem will occur for a specific client? Provide an example.

10

Cross-Tabulation

The term *cross-tabulation* is familiar to most social workers. It is associated with several related statistical tests that analyze the relationship between nominal-level variables. The best known of these is the *chi-square test of association.*

THE CHI-SQUARE TEST OF ASSOCIATION

The chi-square test of association is often referred to simply as *chi-square.* No nonparametric statistical test (and probably no other statistical test) is better known than chi-square. Research articles using chi-square analyses appear frequently in the professional literature. Since we feel comfortable with the test, we are more likely to read reports that use it than studies that employ less widely known and understood statistical tests.

A major reason for the popularity of chi-square is that it requires only nominal-level measurement of the dependent and independent variables. Thus, it is especially well suited for social work research situations. We often want to know, for example, if there is a relationship between certain variables and treatment effectiveness. The independent variables that may be related to treatment effectiveness often are only at the nominal level. They might be, for example, the type of intervention provided (e.g., individual treatment, group treatment), the highest degree completed by the social worker (e.g., BSW, MSW), or various demographic characteristics of the client (e.g., marital status, gender, religious affiliation, ethnicity, sexual orientation, type of disability).

More often than not, measurement of the dependent variable (treatment success) can only produce a nominal-level variable. We frequently can do little more than assign cases to value categories (e.g., found employment, did not find employment; abused again, did not abuse again; was rehospitalized, was not rehospitalized).

Many other variables in social work research studies have yes/no or other dichotomous value categories so that the variable is only at the nominal level. A small research study, for example, might measure whether a piece of social legislation passed *or* did not pass in different states and whether the local chapters of the National Association of Social Workers supported *or* did not support the legislation. Another study could examine whether there is an association between whether candidates for local offices were elected (*or* not) and whether (*or* not) they had taken a pro-choice position on the issue of abortion.

Chi-square, like correlation analyses, is a statistical test of association between variables. Thus, except in those rare situations where a tight experimental design was used, even if a chi-square test demonstrates support for a relationship between variables, it is not appropriate to claim that the different value categories of the independent variable caused the different value categories of the dependent variable. We can only state that a strong pattern or clustering of value categories was found to exist—certain value categories of one variable tended to be found where certain value categories of the other variable were also present. Like all inferential statistical tests of significance, chi-square can also determine whether the association between two nominal-level variables within sample data is so strong that sampling error is an unlikely explanation of it.

A simple hypothetical example illustrates how chi-square works. Suppose that we want to find out if there is a relationship between one nominal-level independent variable, type of treatment (i.e., group, individual), and one nominal-level dependent variable, client outcome (i.e., success, failure), within a large alcoholism counseling program. Based on a review of professional literature and previous practice observations, we feel justified in formulating the following one-tailed research hypothesis:

Alcohol-addicted clients in group treatment are more likely to abstain from alcohol for two months than clients in individual treatment.

The corresponding null hypothesis for our one-tailed research hypothesis would be as follows:

There is no relationship between the type of treatment alcohol-addicted clients receive and whether they abstain from alcohol for two months.

The null hypothesis would assert that although it may seem within a sample that successful treatment is more likely to occur among clients who received group treatment than among those who received individual treatment, there is not a real relationship between the variables within the population from which the sample was drawn. Any difference in success rate within the sample is likely to be due to sampling error, or chance.

When a one-tailed research hypothesis is stated and we are planning to use the chi-square test to accept or reject its null hypotheses, it is helpful to display the research hypothesis in the form of a dummy table. A *dummy table* shows where we would expect to find a disproportionately large number of cases if the results of the chi-square test support the rejection of the *null hypothesis*. In our example, we would

TABLE 10.1   Dummy Table: Type of Treatment by Client Outcome

	Results		
Type of Treatment	**Success**	**Failure**	**Totals**
Group	*		
Individual		*	

expect to find a relatively large number of cases in group treatment who abstained from alcohol (success) and a relatively large number of cases in individual treatment who did not abstain (failure). This is reflected in the placement of the asterisks in the body of Table 10.1. A dummy table created at the time a one-tailed research hypothesis is formulated can later assist in the interpretation of a study's findings.

To conduct the study, we could randomly select a sample of 100 cases ($n = 100$) from the 300 outpatient clients who are currently being seen for alcohol dependency problems. We could then ask each of their social workers to tell us for each client (1) whether the client was in individual *or* group treatment and (2) whether the client abstained *or* did not abstain from alcohol for the previous two-month period.

Type of treatment would have two possible value categories—group and individual. Client outcome also would have two possible value categories—success and failure. (Success would be operationalized as at least two months of alcohol abstention.) Thus, there are four possible combinations of value categories that could be recorded for each client, with every client falling into one, and only one, of the following four classifications:

- Group treatment and client success
- Group treatment and client failure
- Individual treatment and client success
- Individual treatment and client failure

Suppose, for example, that the 100 clients were distributed among each of the four categories as follows:

- Group treatment and client success (40 clients)
- Group treatment and client failure (20 clients)
- Individual treatment and client success (15 clients)
- Individual treatment and client failure (25 clients)

Observed Frequencies

The above data (i.e., 40, 20, 15, 25) could now be placed into what is called a cross-tabulation table. The data in the four cells of Table 10.2 are the actual number of

TABLE 10.2   Observed Frequencies: Type of Treatment by Client Outcome (*n* = 100)

	Results		
Type of Treatment	**Success**	**Failure**	**Totals**
Group	40 (*a*)	20 (*b*)	60
Individual	15 (*c*)	25 (*d*)	40
Totals	55	45	100

clients who possessed each combination of value categories for the two variables. Such a table (also referred to as a *chi-square table, cross-break table,* or *contingency table*) is constructed using the variable labels, value categories, and frequencies drawn from the data.

The areas where the frequencies (i.e., 40, 20, 15, 25) are placed are referred to as cells. Table 10.2 contains two dichotomous (two-value category) variables: type of treatment and client outcome; thus, it has four cells. It is, of course, possible to have variables with more than two value categories. The cross-tabulation table would then have more rows and columns and thus more cells.

By convention, small italicized letters (e.g., *a, b, c, d*) are used to refer to the respective cells. As can be seen from Table 10.2, they are lettered left to right, starting with the top row, then going to the next row, and so on.

In the far right-hand column of Table 10.2, the totals for each row (adding across) are entered. Likewise, the totals for each column (adding down) are entered on the bottom line. These row and column totals are called *marginals* (marginal totals). They indicate the total number of cases that were observed to possess a given value category for each variable: group treatment (60), individual treatment (40), success (55), and failure (45). The grand total of cases (*n*) in the sample entered in the bottom right-hand corner (100). Note that the sum of the row totals equals the grand total, as does the sum of the column totals.

Since the variables are at the nominal-level of measurement, there is no logical sequence in which they should appear in a table. In our example, it would have been equally correct to place individual treatment above group treatment or to place failure to the left of success. By convention, however, we display the dependent variable in the columns and the independent variable in the rows, as seen in Table 10.2. If neither variable is clearly one or the other, it makes no difference which variable's value categories run across the top of the table and which run down the side.

Once the data have been placed in a cross-tabulation table (e.g., Table 10.2), we can compare the outcomes of clients who received group treatment with outcomes of clients who received individual treatment. Such a comparison, however, cannot be easily accomplished using only the observed frequencies as contained in Table 10.2. We cannot simply compare the raw number of clients who had successful outcomes with group treatment (40) directly with the raw number of clients who had successful outcomes with individual treatment (15) and conclude that group treatment is better just because 40 is larger than 15. We would naturally expect to have more successes among those clients in group treatment than among those in individual treatment because more clients (60) were in group treatment and fewer (40) were in individual treatment.

It is possible to compensate for the difference in the number of cases in the two subsamples (individual versus group) by using percentages. Percentages equalize the sizes of groups. Using percentages, we can demonstrate, for example, that 66.7 percent of the 60 clients who received group treatment had successful outcomes, compared with 37.5 percent of the 40 clients who received individual treatment and had successful outcomes. Table 10.3 is a percentage table for the observed data contained in Table 10.2.

If the percentages in cells *a* and *c* and the percentages in cells *b* and *d* had been exactly the same, we would have no reason to believe that the variables are related. The percentages in the cells in Table 10.3 are quite different, however, and thus may not be due to sampling error. They seem to suggest that among clients who are alcohol dependent, type of treatment and treatment success may be related. Yet, at this point, it is difficult to know whether the apparent relationship is only related to sampling error. The null hypothesis would argue that a 29.2 percentage point difference (66.7% − 37.5% = 29.2% points) is not really that large. But is it? How much of a percentage point difference is needed to rule out sampling error as an apparent relationship between the two variables? Percentages alone cannot answer this question.

Expected Frequencies

In order to answer the question, we need to introduce the concept of expected frequencies. *Expected frequencies* are the frequencies we would expect to occur most often in an infinite number of samples if the null hypothesis were correct—that is, if there was no real relationship between the two nominal-level variables. Unlike observed frequencies, which reflect actual data collected (e.g., Table 10.2), expected frequencies are hypothetical numbers; they are derived using simple mathematics from the marginal totals in a cross-tabulation table.

To understand expected frequencies, return to Table 10.2. Let us see how the expected frequencies for a cell are obtained. Look first at cell *a*, which contains the 40 clients who were in group treatment and who had successful outcomes.

TABLE 10.3   Percentages of Clients: Type of Treatment by Client Outcome (*n* = 100)

Type of Treatment	Results		
	Success	Failure	Totals
Group	66.7	33.3	100.0
Individual	37.5	62.5	100.0

The expected frequency for any cell is based in part on the two marginal totals that correspond to that cell; that is, the total for the row in which the cell appears and the total for the column in which the cell appears. For cell *a* in Table 10.2, for example, these two marginal totals are 60 and 55 respectively. For cell *b,* they are 60 and 45 respectively. For cell *c,* they are 40 for the row total and 55 for the column total, and for cell *d,* they are 40 and 45.

The expected frequency for any given cell is computed by multiplying that cell's row total by its column total and then dividing by the grand total for the table or the sample size (*n*). We can express this as a formula:

$$E = \frac{(R)(C)}{N}$$

where:

E = Expected frequency in a particular cell

R = Marginal total for the row in which the cell appears

C = Marginal total for the column in which the cell appears

N = Total number of cases in the data analysis

Using the formula, we can determine the expected frequency for each cell:

$$\text{cell } a = \frac{60 \times 55 = 3300}{100} = 33$$

$$\text{cell } b = \frac{60 \times 45 = 2700}{100} = 27$$

$$\text{cell } c = \frac{55 \times 40 = 2200}{100} = 22$$

$$\text{cell } d = \frac{45 \times 40 = 1800}{100} = 18$$

Table 10.4 displays the expected frequency for each of the four cells in parentheses next to the corresponding observed frequency. Note that there is only one set of marginal totals because they are the same for both the observed frequencies and the expected frequencies.

✦ Chi-square compares the observed frequency for each cell with its respective expected frequency. It uses a formula to produce a chi-square value, which is directly related to the size of these differences. Larger differences between the observed and expected frequencies produce larger chi-square values and vice versa. We will look at how a chi-square value is calculated and interpreted using the data in Table 10.4. Before we do this, however, we will introduce the concept of degrees of freedom and how it relates to a given chi-square value.

TABLE 10.4   Observed and Expected Frequencies: Type of Treatment by Client Outcome (*n*= 100)

	Results				
	Success		Failure		
Type of Treatment	Observed	Expected	Observed	Expected	Totals
Group	40	(33)	20	(27)	60
Individual	15	(22)	25	(18)	40
Totals	55		45		100

Degrees of Freedom

If we were to study the chi-square formula carefully (Box 10.1), we could see why the size of the differences between observed and expected frequencies is not the only thing that generates larger chi-square values. The likelihood of obtaining a smaller or larger chi-square value is also affected by the size of the cross-tabulation table on which it is computed, that is, by the number of rows and columns it contains and, more specifically, by the number of cells in the table.

The larger the table, the more likely it is to have a large chi-square value. Why? The more cells in a table, the more cells available to contribute to the chi-square value and the higher that value is likely to be, even if the difference between individual pairs of observed frequencies and expected frequencies is quite small. Thus a chi-square value must be evaluated in relation to the size of the table from which it was computed. A large chi-square value in itself may not suggest a real relationship between two nominal-level variables within the population. It could have been generated by a large table with many cells, each contributing a small amount (because of small differences) to that value. Conversely, a smaller chi-square value may still reflect a real relationship between variables if the table that produced it had relatively few cells to contribute to its value.

The number of cells in a cross-tabulation table is referred to as its degrees of freedom. The *degrees of freedom* (*df*) for any cross-tabulation table is the number of rows minus 1, times the number of columns minus 1. Using this formula, Table 10.2 (which is referred to as a 2 × 2 or 2-by-2 table since there are two value categories for each of its two variables) has 1 degree of freedom (as will all 2-by-2 tables). A 3-by-3 table would have 4 degrees of freedom $(3 - 1) \times (3 - 1) = 4$, a 2-by-3 table would have two degrees of freedom $(2 - 1) \times (3 - 1) = 2$, and so on. As can be seen in Table 10.5, larger degrees of freedom (tables with more cells) require larger chi-square values to achieve statistical significance at the same rejection level (e.g., .05) than smaller degrees of freedom (i.e., tables with fewer cells). Thus, degrees of freedom are a way of correcting for the number of cells available which contribute to the chi-square value.

BOX 10.1
The Chi-Square Statistic (Without Yates Correction Factor)

Hypothesis: Clients who received group treatment are more likely to abstain from alcohol than clients who received individual treatment.

Null Hypothesis: There is no difference between the type of treatment clients received and whether they abstained from alcohol.

Predictor Variable: Type of treatment—nominal level (group versus individual).

Criterion Variable: Client outcome—nominal level (success versus failure).

Observed Frequencies: See Table 10.2.

Expected Frequencies Formula: $E = \dfrac{(R)(C)}{(N)}$

where: E = Expected frequency in a particular cell C = Total number in that cell's column
         R = Total number in that cell's row N = Total number of cases

Substituting values for letters:

Cell a: $E = (60)(55)/100 = 33$ Cell c: $E = (40)(55)/100 = 22$
Cell b: $E = (60)(45)/100 = 27$ Cell d: $E = (40)(45)/100 = 18$

Chi-Square Formula: $\chi^2 = \Sigma \dfrac{(O-E)^2}{E}$

where: x^2 = Chi-square value E = Expected frequency
         O = Observed frequency Σ = Sum of (for all cells)

Substituting values for letters:

$$\text{cell } a \quad + \quad \text{cell } b \quad + \quad \text{cell } c \quad + \quad \text{cell } d$$

$$\chi^2 = \frac{(40-33)^2}{33} + \frac{(20-27)^2}{27} + \frac{(15-22)^2}{22} + \frac{(25-18)^2}{18}$$

Degrees of Freedom Formula: $df = (r-1)(c-1)$

where: df = Degree of freedom
         r = Number of rows
         c = Number of columns

Substituting values for letters:

$df = (2-1)(2-1)$
$= 1$ (degree of freedom)

Presentation of Results: $x^2 = 8.24$, $df = 1$, $p < .005$

Conclusions: The null hypothesis is rejected and the one-tailed research hypothesis is supported. In short, clients who received group treatment had statistically significant better outcomes than clients who received individual treatment.

TABLE 10.5 Critical Values of χ^2 *(Chi Square)*

	Level of significance for a one-tailed test					
	.10	.05	.025	.01	.005	.0005
	Level of significance for a two-tailed test					
df	.20	.10	.05	.02	.01	.001
1	1.64	2.71	3.84	5.41	6.64	10.83
2	3.22	4.60	5.99	7.82	9.21	13.82
3	4.64	6.25	7.82	9.84	11.34	16.27
4	5.99	7.78	9.49	11.67	13.28	18.46
5	7.29	9.24	11.07	13.39	15.09	20.52
6	8.56	10.64	12.59	15.03	16.81	22.46
7	9.80	12.02	14.07	16.62	18.48	24.32
8	11.03	13.36	15.51	18.17	20.09	26.12
9	12.24	14.68	16.92	19.68	21.67	27.88
10	13.44	15.99	18.31	21.16	23.21	29.59
11	14.63	17.28	19.68	22.62	24.72	31.26
12	15.81	18.55	21.03	24.05	26.22	32.91
13	16.98	19.81	22.36	25.47	27.69	34.53
14	18.15	21.06	23.68	26.87	29.14	36.12
15	19.31	22.31	25.00	28.26	30.58	37.70
16	20.46	23.54	26.30	29.63	32.00	39.29
17	21.62	24.77	27.59	31.00	33.41	40.75
18	22.76	25.99	28.87	32.35	34.80	42.31
19	23.90	27.20	30.14	33.69	36.19	43.82
20	25.04	28.41	31.41	35.02	37.57	45.32
21	26.17	29.62	32.67	36.34	38.93	46.80
22	27.30	30.81	33.92	37.66	40.29	48.27
23	28.43	32.01	35.17	38.97	41.64	49.73
24	29.55	33.20	36.42	40.27	42.98	51.18
25	30.68	34.38	37.65	41.57	44.31	52.62
26	31.80	35.56	38.88	42.86	45.64	54.05
27	32.91	36.74	40.11	44.14	46.94	55.48
28	34.03	37.92	41.34	45.42	48.28	56.89
29	35.14	39.09	42.69	46.69	49.59	58.30
30	36.25	40.26	43.77	47.96	50.89	59.70
32	38.47	42.59	46.19	50.49	53.49	62.49
34	40.68	44.90	48.60	53.00	56.06	65.25
36	42.88	47.21	51.00	55.49	58.62	67.99
38	45.08	49.51	53.38	57.97	61.16	70.70
40	47.27	51.81	55.76	60.44	63.69	73.40
44	51.64	56.37	60.48	65.34	68.71	78.75
48	55.99	60.91	65.17	70.20	73.68	84.04
52	60.33	65.42	69.83	75.02	78.62	89.27
56	64.66	69.92	74.47	79.82	83.51	94.46
60	68.97	74.40	79.08	84.58	88.38	99.61

Source: From Table IV of R. A. Fisher and F. Yates, *Statistical Tables for Biological, Agricultural, and Medical Research,* published by Longman Group, Ltd., London (previously published by Oliver and Boyd, Ltd., Edinburgh) and by permission of the authors and publishers.

Computation of Chi-Square

With easy access to computer software programs, a chi-square analysis is rarely undertaken with pencil and paper anymore. When it is, there are seven fairly simple steps:

1. Place the observed frequencies into a cross-tabulation table, and add the marginal totals.

2. Compute the expected frequencies, and add them to the table.

3. Compare the observed frequencies with the expected frequencies for each cell using the chi-square formula.

4. Compute degrees of freedom for the cross-tabulation table.

5. Go to the appropriate line for the degrees of freedom in a critical values of chi-square table (see Table 10.5), and see where the chi-square would fall (between which two numbers).

6. Go to the number to the left of where the chi-square value would fall.

7. Go to the top of the column in which that number appears and obtain the approximate p-value using the line corresponding to the type of research hypothesis used (one-tailed or two-tailed). The probability that sampling error may have produced the relationship between the two variables can now be described as less than ($<$) that approximate p-value.

The formula needed to compute a chi-square statistic is the general formula contained in Box 10.1. It is appropriate for any cross-tabulation table containing more than four cells. In fact, if there are only four cells, as in our example, we should adjust the formula slightly by reducing the absolute difference between the observed and expected frequencies by .5 for each cell before squaring it (referred to as the *correction for continuity* or, sometimes, the Yates correction factor). This is a mathematical correction designed to avoid the slightly inflated chi-square value (such as that in Box 10.1) that the uncorrected general formula produces when used with 2 × 2 tables.

In order to illustrate the basic chi-square formula (and because most cross-tabulation tables contain more than four cells), we did not use the correction for continuity in Box 10.1. However, the chi-square values displayed in the tables elsewhere in this chapter were derived using the corrected formula for 2 × 2 tables.

Today, any statistical software program that has the capacity to calculate a chi-square value performs it almost instantaneously. The formula for chi-square along with the formulas for expected frequencies and degrees of freedom are all programmed. Once we have entered the data for the cases in our research sample, we would then select cross-tabulation (or, in some cases, chi-square) from the menu. The displayed results would include the chi-square value and the associated p-value for the data.

In our example, we would learn that the chi-square value for the data contained in Table 10.2 is 8.24 (without using the correction for continuity) and that it is reduced to 7.11 when the Yates formula is used. With one degree of freedom, the p-value for the data, using either formula, was less than .005.

Presentation of Chi-Square

The actual presentation of findings of a chi-square analysis is straightforward. First, the cross-tabulation table (containing observed frequencies) is displayed. The actual chi-square value derived from the analysis of the data (χ^2), the degrees of freedom (df), and the probability that sampling error might have produced the chi-square value (p) are placed at the bottom of the cross-tabulation table as in Box 10.1:

$$\chi^2 = 8.24, \, df = 1, \, p < .005$$

Interpreting the Results of a Chi-Square Analysis

Returning to the example, which examined the relationship between type of treatment for clients who were alcohol dependent and client outcome, the corresponding p-value for the chi-square value is very small (i.e., $p < .005$), which is what we had hypothesized we might find. Since we did not specify and justify a different rejection level, our cutoff point for rejection of the null hypothesis would be the customary .05 rejection level, where we would conclude that sampling error would produce that large a difference between the observed and the expected frequencies less than 5 times out of 100.

In fact, since .005 is 10 times smaller than .05, it is safe to reject the null hypothesis that there is no relationship between the two variables. A $p < .005$ means that sampling error would produce that large a difference between the observed and expected frequencies less than 5 times out of 1000 if an infinite number of samples of 100 were drawn and there was not a real relationship between the variables within the population.

Can we now say that we have statistical support for our one-tailed research hypothesis? Not quite yet. Chi-square is just a statistical test; it has no way of knowing what we predicted in our one-tailed research hypothesis. It simply checks to see if the difference between the observed and expected frequencies is large enough that it probably is not the work of sampling error.

In our example, a large chi-square value and a corresponding low p-value would have occurred if clients in group treatment had a much better record of abstinence, or if the better record had been among clients in individual treatment. Our chi-square analysis told us only that the variables probably are related; it did not (and cannot) tell us if the direction of that relationship was what we hypothesized or just the opposite.

To find out if we have statistical support for our one-tailed research hypothesis, we could now compare the dummy table (Table 10.1) that we created to represent our one-tailed research hypothesis with Table 10.4. We would ask, "Where are the disproportionately large observed frequencies?" (A disproportionately large observed frequency is one that is larger than its expected frequency.) Are they in the cells where we predicted they would be (a and d), or are they in the opposite cells (b and c)?

The disproportionately large number of cases are in cells a and d in Table 10.4, just where we predicted they would be. Thus, we can now reject the null hypothesis and claim support for our one-tailed research hypothesis. If the disproportionately large observed frequencies had occurred in cells b and c (where clients in individual treatment who abstained from alcohol and clients in group treatment who did not are displayed), we could not claim support for our research hypothesis. In that case, we would have reason to believe that the variables are related, but in the direction opposite to that we predicted—something worth examining by replicating the study with a different research hypothesis.

Having demonstrated a statistically significant association between the variables in the hypothesized direction, we are still a long way from concluding that clients who are alcohol dependent should be put into group treatment because they are less likely to drink again. True, the difference between the percentages of abstinence in our two subsamples was pretty substantive (66.7% for group treatment versus 35.7% for individual treatment). Before we can claim that we have uncovered a relationship between variables that would hold for all or even any other drug dependency treatment program, however, we would want to be very sure that the alternative explanations for a real relationship between the variables (besides sampling error) did not produce the apparent relationship between the variables.

Perhaps, for example, most of the substance abuse workers in the agency were hired because they are especially adept at working with groups and they have less skill in individual counseling; or perhaps there was an unwritten precedent that only clients with the most severe alcohol problems are assigned to individual treatment. Either fact might explain the relatively high rate of success among clients in group treatment.

The most we can say about our finding of a statistically significant relationship between the variables is that most likely the variables really are associated, at least in the agency from which the sample was drawn. We cannot say with certainty, however, why this relationship occurred, nor can we predict if it will be found again in different agency settings with different staff training, agency policies, type of group or individual treatment used, and so forth. Maybe we are on to something, but only replication and other research studies—perhaps using more powerful research designs and more powerful statistical analyses—will provide evidence that our original one-tailed research hypothesis is, indeed, correct.

Meaningfulness and Sample Size

As mentioned in Chapter 6, when using any statistical test, the larger the sample size, the greater the chance of acquiring statistical support for the decision to reject the null hypothesis. The chi-square test is no exception—large samples are almost certain to produce large chi-square values since they make the test quite powerful, sometimes too powerful. With a very large sample, statistical significance is almost always achieved, even if the actual percentage differences between the expected and observed frequencies are small.

When we see that a chi-square test has demonstrated the presence of a statistically significant relationship between variables, it is easy to be impressed, but we need to look carefully at the sample size (n) that produced it. Like other statistical tests, a chi-square analysis can identify a statistically significant relationship between variables, but it may be a statistically significant weak relationship.

A continuation of the example we have been using will demonstrate the point. Suppose that we tried to replicate the results of our earlier research study. This time, a

TABLE 10.6   Observed Frequencies and Percentages: Type of Treatment by Client Outcome ($n = 200$)

Type of Treatment	Results				Totals	
	Success		Failure			
	Frequency	Percentage	Frequency	Percentage	Frequency	P(
Group	30	60.0	20	40.0	50	
Individual	80	53.3	70	46.7	150	
Totals	110		90		200	

$\chi^2 = .429$, $df = 1$, $p > .10$ (direction predicted)

sample of 200 clients being treated for alcoholism was followed over a 2-month period. The results of the second study are displayed in Table 10.6.

When a chi-square test is computed for the data in Table 10.6, $p > .10$ (for a one-tailed research hypothesis), because the likelihood that chance might have produced the difference between the observed and expected frequency for these data is relatively large, we would lack sufficient statistical support to be able to reject the null hypothesis (i.e., .10 is larger than .05).

Since the evidence in support of our one-tailed research hypothesis is now conflicting, we might want to attempt our study for a third time, this time with a very large sample. Let us suppose that we used data on 10 times more clients 2,000 clients. The data from this third study are displayed in Table 10.7.

TABLE 10.7   Observed Frequencies and Percentages: Type of Treatment by Client Outcome ($n = 2000$)

Type of Treatment	Results				Totals	
	Success		Failure			
	Frequency	Percentage	Frequency	Percentage	Frequency	Percentage
Group	300	60.0	200	40.0	500	100
Individual	800	53.3	700	46.7	1500	100
Totals	1100		900		2000	

$\chi^2 = 4.29$, $df = 1$, $p < .025$ (direction predicted)

A close look at Tables 10.6 and 10.7 reveals that the percentages of the 2,000 clients in the respective cells in Table 10.7 are exactly the same as those within the comparable cells in the sample of 200 cases in Table 10.6. In both hypothetical studies, 60 percent of clients in group treatment abstained from drinking compared with 53.3 percent of clients in individual treatment. Both 2 × 2 tables have 1 degree of freedom. But the chi-square values are very different. The value is 10 times larger in the study using the larger sample than in the one using the smaller sample.

The *p*-value also is very different (less than .025 with the sample of 2,000, compared with greater than .10 with the sample of 200). The relationship between the variables is not statistically significant using the data in the study with 200 cases, but it is statistically significant in the study with 2,000 cases. If we had used 20,000 clients, the chi-square value would be 42.9; if we had used 200,000 clients, it would be 429, and so on. Since the percentages within the tables did not change, the strength of the association would be identical in each instance, but the chi-square values would be very different.

There is a logical reason why we would be more likely to be able to reject the null hypothesis when larger samples are used even though the percentages are the same. When smaller samples are used—the short run mentioned in the discussion of the role of probability in hypothesis testing in Chapter 5—a difference of 6.7 percentage points (60.0% – 53.3% = 6.7% points) may well have been the work of sampling error. With the much larger samples, the law of averages (the long run) should have taken over; any differences in success for the two types of treatment should have disappeared as more and more cases were added if no real relationship between type of treatment and treatment success existed.

The fact that a 6.7 percentage point difference still exists for the very large sample suggests that the relationship between the variables is a real one, so we must reject the null hypothesis. We also should remember, however, that the relationship between the variables is relatively weak, because it shows up only when very large samples are used.

Related Indicators of the Strength of a Relationship

Including actual percentage differences is one way to report the actual strength of relationships between variables when a chi-square test has been used. Reporting a related measure of association is another. When chi-square analysis is performed using a statistical software package, related indicators often are displayed as part of the results of the data analysis. Some of the better known ones are *phi, Yule's Q, lambda,* and *Cramer's V.* Each is designed for a specific data analysis situation. For example, *Q* is designed for use with two dichotomous variables, is easily computed by hand, and produces a correlation coefficient that can be used to describe the strength of the relationship between variables, but it should not be used if one of the cells has an observed frequency of 0.

While both phi and *V* produce a correlation coefficient that can be squared (r^2) to suggest the amount of variation in the dependent variable that is associated with the variation in the independent variable, phi should be used if both variables are dichotomous and *V* if one or both variables contain more than two value categories. If both variables can be regarded at the ordinal level (and chi-square often is still the test of choice in such situations), still other measures of association (for example, *gamma* or one of the nonparametric tests of correlation introduced in Chapter 8 can be used to report the strength of the relationship between the variables. Reporting the appropriate measure of association along with chi-square values and *p*-values helps put research findings into perspective. It is especially recommended if very large sample sizes are used, since statistical significance is so likely that it is almost meaningless as a research finding.

Restrictions on the Use of Chi-Square

We must know what an expected frequency is and how it is calculated in order to understand the important concept that the chi-square statistic compares observed frequencies with expected frequencies. But it is also useful to know how to calculate an expected frequency so that we can determine if we should be using the chi-square statistic at all.

The chi-square statistic is not appropriate for all the analyses of the relationship between two nominal-level variables. Its formula will not produce accurate results and it, therefore, should not be used if either of two situations exists:

1. When, in a 2 × 2 (four-cell) table, at least one cell has an expected frequency of less than 5.
2. When, in a table that is larger than 2 × 2, more than 20 percent of the cells have expected frequencies of less than 5, or any cell has an expected frequency of 0.

A handy check on whether there is a problem with small expected frequencies in any cross-tabulation table can be performed by locating the cell with the smallest expected frequency. To do this, locate the row with the smallest marginal total and the column with the smallest marginal total. The cell with the smallest expected frequency is at the intersection of that row and column. The cell's expected frequency can be determined with the expected frequency formula. If an expected frequency in a 2 × 2 table is 5 or more, it is safe to use the chi-square statistic. If the expected frequency is less than 5, chi-square should not be used.

In larger tables, additional checks will have to be made to see if the second no-go situation exists. (If a computer software package is used, a warning generally appears if all expected frequency requirements have not been met.) If there are problems, it may still be possible to use a chi-square test by combining adjoining cells to form a table with fewer cells with sufficiently large expected frequencies. This process, called collapsing, should be done using common sense and logic and in a way that does not discard any more data than absolutely necessary. Value categories of a variable that are thus combined should possess a strong logical similarity to each other.

An Alternative To Chi-Square: Fisher's Exact Test

If, in examining the relationship between two dichotomous variables, the expected frequency size requirements for the use of the chi-square test cannot be met, *Fisher's exact test.* is an alternative nonparametric test. Like chi-square, it is used with two independent subsamples. The independent subsamples may have resulted from the random sampling of cases that have been categorized as falling into two identifiable groups, such as gender (e.g., male, female) or marital status (e.g., married, not married). Or they may be the experimental and control groups to which cases were randomly assigned in a classic experimental research design.

Because Fisher's exact test can only analyze data using a 2 × 2 contingency table (four cells), if there are more than two value categories of either (or both) of the variables, it is necessary to first collapse the data into a 2 × 2 table (making both variables dichotomous). This results in a loss of available measurement precision, so if feasible, it might be preferable to enlarge the size of the research sample so that the requirements for the use of chi-square can be met.

USING CHI-SQUARE IN SOCIAL WORK PRACTICE

Major changes in the delivery of social work services may have a positive or a negative effect on the lives of clients. Changes based on findings derived from a chi-square analysis alone can be especially risky. After all, as we have noted, the identification of a statistically significant relationship between variables using a chi-square test is usually just evidence of association; causation cannot be implied.

Like any type of statistical analysis, chi-square can also suggest relationships between variables that are spurious, that is, not real ones. They might disappear if the influence of other variables was controlled in some way. For this reason, chi-square analyses are sometimes best used to tentatively identify associations between variables and to formulate critical questions that can subsequently be answered through more high-powered statistical analyses.

Example: Discharge Planning and Readmission

Amelia is a social worker in a state inpatient hospital. Her main duty is to do readmission intake interviews with patients with prior hospital admissions. Over the past 5 years, she observed what appeared to be a disproportionately large number of patients who were readmitted to the hospital who had been previously discharged to live with their relatives. Knowing that her social work colleagues doing discharge planning also made frequent use of boarding homes for discharged patients, she wondered why she was not seeing more readmissions of patients who were discharged to boarding homes. She wondered if there might not be a relationship between patients being readmitted (or not readmitted) to the hospital and the place to which they had been discharged (boarding home versus relatives).

Amelia read all the available related literature. She then designed and implemented a small-scale research study that would gather data to test her one-tailed research hypothesis:

Patients discharged to boarding homes will have a lower rate of readmission to the hospital than patients discharged to live with their relatives.

Amelia received permission from her supervisors to select a 10 percent random sample of all files of patients discharged during the previous 18 months. Using a standardized data collection instrument that she constructed, she gathered data on a wide variety of demographic variables on the 148 patients (10% of 1480 patients = 148 patients) who were discharged to boarding homes and the 250 patients (10% of 2500 patients = 250 patients) who were discharged to relatives. Her total sample (n) was 398 patients (148 + 250 = 398).

Table 10.8 is the findings from Amelia's chi-square analysis. What did she learn from Table 10.8? From her general knowledge of hypothesis testing, she knew that $p < .01$ meant that the differences between the observed and expected frequencies probably were not due to sampling error; the likelihood that chance produced the relationship between the variables within her sample was less than 1 percent. She thus was able to reject the null hypothesis and conclude that there was a statistically significant relationship between the variables.

Amelia also knew that when a one-tailed research hypothesis is tested using a chi-square test, it is necessary to determine whether a statistically significant relationship between variables is in the predicted direction, either by looking for the cells where disproportionately large observed frequencies occurred or by examining percentages. Using Table 10.8, Amelia was able to determine that approximately 17 percent (25 of 148) of patients discharged to boarding homes had been readmitted to the hospital, compared with 28 percent (71 of 250) of those discharged to relatives. These two percentages were consistent with the direction of her hypothesis; patients discharged to boarding homes were less likely to be readmitted than patients discharged to relatives.

**TABLE 10.8   Readmission to Hospital
by Discharge Status ($n = 398$)**

Discharge Status	Readmission?		Totals
	Yes	**No**	
Boarding Home	25	123	148
Relatives	71	179	250
Totals	96	302	398

$x^2 = 6.113$, $df = 1$, $p < .01$ (direction predicted)

Before Amelia drew any conclusions about the meaningfulness of the statistical significance between the variables, she knew that she must acknowledge the limitations of her research design. The validity of the data in the patient records might be a problem; in addition, there might be other factors relating to bias. There was also a long list of other variables that might have affected readmission of the patients in her study. They included patient diagnosis, length of first hospitalization, availability of aftercare services, patient's use of medication, and a myriad of other factors that she had no reason to believe were proportionally represented in the two groups (boarding home/relatives) of patients.

What did her findings really tell Amelia about the relationship between the setting to which patients are discharged and their readmission? The goal of a chi-square analysis is to acquire evidence for or against the existence of an association between variables. Cause-and-effect knowledge was not a possibility from the beginning. This was due partly to the absence of an experimental research design and partly to the limits of the chi-square analysis itself. What Amelia learned was that, for whatever reasons, patients who were discharged to boarding homes from her particular hospital were not as likely to be readmitted as those patients who were discharged to relatives.

Amelia also gathered data on patient diagnosis and length of first hospitalization. She could examine the relationship among these other variables and the dependent variable as well, using the appropriate statistical analysis. The patients' records might have yielded insights into other variables that went into the decision to live with relatives or in a boarding home; these data could be used to enhance the results of her analysis and to shed more light on her original findings.

Given all the limitations that tempered the interpretation of Amelia's findings, it might seem that they were of little value. The likelihood of the existence of many other variables that might have affected whether a patient was readmitted would seem to discount the utility of the findings for social work practice. Yet, despite a less than perfect research design and the use of relatively low-powered nonparametric statistical analysis, several possible practice implications emerged.

Knowing (even without fully understanding why) that patients discharged to boarding homes in Amelia's hospital are less likely to be readmitted than patients discharged to relatives could be valuable to her social work colleagues doing discharge planning. Patients discharged to live with relatives could be perceived as being at higher risk of readmission.

Based on her findings in Table 10.8, Amelia began to ask certain questions:

1. Should I try to find boarding home placements for more of my clients?
2. Should I endeavor as a professional social worker to work toward the creation of more boarding home facilities?
3. Should I endeavor to provide additional sources of support for patients going to live with relatives in order to reduce the likelihood of their being readmitted?

These applications of the research findings are still only questions. None of them indicates that Amelia or the other social workers at her hospital should make drastic modifications in their service delivery methods without careful consideration and, what is more important, without further research studies.

Example: Legislators' Voting Patterns and Tax Issues

Juan is a social worker employed by a legislative committee. He is attempting to assist in the passage of an increase in the state sales tax, which will provide additional revenues for public education. As part of his job, he recently began gathering demographic data on state legislators. He hoped to gain insight into why they might favor or oppose the proposed tax bill.

After he had examined available data and hearsay on 30 legislators, it seemed to Juan that legislators who favored the bill tended to have children currently attending public schools; legislators who were on record as not supporting the bill tended not to have children currently in public schools. Juan wondered whether he could find statistical support for a relationship between the nominal variables support (or nonsupport) of the bill and use (or nonuse) of public schools.

After a discussion with committee members and a review of the literature available on legislators' voting patterns on various tax issues, Juan concluded that he could justify formulation of a one-tailed research hypothesis:

> Legislators who currently have children attending public schools are more likely to support the bill than are legislators who do not have children currently attending public schools.

Juan continued to gather data on the state's legislators, but he made a special effort to learn about and systematically record data on his two variables. He identified 160 legislators who had publicly stated support for or opposition to the tax bill. Of these, he obtained sufficient current biographical data on 125 (78 percent) to conclude with reasonable certainty whether or not they were currently sending their children to public schools. Table 10.9 presents Juan's findings.

TABLE 10.9   Legislators' Support for Tax Bill by Whether They Use Public Schools ($N = 125$)

	Support for Bill?		
Use Public Schools?	**Yes**	**No**	**Totals**
Yes	39	36	75
No	21	29	50
Totals	60	65	125

$x^2 = .834$, $df = 1$, $p > .10$ (direction predicted)

Juan was somewhat disappointed by the findings of his chi-square analysis, yet he was grateful that he had not relied on his subjective hunches in his presentation to the legislative committee. If he had, he might have misled the committee members.

With 1 degree of freedom and a one-tailed research hypothesis, Juan knew his chi-square value should have been at least 2.71 (see Table 10.5) in order to reject the null hypothesis at the customary .05 rejection level. It was only .834. He lacked sufficient evidence to conclude that the legislators' use or nonuse of public schools for their children was associated with their voting preference on the tax bill (which was his original one-tailed research hypothesis).

Perhaps other variables were more closely associated with whether they favored the bill—for example, their voting record on all tax bills, their perceptions of the fairness of a sales tax versus other sources of revenue, a partner who was teaching in the public school system, and so on. Juan also knew that these other variables may have helped obscure the presence of a relationship between the variables whose association he had tested.

The lack of statistical support for Juan's one-tailed research hypothesis in no way negated the value of his study. He avoided drawing an erroneous conclusion based on inadequate evidence that might have resulted in an inappropriate lobbying strategy. Portraying the motivation of legislators who opposed the bill as self-serving would have been a mistake. Juan could now spend his time more efficiently by pursuing other avenues to gain insight into the legislators' positions on the proposed tax.

CHI-SQUARE WITH THREE OR MORE VARIABLES

In the example used earlier in this chapter, we were seeking to document the existence of an association between the variables *type of treatment* and *client success*. Suppose we repeated the research study using 100 clients and again used chi-square to analyze the data. The observed frequencies for this hypothetical study are displayed in Table 10.10.

Despite the presence of a statistically significant association between the variables, we may wonder if a third variable, for example, gender, may explain why clients in group treatment appear to do better than those in individual treatment. We would like to

TABLE 10.10   Observed Frequencies: Type of Treatment by Client Outcome ($n = 100$)

Type of Treatment	Results		
	Success	**Failure**	**Totals**
Group	15	35	50
Individual	25	25	50
Totals	40	60	100

$x^2 = 3.376$, $df = 1$, $p < .05$ (direction predicted)

somehow control for the effects of this third variable (called a control variable) to get a better picture of the true relationship between type of treatment and client outcome.

One way to explore the effect of the third variable might be to divide our sample into its two subcategories, male and female. We could then construct two separate tables—one for female clients and one for male clients. We could use the chi-square test with each of the two subsamples to see if the relationship between type of treatment and client outcome held up within each of the subsamples. But there would be a better and more efficient way to accomplish the same purpose, the use of multiple cross-tabulation tables.

It is possible to examine the association between two nominal-level variables while controlling for a third variable while using a single cross-tabulation table. Multiple cross-tabulation tables can be used to spread the cases in the original cross-tabulation table (e.g., Table 10.10) among a larger number of cells. (This is the opposite of the process of collapsing described earlier.) Two or more variables are displayed along one axis or even along both axes. Table 10.11 is a multiple cross-tabulation table using the same data that were used in Table 10.10, only in Table 10.11 a third variable, gender, has been added.

Notice that the chi-square in value Tables 10.10 and 10.11 are similar—the one in Table 10.11 is actually a little larger. But the p-values displayed in Tables 10.10 and Table 10.11 ($< .05$ and $> .05$ respectively) are different. Before the variable gender is introduced, we would be able to reject the null hypothesis (using the .05 rejection level), but after it is introduced, we cannot. How can we interpret this phenomenon? It may mean that the relationship between type of treatment and client outcome is a spurious one or is so weak that the introduction of gender has obscured it in the sample studied.

Problems with Sizes of Expected Frequencies

It is not always possible to control for one or more variables using multiple cross-tabulation. When data are spread out in larger cross-tabulation tables, size requirements for expected frequencies for using chi-square sometimes cannot be met.

TABLE 10.11   Observed and Expected Frequencies: Type of Treatment and Gender of Client by Client Outcome ($n = 100$)

		Client Outcome				
		Success		Failures		
Treatment	Gender	Observed	Expected	Observed	Expected	Totals
Group	Male	7	(10)	18	(15)	25
Group	Female	8	(10)	17	(15)	25
Individual	Male	13	(10)	12	(15)	25
Individual	Female	12	(10)	13	(15)	25
Totals		40		60		100

$x^2 = 4.334$, $df = 3$, $p. > .05$ (direction predicted)

In Table 10.11, the 100 cases are distributed among eight cells. The expected frequencies of the eight cells would thus be smaller than the expected frequencies of the four cells in Table 10.10. The expected frequencies are, however, over 5 in a sufficiently large percentage (more than 80 percent) of the cells to justify the use of the chi-square test. This happened only because the number of cases in group and individual treatment were equal, there were an equal number of males and females, and the overall number of successes and failures were similar. If the cases had not split so evenly into the value categories, the expected frequencies may have been less than 5 in more than 20 percent of the cells. Then we could not have used the chi-square test.

Because the use of multiple cross-tabulation tables spreads the cases into a larger number of cells, such tables can be used only when relatively large samples are available and cases break fairly evenly among value categories of the variables. Even then, if at least one examined variable has been measured in a way that results in a large number of value categories, the value categories may have to be collapsed so that the cross-tabulation table has fewer cells (and sufficiently large expected frequencies) before we can use the chi-square test.

Only the expected frequency size requirement of the chi-square test prevents the more frequent use of multiple cross-tabulation tables for examining the effect of other variables on the relationship between variables. Theoretically, several variables could be combined along the left of the table and several more could be combined along its top. To do this, however, a very large sample would be required, larger than is found in most social work research situations.

Effects of Introducing Additional Variables

As in the above example, the original association between variables will sometimes disappear when a third variable is controlled. Other times, the relationship between the two original variables will appear stronger when a third variable is controlled. In such instances, the third variable, called a *suppressor* or *obscuring variable,* may cause us to underestimate the actual strength of the association between the two variables.

When a third variable is introduced, a third result also may occur. The relationship between the first two variables may remain statistically significant. But it may be significant in one direction with one or more value categories of the third (control) variable and significant in the opposite direction in its other value categories. When this happens, it is usually not possible to summarize the findings easily; the relationship between the independent variable and dependent variable has to be described for each value category of the control variable. The third variable is said to further specify the relationship between the first two variables, and it is therefore called a *specifying variable.*

The many possible effects of the introduction of one or more additional variables to a *statistical analysis* remind us of the complexity of most relationships among variables. It is because of this complexity that we should exercise extreme caution in drawing conclusions about the effect of one variable on another or even about their association. A statistically significant relationship between variables can still be a spurious one. All that statistical significance tells us is that the relationship is unlikely to be due to sampling error, or chance.

SPECIAL APPLICATIONS OF THE CHI-SQUARE FORMULA

Other statistical tests also rely on the chi-square formula to determine if the relationship between variables is statistically significant. Two of them—McNemar's test and the median test—are sometimes found in the professional literature.

McNemar's Test

One special application of the chi-square test, *McNemar's test*, also called the *test for the significance of changes,* is popular in research situations that employ a one-group pretest-posttest research design. The test entails two measurements of a two-category nominal-level variable using a single research sample. It could be used, for example, to determine if an educational program on the life experiences of Southeast Asian refugees was associated with a desired change in attitudes about them among community members who attended an educational program (the intervention).

In social work practice and research we often wonder whether an intervention (the independent variable) can be demonstrated to be associated with desirable changes in the dependent variable. The McNemar's test offers the opportunity for at least a preliminary insight into this question. It can tell us if the amount of change that occurred in the desired direction in a research sample was statistically significant or likely to be due to sampling error.

For example, Chester is a school social worker. He requested time to address a meeting of a parents' group to present arguments for hiring four additional school social workers for the district, a proposal currently being considered by the school board. Chester believed that parents would reflect a positive change in their attitudes following his presentation.

Since Chester predicted that his presentation would be associated with a positive change in parents' thinking on the issue, he formulated a one-tailed research hypothesis:

Following the presentation, more parents will reflect positive attitudes about hiring additional social workers.

Just prior to his presentation to the parents' group, Chester gave a sheet of paper and a pencil to each parent. On the paper, he asked each parent to include a five-digit identifying number (for anonymity) and to indicate if he or she was in favor of hiring the four additional social workers. Immediately after his presentation, he once again gave all parents a sheet of paper and a pencil and asked them to supply the same identifying number and to again indicate if they were in favor of hiring the additional social workers. Based on pretest and posttest data supplied by the parents, Chester classified each parent into one of four mutually exclusive categories:

1. Favored before, favored after
2. Favored before, did not favor after
3. Did not favor before, favored after
4. Did not favor before, did not favor after

Chester placed his raw data into a 2 × 2 cross-tabulation table (Table 10.12). He then used the basic chi-square formula (with a correction for continuity) to compute a chi-square value. He checked the table of critical values (see Table 10.5) to see whether he had statistical support to reject the null hypothesis.

In Table 10.12, the totals on the right side represent the numbers of parents for and against the proposal before (pretest) Chester's presentation (32 and 18 respectively). The totals along the bottom of the table represent the numbers for and against it after (posttest) the presentation (16 and 34 respectively).

The numbers within the body of the table (its four cells) represent individual cases, as they do in any cross-tabulation table. The 50 cases (parents) were distributed among the table's four cells based on a pair of measurements—whether or not each parent favored the proposal before the presentation and whether or not he or she favored the proposal after it. Thus, if Ms. Aguilar favored the proposal before Chester's presentation, for example, but opposed the proposal after his presentation, she would be one of the 26 cases in cell *b*. Or if Mr. Owens was against the proposal before his presentation and was still against it after the presentation, he would be one of the 8 cases in cell *d*.

The McNemar's test focuses on cells in which change is reflected, in this case, cells *b* and *c*, where parents changed their position. (Cells *a* and *d* contain parents who did not change their position.) When using McNemar's test, the null hypothesis is that some change would be likely to occur with some cases but whatever change occurred probably would be about equal in both directions. These changes would theoretically

TABLE 10.12   Significance of Change Analysis (McNemar's Test): Positions on Proposal before and after Chester's Presentation

	After Presentation		
Before Presentation	**For**	**Against**	**Total**
For	6 (*a*)	26 (*b*)	32
Against	10 (*c*)	8 (*d*)	18
Totals	16	34	50

$x^2 = 5.58$, $df = 1$, $p < .01$

cancel each other out, and the number of parents favoring or opposing the proposal to hire more social workers would remain about the same after the presentation as they were before it.

Using the McNemar's test, the null hypothesis can be rejected only if a very large percentage of the changes that occurred were in one direction (larger than what sampling error normally would be expected to produce). This is reflected in a statistically significant p-value (usually, $p < .05$). In addition, if a one-tailed hypothesis had been formulated (as was the case in Chester's study), most of the changes must be in the direction predicted. In Chester's study, they were in the opposite direction, i.e., from support for the proposal to hire more social workers to opposition to it. Thus, despite a p-value of $< .01$, Chester could not reject the null hypothesis and claim statistical support for his one-tailed research hypothesis.

Only 14 parents failed to change their positions (cells a and d). But of the 36 who changed them (cells b and c), only 10 moved from negative to positive (cell c), while 26 (cell b) who had previously favored the proposal opposed it after the presentation. Chester speculated on the meaning of these findings. Had he said something to turn off the parents? Why had so many of them changed in a negative direction following his presentation? Before he gave any more presentations to parents' groups, he planned to review carefully what he had said and how he had said it.

As can be seen, the McNemar's test is quite limited. It is used in research situations that involve a two-category nominal-level dependent variable that is measured twice for the same sample of cases. Because it is ideal for many one-group pretest-posttest research designs that evaluate practice intervention methods, it can be a useful test for the social work researcher or practitioner.

Median Test

Another related procedure is useful in situations in which one variable (usually the dependent one) is ordinal, interval, or ratio level, but badly skewed. It is the *median test*. It is designed to assess the likelihood that the value categories of the other dichotomous nominal variable (e.g., experimental group, control group) are sufficiently different from each other in regard to the ordinal, interval, or ratio variable to warrant the rejection of the null hypothesis.

The median test is relatively simple. Scores are first rank-ordered, and the median for all scores is computed. Values that fall at the median are dropped or added to one group or the other. Then the number of values or value labels above and below the median are tabulated for both categories of the dichotomous nominal-level variable, and the frequencies are placed in a cross-tabulation table.

Because it uses the median as the cutoff point, the median test divides the sample into two equal-sized subgroups (half above the median and half below the median) based on measurements of the variable. With larger samples (30 or 40 or more total cases) that also reflect a reasonably even split in the number of cases in a dichotomous nominal-level variable (two subsamples), the expected frequencies may be large enough to justify the use of the chi-square test to complete the data analysis. When the total number of cases (both groups) is small, Fisher's exact test is substituted to see if the relationship between the two variables is statistically significant.

The median test is based on the assumption that if the two groups are not really different or if they reflect differences that can be attributable to chance, each will have approximately the same percentage of cases above and below the median of the ordinal-level, interval-level, or ratio-level variable. A clustering above the median by one group and below the median by the other group may indicate a real relationship between the two variables, depending on the strength of the pattern and the degree to which other alternative explanations have been ruled out.

For example, Beulah is a social worker employed in a genetic counseling center. She observed that less than half of pregnant women over 40 years of age who were referred for amniocentesis (a medical procedure that determines if a fetus has certain genetic problems) followed through with the referral. She noticed what she thought might be a factor related to this phenomenon. It seemed to her that women who did not follow through on the referral tended to have more children; those who did follow through seemed to have fewer children. Thus, she formulated a one-tailed research hypothesis:

> Women with more children are less likely to complete a referral than those with fewer children.

Beulah drew a random sample of 100 ($n = 100$) case records that documented referral for amniocentesis. She recorded for each (1) the number of children in the family at the time of the referral, and (2) whether the client completed the referral. The variable *number of children* is at the ratio level of measurement. Beulah knew, however, that the variable is positively skewed. Thus, she decided to use the median test. She computed the median for the variable number of children in her sample (2.14). She then grouped the data into four cells of a contingency table (Table 10.13) based on where each case fell in relation to the two-category nominal-level dependent variable (i.e., did not complete referral, did complete referral) and the ratio-level independent variable *number of children* (i.e., above the median, below the median). The criteria for size of expected frequencies for the chi-square test were met for (the smallest, cell *c,* was 5.76), so she completed her statistical analysis using the formula for chi-square

TABLE 10.13   Median Test Data: Completion of Referral for Amniocentesis and Number of Children ($n = 100$)

Completion of Referral	Number of Children (Md. = 2.14)		
	Above Median	**Below Median**	**Total**
No	28 (*a*)	12 (*b*)	40
Yes	22 (*c*)	38 (*d*)	60
Totals	50	50	100

$x^2 = 9.375, df = 1, p < .005$

(using the correction for continuity). Her initial one-tailed research hypothesis was confirmed by the median test—women with more children were less likely to complete a referral than those with fewer children. She speculated on her findings, wondering whether the possible birth of a child with, for example, Down syndrome was of less concern in larger families because additional child-care help was available from older siblings. She decided to pursue this possible explanation in subsequent research studies.

This example is a little unusual for use of the median test in that the independent variable is at the ratio level of measurement, but badly skewed. More typically, it is the dependent variable that is at the interval or ratio level of measurement, but skewed, while the independent variable (e.g., type of treatment) is at the nominal level of measurement.

All too frequently, researchers observe that the criteria for use of a parametric test (for example, one or more normally distributed interval-level or ratio-level variables) cannot be met and immediately turn to chi-square. The median test takes better advantage of the level of measurement precision that is available. The median test at least treats a skewed interval-level, ratio-level, ordinal-level variable as being more than nominal. Chi-square treats all variables as if they were at the nominal level of measurement. To use chi-square in such situations increases the risk of a Type II error in drawing conclusions about a relationship between variables.

Like the McNemar's test, the median test has no formula of its own. It really would be more accurate to describe both not as tests but as procedures for assigning cases into the cells of a contingency table. Then the formula for chi-square, or Fisher's exact test, can be applied to produce a *p*-value.

CONCLUDING THOUGHTS

Most of this chapter was devoted to the widely used chi-square test of association. The fact that it requires only nominal-level data for both variables means that it is ideally suited to many of hypothesis testing needs in our profession. Unfortunately, there are certain errors commonly made in its use. They usually entail making too much of a finding of statistical significance by (1) implying that the relationship is one of more than just association, (2) overestimating the importance of findings that reflect weak relationships between variables where a finding of significance was virtually inevitable because of the use of very large samples, or (3) failing to consider that the association may be a spurious one and thus attempting to control for other variables that may be creating a false impression about the relationship that has been identified.

Still another common error is made when the chi-square test is used when one or both variables are at the ordinal, interval, or ratio level of measurement. When chi-square is used, the test treats different values as if they are only differences in kind (value categories); it ignores the fact that they reflect quantitative differences in the variable. Unless both variables are only at the nominal level of measurement, there is very likely to be a better (often a more powerful) statistical test that can and should be used. We presented an overview of one of these, the median test.

STUDY QUESTIONS

1. Why is the frequent use of chi-square in social work research both good and bad? How is the test particularly well-suited to social work research?
2. What do the numbers in each of the cells in a cross-tabulation table mean?
3. What is a dummy table, and what does it reflect?
4. Can chi-square tell us whether one variable causes variations in the second variable? Explain.
5. What are expected frequencies, and how are they used in chi-square testing?
6. How do degrees of freedom affect whether a chi-square value of a given size (e.g., 10.00) will be considered statistically significant?
7. What are the minimum expected frequency requirements for the use of chi-square? What other nonparametric alternative is available when the expectation for a 2-by-2 table cannot be met?
8. What is the final step in the process for determining if chi-square has demonstrated support for a one-tailed research hypothesis? Provide examples.
9. How can cross-tabulation (chi-square) be used to examine the relationship between variables while controlling for the effect of a third variable? How can this detect the presence of a spurious relationship between variables?
10. What is a useful test that examines whether the change in a nominal-level variable in a single group of cases is statistically significant?
11. Why is the median test preferable to chi-square when one variable is interval or ratio level but badly skewed?

t Tests and Analysis of Variance

One of our profession's greatest needs is for research studies that evaluate the effectiveness of treatment interventions. We need to know, for example, whether a particular intervention is associated with positive or negative changes in clients' values, knowledge levels, affect levels, or behavioral levels. In addition, we often need to know if one intervention is more effective than another in producing desired changes.

In testing hypotheses related to practice effectiveness, we frequently have reasonably precise measurements of the variable we seek to influence—the dependent variable. Examples of common dependent variables in social work research are client self-esteem, public attitudes toward welfare recipients, client marital satisfaction, and incidence of spouse abuse, to name just a few. Thanks to the work of researchers over the years, many standardized self-report measuring instruments to measure these variables now exist. They are assumed to generate interval-level data that approximate a normal distribution in the population on which they have been developed.

Other dependent variables, such as number of appointments missed, number of stated oppositions to a proposed social service program, or amount of illegal drugs consumed, often are normally distributed at the interval or ratio levels of measurement by their very nature. Many of these variables also tend to be normally distributed within the population, making the mean an appropriate measure of their central tendency and the standard deviation an appropriate measure of their variability (see Chapter 3).

In testing research hypotheses related to practice effectiveness, the independent variable is often at the nominal level of measurement. It may be, for example, type of treatment intervention, gender of the social worker, ethnicity of the social worker, or some other variable that can only be measured by grouping cases into different value categories. Often, the research sample available for a study is small; large samples are not common in social work research, particularly in clinical situations.

The three conditions briefly described above—one nominal-level independent variable, one normally distributed interval-level or ratio-level dependent variable, and a relatively small research sample(s)—are ideally suited to a family of related statistical procedures: (1) *t* tests and (2) simple analysis of variance, or simple *ANOVA*.

THE USE OF *t* TESTS

In many social work research studies, the dependent variable is measured within either a single sample or two samples. In a single-sample situation, for example, we may wish to know if the sample really differs greatly from its population in relation to the dependent variable—that is, how typical is it? On the other hand, in the two-sample situation, we may wish to know if measurements of the dependent variable differ greatly between the two samples in relation to the dependent variable—that is, are the two samples really all that different from one another in relation to the dependent variable?

The various *t* tests are based on the *t* distribution of means referred to briefly in Chapter 6. There is actually a different *t* distribution for each sample size under 30. As sample sizes approach $n = 30$, they start to look more and more like a normal distribution curve.

Both normal distributions (Chapter 5) and sampling distributions (Chapter 6) rely heavily on knowledge of the amount of variation (standard deviation) of a variable in the population. With this knowledge, it is possible to compute a confidence interval that can then be used to determine just how large (or small) a sample mean would be required in order to achieve statistical significance—that is, to conclude with reasonable certainty that the difference between the sample's mean and its population is unlikely to be due to sampling error.

But what if the amount of variation in the population is not known? This is true for many dependent variables that we attempt to influence. We are unlikely to know, for example, a population's standard deviation for variables such as number of unsafe sexual contacts per month in a given community or weekly number of bullying incidents within a middle school. Then we must rely on the *t* distribution. It allows us, based on measurements of the variable in a sample and the size of that sample, to compute a confidence interval for interval-level and ratio-level variables whose standard deviations in the population are unknown.

Because *t* tests are classified as parametric, they are designed for use in situations where the dependent variable is interval or ratio level and normally distributed. They are, however, quite robust; that is, if we use them with interval-level or ratio-level variables that are only somewhat skewed, they produce findings that are quite accurate.

As with the chi-square test, the popularity of *t* tests sometimes can lead to their misuse. The tests are familiar to us, easily understood, and relatively nonthreatening. Consequently, there may be a tendency to want to use them in situations in which they are inappropriate and in which other, more appropriate tests should be used. Two common misuses are (1) ignoring the shape of the distribution of the interval-level or ratio-level dependent variable in the population and (2) using the "shotgun" approach to data analyses.

As noted earlier, *t* tests are designed for use in situations where the interval-level or ratio-level dependent variable is considered to be normally distributed in the population. If a variable is badley skewed in the population, other tests (such as the nonparametric alternatives discussed later in this chapter) should be used in their place. The value of research findings can be seriously jeopardized if *t* tests are used with interval-level or ratio-level data that are badly skewed in the population from which the samples were drawn.

A second common misuse of two types of *t* tests (the two sample independent and dependent *t* tests) involves calculating a large number of the tests using a single dependent variable and a long list of dichotomous independent variables. In some particularly glaring examples of this "shotgun" approach to data analyses, researchers have run hundreds of tests with little basis in the professional literature for believing that any of the independent variables might be related to the dependent variable. To their delight, this fishing expedition has produced a statistically significant relationship between a few of the independent variables and the dependent variable.

Findings of a few statistically significant relationships between variables when a large number of pairs of variables have been tested should not be surprising. In fact, we would probably be more surprised if none of the relationships between the variables proved to be statistically significant. Probability theory alone suggests that we will uncover one or more spurious relationships this way. It is nothing more than the mathematical principle that "with an infinite number of monkeys, an infinite number of computers, and an infinite amount of time, some monkey, sometime, somewhere, will write a Pulitzer Prize winning novel."

Expressed another way, by trying enough combinations, a researcher is almost certain to stumble onto one of those rare times that sampling error caused two variables to be strongly related within a research sample, even if the variables really are unrelated. Statistically examine the relationship between 100 different pairs of variables that have no relationship to each other whatsoever, and the laws of probability tell us that the most likely result is that perhaps 4 (4 is less than 5) of the combinations will reflect a statistically significant relationship at the .05 rejection level. Making too much of a "finding" from such a misuse of a statistical analysis can result in a Type I error, since the results are unlikely to be replicated in a second pair of samples. In situations in which there is reason to believe that many different independent variables may be related to the dependent variable, multivariate statistical tests that are specifically designed for such situations should be used.

Of course, the two common misuses of two-sample *t* tests that we have just described can occur when other inferential tests are used, too. For example, we can mistakenly use Pearson's *r* (Chapter 8) when one or both variables reflects a skewed distribution in the population. Or we could use a series of 100 bivariate chi-square tests (Chapter 10) and then make far too much of what might be a spurious relationship when a statistically significant relationship is found between a few of the pairs of variables.

THE ONE-SAMPLE *t* TEST

The *one-sample* t *test* is used when a research study employs only one randomly selected sample. It compares the mean of an interval-level or ratio-level variable in a
sample with its corresponding population mean. The formula for the test produces a *t*-
value, which is then compared with a table like Table 11.1 to find the *p*-value, the likelihood that sampling error might have produced the sample mean of the dependent
variable, given the size of the sample that was employed. When a computer is used, the
output displays both the *t*-value and the corresponding *p*-value, along with the degrees
of freedom for the sample size that was used. With *t* tests, degrees of freedom adjust
for the sample size that produces a *t*-value. For the one-sample *t* test, the degrees of
freedom are the number of cases in the sample minus one.

The one-sample *t* test is used for two different purposes: (1) to determine whether
a sample is sufficiently representative of its population in relation to some variable for
use in a research study (a design issue) and (2) to test hypotheses (for inference).

Comparing a Sample's Mean
to a Population's Mean

When using the one-sample *t* test to evaluate the representativeness of a sample in relation to an interval-level or ratio-level variable, we generally hope *not* to be able to
reject the null hypothesis. Why? If we get a high *p*-value such as .10, .50 or even .75,
this provides support for the position that any difference between the two means is so
small that it is very likely to be due to sampling error—that is, our sample is indeed
representative of its population.

For example, suppose we want to conduct a simple research study to examine the
relationship between the variables *age* and *job satisfaction level* among child protection social workers (using Pearson's *r*). We have been told by the program's director
that we can draw only a small random sample ($n = 25$) of workers since we need to
conduct extensive interviews with them. We would like the sample to be representative
of the population of all child protection workers in relation to what logically may be an
intervening interval-level variable, size of a worker's caseload. We have been told by
the director that the average caseload for all child protection workers is normally distributed and about 50 cases.

We could draw the sample of 25 and then, use the one-sample *t* test to compare the
sample's mean caseload size with the population's mean caseload size of 50. If the results of our analysis suggest that the difference between the two means is likely to be
the work of sampling error (say, $p > .20$), we would *not reject* the null hypothesis. The
sample would be not all that different, probably close enough to be considered representative of its population in regard to the variable *size of worker's caseload*. We
would proceed to interview the 25 cases in the sample.

If, however, a one-sample *t* test analysis compared our sample's mean with its
population's mean and concluded that the difference between the two means was not
likely to be the work of sampling error ($p < .05$), we would reject the null hypothesis.
From this, we could conclude either (1) that our sample and its population really are

more than

TABLE 11.1   Critical Values of *t*

less than

	Level of significance for a one-tailed test					
	.10	.05	.025	.01 99	.005 99.5	.0005 99.9

	Level of significance for a two-tailed test					
df	.20	.10	.05	.02	.01	.001
1	3.078 3.	6.314	31.821	31.821	63.657	636.619
2	1.886	2.920	4.303	6.965	9.925	31.598
3	1.638	2.353	3.182	4.541	5.841	12.941
4	1.533	2.132	2.776	3.747	4.604	8.610
5	1.476	2.015	2.571	3.365	4.032	6.859
6	1.440	1.943	2.447	3.143	3.707	5.959
7	1.415	1.895	2.365	2.998	3.499	5.405
8	1.397	1.860	2.306	2.896	3.355	5.041
9	1.383	1.833	2.262	2.821	3.250	4.781
10	1.372	1.812	2.228	2.764	3.169	4.587
11	1.363	1.796	2.201	2.718	3.106	4.437
12	1.356	1.782	2.179	2.681	3.055	4.318
13	1.350	1.771	2.160	2.650	3.012	4.221
14	1.345	1.761	2.145	2.624	2.977	4.140
15	1.341	1.753	2.131	2.602	2.947	4.073
16	1.337	1.746	2.120	2.583	2.921	4.015
17	1.333	1.740	2.110	2.567	2.898	3.965
18	1.330	1.734	2.101	2.552	2.878	3.922
19	1.328	1.729	2.093	2.539	2.861	3.883
20	1.325	1.725	2.086	2.528	2.845	3.850
21	1.323	1.721	2.080	2.518	2.831	3.819
22	1.321	1.717	2.074	2.508	2.819	3.792
23	1.319	1.714	2.069	2.500	2.807	3.767
24	1.318	1.711	2.064	2.492	2.797	3.745
25	1.316	1.708	2.060	2.485	2.787	3.725
26	1.315	1.706	2.056	2.479	2.779	3.707
27	1.314	1.703	2.052	2.473	2.771	3.690
28	1.313	1.701	2.048	2.467	2.763	3.674
29	1.311	1.699	2.045	2.462	2.756	3.659
30	1.310	1.697	2.042	2.457	2.750	3.646
40	1.303	1.684	2.021	2.423	2.704	3.551
60	1.296	1.671	2.000	2.390	2.660	3.460
120	1.289	1.658	1.980	2.358	2.617	3.373

Source: From Table III of R. A. Fisher and F. Yates, *Statistical Tables for Biological, Agricultural, and Medical Research,* published by Longman Group, Ltd., London (previously published by Oliver and Boyd, Ltd., Edinburgh) and by permission of the authors and publishers.

different in regard to the variable *size of caseload* or (2) that the director gave us mis-information about the average caseload size in the population.

If we were to proceed to the interviewing stage of the study using a sample that may be different from its population, we would jeopardize our ability to generalize our study's findings to the population from which the sample was drawn. It might be better to draw two or three more random samples and repeat the statistical analysis using the one-sample *t* test. If the other samples all produce a relatively large *p*-value (we cannot reject the null hypothesis) and their means are similar, it is probably safe to use one of them for our study and conclude that the first sample was just a fluke. However, if re-peated sampling continues to generate *p*-values of < .05 and the means are all similar, it is altogether possible that the director gave us misinformation since, with samples of 25, most samples should have mean caseloads quite close to the population mean. The average caseloads in the samples, especially if they are quite similar to each other, may indeed be representative of the true population and therefore any one of them may be appropriate for use.

Hypothesis Testing

When we use the one-sample *t* test to attempt to gain support for a one-tailed or two-tailed research hypothesis, we hope to demonstrate that our sample is so different from its population in regard to an interval-level or ratio-level dependent variable that the difference is not likely to be due to sampling error. Thus, we hope to be able to reject the null hypothesis.

A one-sample *t* test can determine if an intervention may have made a real differ-ence. We could, for example, select a random sample of clients with low frustration tolerance (as measured by a standardized scale) and offer a supplemental treatment to them (such as a special workshop on frustration management). We could then measure their frustration tolerance levels and compare their mean frustration tolerance level with the mean frustration tolerance level of all clients who have a similar diagnosis using a one-sample *t* test.

The one-sample *t* test also can be used for hypothesis testing when using nonex-perimental research designs. Suppose, using child protection caseworkers as research participants, we hope to demonstrate statistical support for our belief that child protec-tion workers in our county agency do better overall on the state licensure examination than most other child protection caseworkers. Our one-tailed research hypothesis would be stated as follows:

> Social workers at ABC county office score higher than their peers on the state licensure examination.

We could collect the scores from all 25 of our workers who took the examination during the past 5 years and, using the one-sample *t* test, compare their mean score with the mean score of all child protection workers who took the examination during the past 5 years. Perhaps our sample's mean score did turn out to be higher than the population's mean. That alone would not be sufficient to lend support to our one-tailed research hypothesis.

The question remains, was it that much higher? Would we be safe in concluding that our sample's higher mean score was not just due to sampling error? The results of a one-sample t test analysis would answer this question. It would result in both a t-value and a corresponding p-value, which would be based on the t-value and the degrees of freedom ($25 - 1 = 24$). If we had used .05 as our rejection level, a low p-value (i.e., $p < .05$) would support a decision to reject the null hypothesis and would lend support for our one-tailed research hypothesis. A higher p-value (i.e., $p > .05$) would support a decision not to reject the null hypothesis. It would suggest that the difference between the two mean scores is probably just the work of sampling error and that there is no reason that, in the long run, our child protection workers would tend to score higher on the examination than the population.

Presentation of Findings

Using our example, Table 11.2 shows how the findings of one-sample t tests are presented in a research report. It displays the population mean (80.42), the mean of the research sample (85.42), the number of cases in the research sample and in the population (25 and 100 respectively), the t-value (2.620), the degrees of freedom (24), and the corresponding p-value ($p < .01$).

By glancing at Table 11.2, we can see that the 25 workers who took the examination in ABC county scored, on the average, 5 points higher than the population ($N = 100$) as a whole. This 5-point difference is statistically significant at the .01 level (one-tailed test). This means that a 5-point difference would happen because of sampling error less than 1 time out of 100 with this size sample and the standard deviation for the scores in the research sample.

A Nonparametric Alternative: The Chi-Square Goodness-of-Fit Test

There is a useful alternative to the one-sample t test, the chi-square goodness-of-fit (often referred to as simply goodness-of-fit), that performs the same two functions

TABLE 11.2   Reporting Results of t Analyses: State Licensure Examination Scores

Research Participants	Mean
Sample ($n = 25$)	85.42
Population ($N = 100$)	80.42

$t = 2.620, df = 24, p < .01$

when the dependent variable is only nominal level. The major limitation of the goodness-of-fit test is that it can be used only if we have accurate central tendency data about the population from which a sample was drawn.

Unlike the one-sample *t* test, goodness-of-fit does not compare the sample's mean with its population's mean. It is, of course, impossible to compute a mean with nominal-level data. What the goodness-of-fit test does, however, is compare the *percentage* of cases in a given value category of a nominal-level variable for a sample with the known percentage of cases in that variable's value category in its population.

For example, say we know that the percentage of left-handed people in a specific population is 12 percent. We could use a chi-square goodness-of-fit test to determine if the percentage of left-handed people in a sample drawn from this population differs significantly from that in the population—that is, from 12 percent.

Based on sampling distributions (Chapter 6) and how other statistical tests work, we would probably not be surprised if the percentage of left-handed people in our sample of 25 was, say, 11 percent or 13 percent. We would not expect the difference between either of these two sample percentages and the population's 12 percent to be statistically significant. We would not expect to be able to reject the null hypothesis, which would state that any difference between the percentages is probably just due to sampling error. After all, if nothing unusual were going on, we would expect our sample to contain about the same percentage of left-handed people as contained in the population from which it was drawn, and either 11 percent or 13 percent is very close to 12 percent.

But what if the percentage of left-handed people in our sample was, say, 5 percent or 19 percent? Then we would need help to determine whether to reject the null hypothesis—that is, to determine the likelihood (*p*-value) that sampling error might have produced the percentage of left-handed people in a sample of this size.

By applying a simple formula (contained in most statistical software packages), the chi-square goodness-of-fit test can compare our sample's percentage of left-handed people with its population's known percentage of left-handed people. Taking into consideration the size of the sample, a *p*-value is produced, which then tells us the likelihood that the percentage of left-handed people in the sample could have been due to sampling error.

How might we use this test? We probably would not care if a sample had a disproportionate number of left-handed people in it. But we might want (1) to determine whether a sample drawn is sufficiently representative of its population in relation to some potentially intervening nominal-level variable for use in a research study (a design issue) and (2) to test hypotheses (for inference). The chi-square goodness-of-fit test can do either of these. They are the same tasks that a one-sample *t* test performs using interval-level or ratio-level data.

Example: Assessing the Representativeness of a Research Sample—Family Support and Longevity.

Mable wanted to examine the relationship between an independent variable *number of living siblings* and a dependent variable, *length of client survival* among the residents of a large long-term care facility. Her literature review, however, had suggested that gender may be an intervening or extraneous variable in the relationship between the independent and dependent variables. Using case files, she drew a simple random sample of 50 ($n = 50$) residents from the facility's population of 1000 ($n = 1000$).

Mable determined from the home's weekly census that its percentage of females was 72 percent (720 women). Before she conducted a statistical analysis using Pearson's *r*, she wanted to know if her sample (which consisted of 37 females, or 74% females) could be considered representative of the home's population for the potentially intervening variable *gender*. She hoped to not be able to reject the following null hypothesis:

> The percentage of females in the research sample does not differ significantly from the percentage of females in the population from which the sample was drawn.

To accept or reject her null hypothesis, Mable used the chi-square goodness-of-fit test to compare her sample's percentage of females (74%) with the home's actual percentage of females (72%). The test produced a *p*-value of $> .05$. Thus, she was not able to reject the null hypothesis—the percentage difference between her sample (74%) and its population (72%) was relatively small (2 percentage points) and may well have been attributable to sampling error. In other words, her sample was sufficiently representative of the population for the variable *gender*. She went on to conduct her primary data analysis, assured that if she found a relationship between the independent variable and the dependent variable, at least it did not occur because the sample contained a disproportionately large number of females.

Example: Hypothesis Testing—Involvement in the Political Process.
Max works for a community agency located in his precinct, a very low socioeconomic neighborhood in the inner city. One of his agency's goals is to get local residents more involved in the political process in order to work for better public services. Recent election data revealed that only 22 percent of eligible voters in the inner city voted in the last several county council elections. Max selected a random sample of 100 ($n = 100$) eligible voters in his precinct from voter registration lists and visited all of them in their homes. He stressed the importance of voting in the next month's county council election. After the election, he determined that 35 of those he had visited, or 35 percent, had voted, while the overall percentage within the precinct remained constant at 22 percent.

Max used the chi-square goodness-of-fit test to determine whether the difference between the voting percentage in his sample of 100 people (35%) and the usual percentage of those voting within the population (22%) was likely to be due to sampling error. After all, there was a 13-point percentage difference (35% – 22% = 13% points).

The results of his analysis were that the probability (*p*) of a difference of that magnitude occurring with a sample of 100 just because of sampling error was very low ($p < .05$). Max believed that he could safely reject the null hypothesis. Apparently, his sample was really different in its voting record following his intervention. He was hopeful that his home visits had made the difference, and that it was not just the work of some rival hypothesis.

THE DEPENDENT *t* TEST

The *dependent* t *test* is also called the *paired groups* t *test, matched groups* t *test, dependent groups* t *test,* or *correlated groups* t *test.* Unlike the one-sample *t* test, a dependent *t* test does not compare a sample's mean for an interval-level or ratio-level variable with its population's mean. It does, however, compare mean scores from two samples. The two samples may be two different but related samples (naturally related or matched in some way) that are both measured once, or the same sample measured on two separate occasions.

Use with Two Connected (or Matched) Samples Measured Once

In this application of the dependent *t* test, research participants or cases are matched in some way and put into two distinct samples, or groups. The two samples may consist of, for example, pairs of siblings in which one sibling is assigned to sample A and the other is assigned to sample B, or two groups of people that have been deliberately matched in relation to one or more variables (often, potentially extraneous or intervening ones) so that both samples are believed to be comparable. Once the samples are thus constituted, we could, for example, administer a treatment intervention to one of the samples (but not the other) and use the dependent *t* test to see if there is a statistically significant difference between the two samples in relation to an interval-level or ratio-level variable, such as life satisfaction.

Use with One Sample Measured Twice

When the dependent *t* test is used with a single sample consisting of the same people measured at two different times, we have what is called a *one-group pretest-posttest research design.* Suppose we wanted to test the effectiveness of a smoking cessation program. We could draw a random sample of clients who smoke and ask them to record the average number of cigarettes they smoked one day before enrolling in a smoking cessation program (pretest). We could record the number of cigarettes they smoked the day after they completed the program (posttest). We then could compare the mean number of cigarettes the group smoked one day before the program with the mean number they smoked one day after the program.

Like all statistical tests of inference, a dependent *t* test produces a corresponding *p*-value. In our example, it would allow us either to claim a statistically significant relationship between having been in the group and mean number of cigarettes smoked (i.e., $p < .05$) or to not claim it (i.e., $p > .05$).

If we were able to reject the null hypothesis, we would also want to rule out the possibility that something else may have created the relationship between variables within the research sample. The time lapse between the day on which the data for the pretest were collected, for example, and the day on which the data for the posttest were collected (and what may have occurred for our participants in the interim) may be a more plausible explanation than the intervention for any reduction in cigarette smoking.

To use another example, suppose we wished to attempt to find support for the following one-tailed research hypothesis:

Pregnant teenagers will have increased knowledge of child development after they undergo a child development workshop.

A 5-day child-rearing skills workshop could be offered to 22 pregnant high-school students. The group's mean child-rearing skills score could be calculated before the workshop (pretest) and after it (posttest).

Table 11.3 provides an example of how the results of this hypothetical research study might be displayed. Notice that the students had a pretest mean score of 4.8 and a posttest mean score of 5.8. The difference between the two means was 1 point (5.8 − 4.8 = 1). This 1-point difference is statistically significant at the .01 level with 21 degrees of freedom (the number of pairs of scores −1 for the dependent t-test). This means that a 1-point difference would happen because of sampling error less than 1 time out of 100 with this size sample even if the workshop had no real effect on child-rearing skills. Thus, we can reject the null hypothesis and, if all other competing explanations for the apparent relationship can be ruled out, we can claim support for the one-tailed research hypothesis.

A Nonparametric Alternative: The Wilcoxon Sign Test

Sometimes we find ourselves with two related samples (naturally or through matching) and measurements of a dependent variable that are more than ordinal-level but not quite interval-level measurement. The measurements can be rank-ordered based on the absolute amount of the variable that they contain. This is frequently the case with newly developed measuring instruments that measure attitudes, perceptions, or beliefs. Sometimes the amorphous nature of the concept being measured prevents us from claiming that the values we assign reflect precise intervals—that is, equal difference in quantity of the variable.

The *Wilcoxon sign test* is useful in those situations in which, for example, we know that a score of 65 on an anxiety scale reflects more anxiety than a lower score of

TABLE 11.3   Child-Rearing Skill Scores for Pregnant Teenagers Before and After a Child-Rearing Skills Workshop ($n = 22$)

Pretest	Posttest	Difference
4.8	5.8	1

$t = 2.53$, $df = 21$; $p < .01$

60 and where we also believe that this difference is greater than the difference in anxiety between, say, scores of 62 and 60. If this latter determination can be made, we would be throwing away available measurement precision if we were to look at only the direction of difference (more, less, or the same) between pairs of related cases that constitute two subsamples.

In using the Wilcoxon sign test to evaluate the relative effectiveness of two forms of social work intervention, an assumption is made: If the form of intervention used makes no difference, there will be essentially no difference in regard to the dependent variable among the cases in one group and the cases in the other group (the null hypothesis). Specifically, the null hypothesis would state that, for either of the two matched groups, the sum of the overall ranks of positive cases (cases with higher scores than their counterparts in the other group) will equal the sum of the ranks of negative cases (cases with lower scores than their counterparts in the other group).

The ideal situation for using the Wilcoxon sign test involves the use of perfectly matched pairs of cases. Since this is rarely possible, however, cases are usually matched based on a pretest measurement of one or more of the most likely intervening variables.

Once matched pairs are identified, one member is randomly assigned to one group; the second goes to the other group. After the intervention, the Wilcoxon sign test examines the direction and amount of difference between each. In the process, the differences between pairs are themselves rank-ordered (without regard to direction). If the preponderance of differences suggests higher scores for one group and the greatest differences are also among those cases, the Wilcoxon sign test is likely to suggest a statistically significant difference between the two groups. The stronger the pattern, the more likely the null hypothesis can be rejected and vice versa.

For example, Katie is a social work counselor in a student health center. Over the years, she has wondered whether college students having social adjustment problems benefit more from counseling by untrained student volunteers (peers) or by professional social work staff. Using standard intake screening measurements over a 1-month period, she identified a group of prospective clients who were all diagnosed as having moderate social adjustment problems. Before assignment for counseling, she identified 15 matched pairs (matched on such key variables as gender, grade point average, and the like) and randomly assigned one member of each pair to be seen by a student volunteer and the other member to be seen by a social worker. After six 1-hour counseling sessions, all clients were administered a standard measuring instrument that measured the dependent variable *social adjustment*.

The measuring instrument, which Katie considered to be an indicator of college students' social adjustment, was deemed to be capable of generating the "ordinal plus" level data required for use of the Wilcoxon sign test. Data were compared for each pair, and the direction and amount of the differences were noted. The differences were then rank-ordered without regard to the direction of the difference.

Katie was pleased to learn that almost all of the students who were seen by the social workers scored much better on the measuring instrument than did those seen by student volunteers. She analyzed her data using the Wilcoxon sign test. It allowed her to reject the null hypothesis ($p < .05$).

Katie was, of course, not ready to discount student volunteers as effective counselors based on this single small-scale research study. She wondered, however, whether student volunteers might benefit from closer supervision by social work staff or whether they might be used more effectively with students having other problems. She also decided to replicate her study, using another standardized measurement of social adjustment, to see if consistent findings would be obtained.

THE INDEPENDENT *t* TEST

Another variation of the parametric *t* test, the *independent t test,* is especially useful in research studies that employ experimental or quasi-experimental research designs. Like the dependent *t* test, it also compares the means of two samples. But to use the independent *t* test correctly, the two samples must be independently drawn from a population—that is, the random selection of one case does not increase or decrease the likelihood of any other case being selected. This is not the case when the dependent *t* test is used.

The two groups do not have to contain an equal number of cases, which often is the situation in social work evaluations of treatment effectiveness. Often two subsamples (e.g., clients in group treatment, clients in individual treatment) are unequal in size. Even in experimental research studies where it is considered ethical to randomly assign an equal number of cases to two subsamples, clients are likely to drop out of treatment before the study is completed. Any resulting discrepancy between the sizes of the two subsamples presents no problem for the independent *t* test. The formula for the test automatically controls for it.

When using the independent *t* test, the two samples often consist of cases with one or the other measurement of a dichotomous independent variable (e.g., intervention A or intervention B; female therapist or male therapist). In experimental research designs, the two samples would consist of cases assigned to either the experimental group (sample 1) or the control or comparison group (sample 2).

Using the formula for the independent *t* test, mean scores of the two samples are compared to produce a *t*-value and a corresponding *p*-value. On the basis of sampling error, the means of the two samples are almost certain to be somewhat different. The independent *t*-test examines the amount of that difference and determines how likely sampling error is to have produced it if, in fact, the variables are unrelated.

If the difference turns out to be so small that sampling error is a likely explanation for this difference, the *p*-value will be relatively high and the null hypothesis cannot be rejected. We can conclude that the difference between the means of the two groups is too likely to be a function of sampling error and does not reflect a real relationship between the independent and dependent variables.

On the other hand, if the results indicate that the difference is large enough that it is very unlikely to be the work of sampling error (a low *p*-value), we can reject the null hypothesis and conclude that the difference observed in the sample indeed reflects a real relationship between the two variables. Sampling error will have been effectively discounted as a possible explanation for the apparent relationship between them.

As should be evident by now, with small samples such as those often used in social work practice research, even a fairly large difference between two means may be due to sampling error—that is, it may not be statistically significant. Conversely, even small differences between means may suggest a real relationship between variables if the samples are quite large. As with the other *t* tests, degrees of freedom are a way of examining differences in means within the two groups while factoring in the size of the sample that produced them. For the independent *t* test, the degrees of freedom are the total number of cases in both samples, minus 2. Using the *t*-value produced by the *t* test and the appropriate degrees of freedom, we can determine if the difference between the means of two independently formed groups is sufficiently large that sampling error alone is unlikely to have produced it. Generally, we conclude that this is the case when the corresponding *p*-value (described as level of significance in Table 11.1) is < .05.

If data have been computer-analyzed, the *t*-value, the degrees of freedom for our data, and *p*-value are all displayed, along with, among other results, the actual means for each of the two groups. A comparison of the means is a good indicator of effect size—that is, how much difference an intervention really made in a tightly controlled experiment. If the actual difference in the means is quite small but statistically significant (as can easily happen with larger samples), then common sense and practice knowledge might lead us to conclude that the time, effort, and money of any changes in our practice might not be justified.

Example: Study Guide for the State Merit Exam

Dave has developed a new study guide to help social workers prepare for the state merit exam. To evaluate the effectiveness of such a study guide, he randomly selected 15 of the 30 social workers who planned to take the exam the next month and provided them with a copy of it. He asked them to spend part of their study time each night using the guide as instructed.

The 15 social workers who used the guide could be regarded somewhat loosely as the experimental group; the remaining 15, who did not use it, could be regarded as the control group. After all 30 social workers took the state merit exam, their results were compared. Dave compared the mean exam score of the 15 social workers who used the guide (the experimental group) with the mean exam score of the 15 social workers who did not use it (the control group).

In comparing the means for the two groups using the independent *t* test, Dave found a statistically significant ($p < .05$) relationship between the two variables. He was thus able to answer several questions:

1. Is the mean difference between the two groups large enough to allow me to reject the null hypothesis (that any apparent relationship between using or not using the guide and the social workers' scores on the exam is the work of sampling error)? Yes.

2. How confident can I be that the difference was not due to sampling error? At least 95 percent confident.

3. Is the difference in the direction that I predicted, that is, did those using the study guide do better on the exam than those who did not use it? Yes.

4. Does the data analysis suggest that the use of the study guide might help other social workers taking the state merit examination, not just those in the experimental group? Yes.

Dave knew, however, that there are other possible explanations for his research finding. Perhaps, for example, the guide merely served to remind the social workers to prepare for the exam. Consequently, they may have put more time and energy into studying than did those in the control group. Maybe the guide itself was of no direct help at all.

Even if other possible alternative explanations could be ruled out (in addition to sampling error), another question still would have to be addressed: Is the relationship between the variables a meaningful one? Did the size of the difference in the mean scores on the exam, for example, justify the purchase price of the guide for social workers planning to take the exam?

The answer to this question, like others related to the practical value of any research findings, might be a difficult one, even a very individual one. For example, suppose that Dave had found that the people in his study who used the study guide scored an average of five points higher on the exam than those who did not use it. Remember, first, that the average score in each of the two groups was calculated by a group of scores that may have ranged widely. A few social workers in his experimental group might have done quite poorly on the exam, perhaps, worse than if they had not used the study guide. So, just because the group did better on the exam overall, there is no guarantee that Phil and Marylea will do better if they use it; one or both might do worse. In addition, not only is assuming that the study guide might increase scores by an average of five points a big assumption at this point, but five points might not be as meaningful for one person as for another. For Kim, it could be the difference between failing or passing; it might be meaningless for Jennifer who would easily pass without the study guide. Of course, the cost of the study guide and the different financial situations of individuals would also factor into whether an average difference of five points would be more or less meaningful for any one individual.

Example: Treatment of Marital Problems

Rose is a social worker in a large family service agency. In her agency's orientation procedure, she was taught that the best format for marital counseling is to see both the husband and wife together. Five years ago, she treated 20 couples, all of whom could only be seen individually (husband *or* wife) because of their work schedules. She was surprised to observe that although they were never seen as couples after their initial interviews, all 20 couples seemed to make excellent progress in solving their marital problems.

Over the years, Rose saw more and more couples on an individual basis. Since she believed she was having good client outcomes, she encouraged six of her colleagues to also counsel couples with marital difficulties by seeing them separately rather than together. The other social workers were also pleased with their clients' progress.

Rose was not ready to conclude that the individual counseling format was really preferable to couple counseling without conducting some research on the issue. She decided to see if she could find statistical support for her hunch that couples seen individually make better progress toward solving their marital problems than couples seen together.

As Rose began to search the social work literature, she found considerable support for the position that marital satisfaction is best enhanced when couples are treated in counseling together, not individually. But as she ventured into the literature from other fields, such as psychology and pastoral counseling, Rose found a fair amount of support for the belief that success in marital counseling may be more likely to result from individual counseling. A reason sometimes given is that clients tend to discuss areas of dissatisfaction more readily and candidly when the spouse is not present.

Rose concluded that the professional literature was conflicting. She felt that her own observations, however, and those of her colleagues were sufficient to tip the balance enough to justify a one-tailed research hypothesis:

Among couples receiving marital counseling for ten weeks, those seen individually will reflect a higher level of marital satisfaction than those seen together.

Rose designed a small-scale research study to test her one-tailed research hypothesis. She received permission from the agency director and her clients to randomly assign new clients who requested marital counseling during a 3-month period to either individual counseling or couple counseling. In a research sense, the clients were randomly assigned to one of two groups. All six social workers who had previously used, and were experienced with, both couples counseling and individual counseling participated as counselors in Rose's study.

Beginning the next month, every other couple seen at intake was assigned to one of the six social workers to be seen together for counseling, 50 minutes per week; the remaining couples were assigned to be seen individually for 25 minutes each per week. Those who could not agree to this arrangement were also seen but were not included as research participants in the study.

The counseling method (i.e., individual, couple) was the independent variable. The dependent variable, *marital satisfaction* (was measured after 10 consecutive weeks of counseling) using a widely used standardized measuring instrument that measures marital satisfaction. The measuring instrument produces interval-level data.

Fourteen couples were assigned to individual counseling sessions, and 14 were assigned to be seen as couples. Twelve couples assigned to individual counseling completed 10 weeks of treatment, and 13 in couples counseling completed 10 weeks of treatment. After all 25 couples completed the marital satisfaction measuring instrument, Rose took the score for each partner and averaged it with that of his or her spouse to get a couple score.

Then she computed the mean couple score of those who were seen individually (experimental group) and compared it with the mean couple score of those who were seen together (control group) using the independent *t* test. The variable *marital satis-*

faction has been found to be normally distributed, so Rose felt justified in using this test for her statistical analysis. She was attempting to determine whether the difference between the mean scores for the two groups was sufficiently large to allow her to reject the null hypothesis. She hoped to be able to conclude that a real relationship between the two variables was the likely explanation for any difference in the mean marital satisfaction scores of the two groups of clients.

The *t*-value for Rose's data was 1.312. From a table of critical values of *t* (Table 11.1), she learned that she needed a minimum *t*-value of 1.714 to be able to reject the null hypothesis using a rejection level of .05, a sample of 25 (23 degrees of freedom), and a one-tailed research hypothesis.

Rose noted that if she were to reject the null hypothesis based on the analysis of her data, she would have slightly more than a 1 in 10 (10%) probability of committing a Type I error (1.312 is slightly smaller than 1.319). Thus, she lacked statistical support for her one-tailed research hypothesis. Her initial disappointment was made even worse when she looked at the mean score for both groups.

The clients who had participated in individual counseling scored somewhat worse in marital satisfaction, on the average, than did the clients seen together. Rose studied her findings some more. She then realized that her lack of demonstrated support for a relationship between counseling method and marital satisfaction might reflect a useful finding in and of itself. Her inability to reject the null hypothesis could be interpreted to mean that it makes little difference which counseling method is used. Perhaps client convenience should play a larger role in determining which format should be used.

Rose also wondered how she could have been mistaken. The findings from her study were inconsistent with her previous impressions. She wondered whether, in the past, she and the other social workers had perhaps merely perceived their individual counseling clients as doing better because of their surprise at how much progress they made using a counseling format that was not believed to be as effective.

Of course, Rose also wondered whether her initial one-tailed research hypothesis might still be correct (she had committed a Type II error). Perhaps the true relationship between the independent variable and the dependent variable had been hidden by biased measurements or the influence of rival hypotheses (e.g., the social workers' greater experience with couple counseling). As she thought about it, Rose concluded that additional studies employing more rigorous research designs were indicated.

In the interim, before further research studies could be conducted, Rose wondered what practical use she could make of her findings. She presented the results of her study at the next agency staff meeting. She was able to draw implications for social work practice within the agency. As frequently happens in social work research, her research study generated more questions than answers. These questions, however, served to focus the staff's attention on potentially productive areas of inquiry. Based on her findings, Rose and other staff members began to ask the following questions:

1. Since type of counseling (individual or couple) may have little or no effect in enhancing marital satisfaction, should continued attempts be made to encourage clients to enter couple counseling if they resist or if it causes a scheduling difficulty for them?

2. Should funds be allocated for a staff development program to enhance the social workers' use of individual counseling in treatment of marital problems?

3. Should the staff develop a single treatment model that combines individual and couple counseling, or should the professional staff members be allowed freedom to select the counseling format they prefer to use?

These three questions, along with others, range from issues that affected the individual social work practitioner to those that are related to agency policies. The principal value of Rose's study was to call into question certain previously unchallenged practices and to encourage the staff either to justify or to discard them based on further examination.

Example: Staff Turnover

Antonia is the director of social services for a large state health agency. In her professional role, she oversees social work services offered in the 50 district offices throughout the state. It was recently brought to her attention that her agency was having a serious problem with social work staff turnover. A preliminary examination of agency data revealed that the problem was statewide and appeared to be normally distributed among the 50 district offices.

Antonia spoke with the personnel officer responsible for conducting exit interviews with employees leaving the agency. At first he preferred not to suggest possible reasons why so many social workers were resigning. But after Antonia assured him that she did not plan to ask him to identify workers who made complaints to him, he volunteered that the reasons given by many of the social workers for leaving appeared to be amazingly similar. He recalled that many of them seemed totally frustrated with their lack of autonomy in decision making. While they recognized that in some professional and administrative matters the final decision had to be made by their supervisors, they saw no reason why many other decisions could not be made by them and their fellow professionals through a more democratic process.

Antonia thought about what she had been told. While her first inclination was to be annoyed with the district supervisors for their apparent autocratic approach to decision making, she quickly realized that she had to take much of the responsibility for their supervisory styles. She herself was autocratic when it came to decision making. Because it seemed to work so well for her, she had regularly encouraged her supervisors to be more autocratic. Apparently, the supervisors were responding to Antonia's message that an autocratic management style is a sign of good supervision.

Antonia knew that she needed an objective way to determine whether management style was related to staff turnover. She did not want to merely trust the impressions of the personnel officer without further data. She might need to help all her supervisors become more democratic in delegating decision making, but she did not want to do so until she could be reasonably certain that a relationship existed between the two variables.

Antonia decided to conduct a small-scale research study to test the following one-tailed research hypothesis:

> There will be a lower rate of staff turnover in units where a democratic decision-making style is used than in units where a more autocratic style is used.

Antonia knew that management literature stressed the use of quality circles as a promising way to solve some administrative problems by arriving at decisions via the group process. Antonia had been considering the use of quality circles anyway and saw this as a good time to try them. Quality circles seemed to her to be a good way to create a more democratic approach to decision making in the district offices.

Antonia randomly selected 10 districts to serve as her experimental group. She then provided release time to the 10 district supervisors to attend an out-of-state workshop on the use of quality circles. She told the supervisors that she expected them to implement quality circles in their supervision, and she requested a report on their methods of implementation to ensure that this had been done. They were asked not to share their experiences with other district supervisors.

At the same time, Antonia randomly selected 10 other districts as her control group. These district supervisors were given no additional training and no new instructions on how they should handle decision making in their district offices.

After 1 year, Antonia computed a mean rate of turnover for districts in the experimental group and for those in the control group. She had two value categories of the dichotomous nominal-level independent variable *decision-making environment* (i.e., democratic, autocratic). Her dependent variable (staff turnover rate) was at the ratio level of measurement. The situation seemed to be well-suited to the use of the independent *t* test to determine whether there might be statistical support for her one-tailed research hypothesis.

Antonia compared the mean turnover rate for the two groups using the independent *t* test. The mean turnover rate of the experimental group was lower than the mean turnover rate of the control group, exactly as she had hypothesized. The *t*-value was 1.992. She concluded that there were 18 degrees of freedom ($10 + 10 = 20$; $20 - 2 = 18$). Using a table like Table 11.1, she noted that, for the row corresponding to 18 degrees of freedom, the *t*-value from her statistical analysis fell between 1.734 and 2.101. She moved to the left (1.734) and observed that it was in the column headed by .05 for one-tailed tests and .10 for two-tailed tests. The *p*-value corresponding to her data under the one-tailed research hypothesis was therefore less than .05.

From her knowledge of statistics, Antonia knew that she had found support for a statistically significant relationship between the independent variable and the dependent variable. She knew that if she were to reject the null hypothesis, she would have less than a 5 percent probability of committing a Type I error on the basis of statistical probability alone.

Because her study had been very limited in scope, Antonia was reluctant to view her findings as an unequivocal endorsement of the expanded use of quality circles (or other more democratic methods of decision making) as a way to reduce staff turnover. She recognized that it would be precipitous on her part to proceed to implement her findings based solely on a finding of statistical significance. Her study's research design had certainly not eliminated the two alternative explanations (i.e., rival hypotheses, design bias) as possible explanations for the difference between the two staff turnover rates.

Certain methodological questions remained. How much did the opportunity to go out of state for training, for example, positively affect the morale of the supervisors in the experimental group? Perhaps the break from their regular duties put them in a better mood and thus they were more inclined to be more considerate of their workers. If so, this may have been a better explanation than the implementation of quality circles for their lower mean staff turnover rate. Or did the workers view the supervisors in the experimental group as more considerate simply because they made an effort to try something new (a kind of Hawthorne effect)? If so, this might have been a major factor in the lower mean turnover rate.

Despite the fact that Antonia's findings would have to be viewed as tentative, she was still able to use them both to better understand the problem of staff turnover and to begin to address it through her actions. In light of her findings, she asked herself the following six questions:

1. How can I avoid unintentionally communicating to the district supervisors that I expect them to adopt my autocratic management style?

2. How can I help district supervisors identify decisions that are more appropriately made using the democratic process? How can I make them feel more comfortable using this process?

3. How can I help district supervisors identify decisions that are inappropriate for the democratic process (e.g., personnel matters)?

4. What use of the democratic process, besides quality circles, would help social workers feel that they have more input into decisions if they possess the necessary expertise?

5. Would it be advisable to send all district supervisors to quality circle training out of state?

6. What further research studies can be designed to provide additional support for the finding that democratic decision making may be associated with lower staff turnover?

After thinking about these six questions and others that emerged from her study, Antonia discussed her ideas for implementing her findings with social work administrators in other large social service agencies. She then settled on a plan of action.

At the next meeting of all district supervisors, Antonia shared the findings of her research study. She reiterated her support for the use of staff authority in certain situations but also stated her belief that social workers at all levels are professionals and need to be involved in decision making. She emphasized that she believed that overreliance on autocratic supervisory approaches can hurt morale and, even more important, does not take advantage of the expertise of other staff in addressing problems.

She supported these contentions by asking a former district supervisor of the experimental group to use part of the next supervisors' meeting to teach all the supervisors (including herself) the basic principles of quality circles. In the meeting, the other 9 district supervisors who had used quality circles were asked to share their experiences as well.

Antonia was convinced that district supervisors should share decision making in certain situations with their respective workers. In another meeting, she emphasized this belief to the supervisors. Consistent with it, she allowed them to decide individually whether they preferred to receive training in quality circles so as to implement that technique in their district offices or to develop their own plans (with her approval) for introducing ways to increase democratic decision making among their supervisees.

Finally, Antonia set aside time to develop a more comprehensive and larger-scale study of staff turnover. This study would examine factors other than approaches to decision making that the literature suggests are related in some way to staff morale and turnover. She hoped that the findings from this larger-scale study could ultimately be generalized to other social work settings and that a report of the findings would have the potential for publication in a professional social work journal.

Nonparametric Alternatives: *U* and K-S

Several nonparametric options are available if all of the conditions for independent *t* tests cannot be met. Two of the better known ones are the *Mann-Whitney U test* and the Kolmogorov-Smirnov Two Sample Test.

The *Mann-Whitney* U *test* (hereafter called *U* test), is used with a dichotomous nominal-level independent variable and an ordinal-level, interval-level, or ratio-level dependent variable that need not be normally distributed (as required for use of the independent *t* test). Like the independent *t* test, the *U* test determines whether the differences between two independent subsamples with respect to the dependent variable are the work of sampling error.

The *U* test is ideally suited for research studies involving two small independent subsamples consisting of the two different measurement of a dichotomous independent variable. Like the independent *t* test, it is frequently used in experimental and quasi-experimental research situations to determine whether a treatment given to an experimental group, but not to a control group, appears to produce different results.

Like the independent *t* test, the *U* test does not need two groups of identical size (or subsamples). The same formula is used with very small samples (under eight) or larger ones, but we must be careful in interpreting results to use the table of critical values (not included in this book) that is designed to adjust for sample size.

A *U* test is easily computed. It is based on the assumption that a good indicator of the difference between the two groups is the number of cases in one group that fall below each respective score of the other group when all scores are rank-ordered.

The logical premise underlying *U* is that the presence of a disproportionate number of higher scores drawn from one group and of lower scores drawn from the other group probably suggests that, on the whole, the two groups really are different in regard to the dependent variable. The *U* test is a mathematical way of determining whether this pattern is sufficiently strong to reject the null hypothesis, which would state that scores from the two groups will be pretty much evenly distributed when all scores are rank-ordered to form an array.

For example, Shanti is a social worker employed by a large corporation. During July he had 17 referrals of workers identified as having attitude problems on the job. He asked each of their supervisors to name another worker at the same level whom they would describe as having a very good attitude who might participate with him when the problem worker was being counseled. Seven of the supervisors complied with his request; the other 10 did not.

Shanti saw all 17 workers (7 with their coworkers and the other 10 alone) for five sessions. After the fifth interview, he asked their supervisors to complete a standardized measuring instrument that measures an employee's attitude toward work. He then rank-ordered the scores of all 17 workers and used the U test formula to test his one-tailed research hypothesis:

> Members of the experimental group (those receiving counseling with a coworker participating) will have higher job attitude scores than members of the control group (those receiving the usual counseling involving only the supervisor).

Shanti quickly noted that three of the top four attitude scores were achieved by members in the experimental group. However, as he examined the data in more detail, he noticed that two of the lowest scores also came from experimental group members. The U test produced a p-value $> .10$; it did not support a decision to reject the null hypothesis. Even if the U test had achieved statistical significance, alternative explanations for a true relationship (e.g., lack of random assignment to groups, the effect of other variables) could not have been ruled out because of the lack of rigor of Shanti's research design. Shanti decided to tighten up the design and to pursue his inquiry further by using a larger randomly selected sample.

The *Kolmogorov-Smirnov Two Sample Test* (hereafter called the K-S test), has some similarities with the median test discussed in Chapter 10 as a procedure for assigning cases to cross-tabulation tables prior to using the chi-square or Fisher's exact tests. But K-S compares more than just central tendency data, that is, where scores fall in relation to the median. It compares (between two samples) the dispersion, skewness, and other characteristics of the distribution of values of an ordinal-level variable or a skewed interval-level or ratio-level variable. To express this another way, it compares the entire shape of the distribution of the dependent variable in one sample with the shape of its distribution in the other sample.

The K-S test is based on the assumption that if two subsamples are randomly drawn from the same population and the null hypothesis is correct, the overall shape of the distribution of the ordinal-level variable (or skewed interval-level or ratio-level variable) should be the same for the two subsamples. If differences in the distribution of the variable are considerable, they probably are not just the work of sampling error. They indicate a real relationship between the two independent and dependent variables. Thus, the K-S test is a way of determining whether the differences in the distribution of the values of the ordinal-level variable (or skewed interval-level or ratio-level variable) are large enough to rule out sampling error and to reject the null hypothesis.

K-S relies on cumulative frequencies (Chapter 2) to compare the two distributions and to identify at what points in an array of measurements of the dependent variable they differ or are similar to each other. It focuses on the point or points at which the cumulative frequency difference between the two subsamples is the largest. If the dependent variable is interval or ratio level, it might, for example, focus on the fact that a life-satisfaction score of 50 falls at only the 65th percentile in the experimental group, but it at the 95th percentile in the control group. If the dependent variable is only ordinal level, the K-S test compares the cumulative frequencies for intervals in the variable (e.g., what percent of cases were rated either not improved or slightly improved for the control group versus the experimental group).

K-S is equally useful for analyzing the relationship between variables when the independent variable falls naturally into two value categories (rather than being assigned to them by the researcher, as occurs in an experiment). For example, Roosevelt is a county director in a state public welfare agency. Several of his African American workers had complained that Caucasian workers seemed to have excessively suspicious attitudes toward some of their African American clients. Specifically, they told him that they believed that the African American clients who were being seen by Caucasian workers were assumed by them to be liars and cheats.

No valid and reliable measuring instrument for the variable *suspicious attitudes* was immediately available. Roosevelt concluded, however, that the variable *number of referrals for fraud investigation* was an acceptable way to operationalize the variable. Although an exact count of referrals was possible, when used as an indicator of suspicious attitudes (the real dependent variable), ordinal measurement of the variable was all that could be claimed.

Roosevelt compiled a count of fraud referrals for each worker during the previous 3 months. Referrals ranged from 0 to 23. He then assembled a cumulative frequency distribution for African American workers and for Caucasian workers (the two value categories of the independent variable), using eight intervals of number of referrals (for example, 0–2, 3–5, 6–8, and so forth) as his ordinal-level value categories. The decision to use eight intervals was made in an effort to conserve some of the precision of measurement available (using only two or three intervals would throw away too much data) while not cutting too thin.

Using the K-S test, Roosevelt compared the cumulative frequencies for the dependent variable of one group of workers (African American) with that of the other group (Caucasian) and identified the interval at which the cumulative frequency distributions were most different from each other. He learned that, in fact, there was little real difference between the two groups for the measurement of the variable, at least not enough to rule out sampling error and to be able to reject the null hypothesis ($p > .50$).

While Roosevelt did not totally discount the complaints of the African American workers, since a better method of operationalizing the dependent variable might have revealed an attitudinal difference, he concluded that he lacked sufficient evidence to confront his Caucasian workers about what some of his fellow African American workers perceived as a problem. He chose instead to remind all his staff about the need for nonjudgmental attitudes while gathering necessary data about clients.

The K-S test is useful in looking at the relationship between an ordinal-level dependent variable (or skewed interval-level or ratio-level variable) and a nominal-level dichotomous independent variable when just a comparison of central tendency may be insufficient. By examining the whole distribution of values of the dependent variable, we get a fairly complete picture of the similarity or difference between two subsamples.

A variation, the K-S one-sample test, works similarly, except that it compares the distribution of a variable within a sample with another, theoretical distribution of the variable. Thus, it should be regarded as another nonparametric alternative (along with the chi-square goodness-of-fit test) to the one-sample *t* test.

Another test, the Wald-Wolfowitz runs test, goes even farther than the K-S test in that it identifies some of the more subtle differences in distributions of a variable that the K-S test does not detect. There is a test for just about any situation that we can imagine. Still another nonparametric alternative, the Moses test of extreme reactions, is the test of choice for those relatively rare research studies where the presence of a treatment in the experimental group (but not in the control group) might be predicted to create extreme, opposite reactions in the experimental group. For example, a very confrontational form of intervention might make some clients in a group much more assertive; it might make others in the group much less assertive. It might seem that the intervention had no effect (these opposite reactions would cancel each other out) if we were to use tests that rely on a comparison of central tendency (such as the median) to compare the experimental and control groups. If we used the Moses test, however, we would be less likely to be misled by the results of our data analysis.

SIMPLE ANALYSIS OF VARIANCE (ONE-WAY *ANOVA*)

Simple analysis of variance, hereafter called *simple ANOVA,* is also sometimes called *one-way analysis of variance.* Like the independent *t* test, it is appropriate for examining the relationship between variables when there is a nominal-level independent variable and a normally distributed interval-level or ratio-level dependent variable. But, unlike an independent *t* test, which requires the independent variable to be dichotomous (have only two value categories), simple *ANOVA* is used when the independent variable contains three or more value categories.

While *t* tests produce a *t*-value that can be compared with a table (i.e., Table 11.1) to determine whether it is justifiable to reject the null hypothesis, simple *ANOVA* produces an *F*-ratio with its own table (not included in this book) that allows us to make this same determination. When computer software is used for data analyses, the displayed results of both *t* and simple *ANOVA* analyses include *p*-values along with their respective *t*-values or *F*-ratios.

An example illustrates how simple *ANOVA* works. In a large psychiatric outpatient clinic, there are 20 people with the job title case manager. They all (theoretically, at least) perform the same case management functions, even though some are psychologists, some are social workers, and some are nurses by training. The case managers work on one of three teams. One is led by a social worker, one by a psychologist, and one by a psychiatric nurse. We want to know if there are differences in client satisfaction among the three teams. To attempt to find out, we formulate the following one-tailed research hypothesis:

> Client satisfaction will be higher among clients served by the team led by a social worker than among clients served by the other two teams.

We could use a standardized measuring instrument that yields interval-level or ratio-level data to measure the dependent variable *client satisfaction*. Since there are three categories of the independent variable *professional discipline of team leader*—(1) psychologist, (2) social worker, and (3) psychiatric nurse—we could compare the three possible combinations of pairs of means (client satisfaction) using three independent *t* tests—that is, (1) psychologist and social worker, (2) psychologist and nurse, and (3) social worker and nurse. But, why conduct three separate statistical analyses when one will do nicely? Using simple *ANOVA* would tell us if any differences among the three mean client satisfaction levels are related to the discipline of the team leader. Specifically, simple *ANOVA* would tell us the probability (*p*), considering degrees of freedom (based on the size of the samples), that any differences in mean client satisfaction levels among the three teams might have been produced by sampling error.

Computation

In our example, simple *ANOVA* would compare the mean client satisfaction level for each of the three subsamples (i.e., for each team) with the grand mean—the mean client satisfaction level for all clients studied. Thus, simple *ANOVA* examines how much the mean of each subsample (each individual value category of the independent variable) differs from the means of the other subsamples as well as from the grand mean. Simple *ANOVA* examines these differences (referred to as the between groups variance) as well as the amount of variability of client satisfaction within each subsample (referred to as the within groups variance).

As with an independent *t* test, the subsamples used in simple *ANOVA* need not be of equal size. It should be pointed out, however, that simple *ANOVA* does not tell us which subsample mean is statistically different from the other sub-samples' means. It only tells us whether there is a statistically significant relationship among the subsamples' means. If there is a statistically significant relationship among them, then we still need to identify which subsample mean is the most different from the other subsamples' means and, if a one-tailed research hypothesis was used, whether the difference is what we hypothesized. There are statistical procedures that also can help us interpret the results of *ANOVA* analyses. One commonly used procedure is called the *Duncan test*. It often is performed automatically along with simple *ANOVA* analysis when a statistical software package is used. Its results are displayed (along with the *p*-value and the *F*-ratio).

Simple *ANOVA* is a powerful parametric test. It can easily identify relationships between variables that less-powerful statistical tests might miss. As a general rule, however, more-powerful tests also are more restrictive than less-powerful tests—that is, more conditions for their use must be met. Simple *ANOVA* is no exception.

In addition to the requirements of the other parametric statistical tests, simple *ANOVA* should be used only when the amount of variance for the dependent variable within each subsample is approximately equal. In our hypothetical study, we could not use simple *ANOVA* if, for example, the amount of variation in satisfaction among clients served by the team led by a social worker tended to be much greater than among clients served by either of the other two teams.

A Nonparametric Alternative: The Kruskal-Wallis Test

As suggested earlier, the Mann-Whitney *U* test is useful for comparing the rankings of a skewed interval-level or ratio-variable within the two variable categories of a nominal-level variable (a dichotomous variable). However, if there are more than two subsamples (value categories of the nominal-level independent variable), there is a related nonparametric test, the *Kruskal-Wallis test,* a useful nonparametric alternative to *ANOVA.* It works very much like the *U* test, ranking all scores, sorting the rankings into subsamples, and then examining how many cases in other subsamples are ranked below each case in a given subsample (or value category). An extension of the median test (Chapter 10) also is sometimes used in situations in which we wish to examine the relationship between a nominal-level independent variable (with more than two value categories) and an interval-level or ratio-level dependent variable that is skewed.

MULTIPLE ANALYSIS OF VARIANCE

Multiple analysis of variance (MANOVA) is designed for situations in which we wish to test for a relationship that involves two or more dependent variables. Like simple *ANOVA,* a *MANOVA* entails a comparison of means, but it compares the means of the two or more interval-level or ratio-level dependent variables across the value categories of the independent variable. Thus, it compares groups (sets) of means compiled from several dependent variables.

In situations where *MANOVA* is used, a series of simple *ANOVAs* could be used instead. But to do so would fail to address the importance of intercorrelation among the two or more dependent variables. The formula for *MANOVA* takes this into consideration.

Other variations of analysis of variance, called *factorial designs,* are available for situations in which we wish to examine the relationship among two or more nominal-level or ordinal-level independent variables and one interval-level or ratio-level dependent variable. We could, for example, examine the relationship among the discipline of the worker and the gender of the worker (independent variables) and the dependent variable *client satisfaction.* The relationship would be a complex one, and the formula is correspondingly complex

Three-way analysis of variance is used, not surprisingly, to examine the relationship among three nominal-level or ordinal-level independent variables and one interval-level or ratio-level dependent variable. Still another type of test altogether, *Hottelling's T²*, is appropriate when there are two or more independent variables as well as two or more dependent variables. A discussion of the complexities of this test and of the special uses and requirements of factorial designs is beyond the scope of this book. An advanced text is recommended for readers who wish to go beyond our brief mention of multivariate alternatives to *t* tests and simple *ANOVA*.

CONCLUDING THOUGHTS

The family of related tests in this chapter are well suited to social work research. They are versatile and powerful. The *t* tests (for use with two means) and simple *ANOVA* (for use with three or more means) and their nonparametric alternatives are among the most commonly used tests for seeking support for research hypotheses in social work research and practice. While these tests often are used in major research projects that have extensive funding and use sophisticated research designs, they also are valuable for more preliminary limited efforts.

As illustrated in this chapter and elsewhere in the book, while statistical findings that can be used in support of research hypotheses are of practical value at many different levels for the social work practitioner, a lack of statistical support for research hypotheses can be of equal value. If a research study is designed and implemented well and statistical testing is conducted correctly, we can advance the body of knowledge available to social work practitioners, whether statistical support for a research hypothesis is found or not. Hopefully, this text has contributed to readers' understanding of statistical analyses and increased the likelihood that such analyses will be used appropriately to advance knowledge in the profession of social work.

STUDY QUESTIONS

1. What is the appropriate combination of levels of measurement of two variables for using either an independent *t* test or a dependent *t* test?
2. Why do the sample size and subsample size comparability requirements of the independent *t* test frequently make it ideally suited for social work research?
3. If using the independent *t* test, the null hypothesis were correct, would the mean value of a variable in one sample be very similar to or very different from the mean value for that variable in the other sample?
4. What is a nonparametric alternative to the one-sample *t* test that might be used if the variable can be regarded as only nominal level?
5. What is a nonparametric alternative to the dependent *t* test that might be used if the dependent variable can be regarded as a little less than interval level?
6. What additional step is required in determining whether a *t*-value that is statistically significant reflects support for a one-tailed research hypothesis?
7. Explain why a *t* test that does not result in a finding of statistical significance may still produce a finding that is useful for the social work practitioner. Provide an example.

8. Provide an original example of how one could use a one-sample *t* test to evaluate practice effectiveness in a social agency with which you are familiar.

9. Find an article in a professional social work journal that reports on the use of the dependent *t* test. What was the study's hypothesis? How did the author interpret the study's results? Do you feel the test was used appropriately? Why? What contribution did the article make to the profession's knowledge base?

10. What conditions for use of the Mann-Whitney *U* test make it particularly well suited for the individual practitioner who wishes to evaluate the effectiveness of a new treatment method? Provide an original example in your discussion.

11. What test is a good a nonparametric alternative to one-way ANOVA?

References and Further Reading

Anderson, D. R., Sweeney, D. J., & Williams, T. A. (1986). *Statistics: Concepts and applications.* St. Paul, MN: West.

Andrews, F. M., Klem, L., Davidson, T. N., O'Malley, P. M., & Rodgers, W. L. (1994). *A guide for selecting statistical techniques for analyzing social science data* (3rd ed.). Ann Arbor, MI: Institute for Social Research, University of Michigan.

Blalock, H. M., Jr. (1979). *Social statistics* (2nd ed.). New York: McGraw-Hill.

Bohrnstedt, G. W., & Knoke, D. (1988). *Statistics for social data analysis* (2nd ed.). Itasca, IL: Peacock.

Brown, R. W. (1992). *Graph it! How to make, read, and interpret graphs.* Englewood Cliffs, NJ: Prentice-Hall.

Cohen, J. (1977). *Statistical power analysis for the behavioral sciences* (2nd ed.). New York: Academic Press.

Darlington, R. B., & Carlson, P. M. (1987). *Behavioral statistics: Logic and methods.* New York: Free Press.

Davidson, F. (1996). *Principles of statistical data handling.* Thousand Oaks, CA: Sage.

Evans, J. D. (1996). *Straightforward statistics.* Pacific Grove, CA: Brooks/Cole.

Foddy, W. H. (1988). *Elementary applied statistics for the social sciences.* New York: Harper & Row.

Freund, J. E. (1988). *Modern elementary statistics* (7th ed.). Englewood Cliffs, NJ: Prentice-Hall.

Grinnell, R. M., Jr. (Ed.). (1997). *Social work research and evaluation: Quantitative and qualitative approaches* (5th ed.). Itasca, IL: Peacock.

Guilford, J. P. (1950). *Fundamental statistics in psychology and education* (2nd ed.). New York: McGraw-Hill.

Heyes, S. (1986). *Starting statistics in psychology and education.* London: Weidenfeld & Nicolson.

Howell, D. C. (1987). *Statistical methods for psychology* (2nd ed.). Boston, MA: Duxbury Press.

Kachigan, S. K. (1991). *Multivariate statistical analysis* (2nd ed.). New York: Radius Press.

Khazanie, R. (1986). *Elementary statistics: In a world of applications* (2nd ed.). Glenview, IL: Scott, Foresman.

Kiess, H. O. (1989). *Statistical concepts for the behavioral sciences.* Needham Heights, MA: Allyn & Bacon.

Knoke, D., & Bohrnstedt, G. W. (1994). *Statistics for social data analysis* (3rd ed.). Itasca, IL: Peacock.

Krishef, C. H. (1987). *Fundamental statistics for human services and social work.* Boston, MA: Duxbury Press.

Lewis-Beck, M. S. (1995). *Data analysis: An introduction.* Thousand Oaks, CA: Sage.

Loether, H. J., & McTavish, D. G. (1993). *Descriptive and inferential statistics: An introduction* (4th ed.). Needham Heights, MA: Allyn & Bacon.

Maxim, P. S. (1999). *Quantitative research methods in the social sciences.* New York: Oxford University Press.

Miller, E. L. (1986). *Basic statistics: A conceptual approach for beginners.* Muncie, IL: Accelerated Development.

Reid, S. (1987). *Working with statistics.* Cambridge, MA: Polity Press.

Shavelson, R. J. (1988). *Statistical reasoning for the behavioral sciences* (2nd ed.). Needham Heights, MA: Allyn & Bacon.

Siegel, S. (1956). *Nonparametric statistics for the behavioral sciences.* New York: McGraw-Hill.

Stahl, S. M., & Hennes, J. D. (1980). *Reading and understanding applied statistics* (2nd ed.). St. Louis: Mosby.

Tutty, L. M., Grinnell, R. M., Jr., & Williams, M. (1997). Quantitative data analysis. In R. M. Grinnell, Jr. (Ed.), *Social work research and evaluation: Quantitative and qualitative approaches* (5th ed., pp. 475–500). Itasca, IL: Peacock.

Unrau, Y. A., Krysik, J. L., & Grinnell, R. M., Jr. (1997). *Student study guide to accompany the fifth edition of Social work research and evaluation: Quantitative and qualitative approaches.* Itasca, IL: Peacock.

Weinbach, R. W., Grinnell, R. M., Jr., Taylor, L. M., & Unrau, Y. A. (1999). *Applying research knowledge: A workbook for social work students* (3rd ed.). Needham Heights, MA: Allyn & Bacon.

Wilcox, R. R. (1987). *New statistical procedures for the social sciences: Modern solutions to basic problems.* Hillsdale, NJ: Lawrence Erlbaum.

Williams, M., Unrav, Y. A., & Grinnell, R. M., Jr. (1995). *Introduction to social work research.* Itasca, IL: Peacock.

Wright, S. E. (1986). *Social science statistics.* Needham Heights, MA: Allyn & Bacon.

Yegidis, B., Weinbach, R. W., & Morrison-Rodriguez, B. (1999). *Research methods for social workers* (3rd ed.). Needham Heights, MA: Allyn & Bacon.

Glossary

This glossary is designed as a general reference for the student of statistics. Many of the terms are discussed in detail in the text. Others that sometimes appear elsewhere in the statistical literature also have been included.

Absolute frequency distribution: A table that displays the frequencies for various measurements of a variable.

Acceptance region: The outcome of a statistical test that leads to the acceptance of the null hypothesis.

Allowance factor: Used in constructing confidence intervals, it is the distance (on the measurement scale) between the sample statistic and the limits of the interval. We both add and subtract the allowance factor to find, respectively, the upper and lower limits of the confidence interval.

Alpha error: See Type I error.

Alternative hypothesis: See research hypothesis.

Analysis of variance: A statistical technique by which it is possible to partition the variance in a distribution of scores according to separate sources or factors; a statistical measure to test the differences among the means of three or more groups; sometimes referred to as *ANOVA*.

ANOVA: The abbreviation for the statistical procedure known as analysis of variance.

Antecedent variable: A variable that precedes the introduction of the independent variable.

A priori probability: The probability of a future event calculated from prior knowledge of the number of possible outcomes and their relative frequencies.

Arithmetic mean: See mean.

Axes: Reference lines that delineate the two (or sometimes three) dimensions of a graph; the horizontal and vertical lines in a graph on which values of a measurement or the corresponding frequencies are plotted.

Bar graph: A graphical technique of descriptive statistics that uses the heights of separated bars to show how often each score occurs; graphical representation of a frequency distribution table in which each measurement category is represented by a bar that extends to the appropriate distance in the frequency dimension; usually has spaces between bars to represent nominal-level data.

Beta coefficient: When using multiple regression, a mathematically derived indicator of the amount of prediction of the criterion variable that is attributable to any one predictor variable.

Beta error: See Type II error.

Beta weight: When using multiple R, a mathematically derived indicator of the amount of variation in the criterion variable that is attributable to any one predictor variable.

Biased sample: A sample selected in such a way that some members of the population are more likely than others to be picked for sample membership; if we wish to make generalizations about the population based on sample observations, it is desirable to avoid biased samples.

Bimodal distribution: A frequency distribution with two modes reflecting equal or nearly equal frequencies.

Binary variable: A dichotomous variable whose values are 0 (reflecting absence of any quantity of the variable) and 1 (reflecting presence of the variable).

Bivariate analysis: A statistical analysis of the relationship between two variables.

Box plot: A graph that reflects both the central tendency and variability of the distribution of a variable. In one of its most common variations, lines are used to indicate the five-number summary, that is, the minimum value, the 25th percentile, the median, the 75th percentile, and the maximum value.

Canonical correlation: A statistical procedure that simultaneously examines the correlation between a weighted group of criterion variables (a derived predictor variable) and a weighted group of criterion variables (a weighted criterion variable).

Causality: A relationship of cause and effect; the effect will invariably occur when the cause is present; causality is usually statistical; changes in the causal variable (independent variable) will, on the average, alter values of the affected variable (dependent variable).

Causal relationship: A relationship between two variables for which we can say that the presence or absence of one variable determines the presence or absence of the other or that values of one variable result in specific values of the other variable.

Cell: A compartment in a matrix or table, such as in a cross-tabulation table.

Central limit theorem: The assumption underlying mathematically derived sampling distributions. It states that for a skewed distribution of a variable in a population, the distribution of means from samples of fixed sizes drawn from the population will approach a normal distribution if the sample sizes are large (generally defined as more than 30). The sampling distribution will have the same mean as the population mean, and its variance will be the population variance divided by the sample size.

Central tendency: A typical value for a variable within a data set; one of several descriptive statistics used to reflect a middle value in an array of case values.

Chance: The probability of an event occurring because of some random variation; sometimes referred to as sampling error.

Chi-square table: See Cross-tabulation table.

Chi-square test of association: A common statistical procedure used to analyze the association between two nominal-level variables. It is usually referred to as *chi-square*.

Class frequency: Number of observations falling in a class (referring to a frequency histogram).

Cluster analysis: A multivariate statistical procedure that, among its other uses, groups together cases that have similar measurements (values) in relation to certain variables.

Coding: The act of categorizing raw data into groups or giving the data numerical values.

Coefficient of determination: The proportion of variation in a scattergram that is explained—that is, the proportion of variation of the criterion variable accounted for by the predictor variables; the coefficient of determination is equal to r^2, where r is the correlation coefficient summarizing the degree of association between the two variables.

Coefficient of nondetermination: Equal to $1 - r^2$; the proportion of the variation of the criterion variable that is not accounted for by the predictor variable.

Conceptualization: The first step in the measurement process, in which the researcher selects the variables to be measured; delineating the exact meaning of the independent and dependent variables.

Concomitant variation: The case in which two variables vary together; individuals who differ with respect to variable x will also differ with respect to variable y.

Confidence interval: A range of values within which we are willing to assert with a specified level of confidence that an unknown parameter value lies; computed from sample statistics, the width of the confidence interval depends on the rejection level stated, the sample size, and the variability in the sample.

Confidence level: The probability that a population parameter lies within a given confidence interval.

Confidence limits: Upper and lower boundaries of confidence intervals.

Confounding variables: Variables operating in a specific situation in such a way that their effects cannot be separated; they occur when the effects of an extraneous variable cannot be separated from the effects of the dependent variable; the effects of the extraneous variable thus confound the interpretation of research results.

Confusion matrix: A table that displays the type and number of errors that a given group of predictor variables have produced; a product of discriminant analysis.

Constant: A characteristic that has the same value for all individuals in a research study.

Contingency table: See cross-tabulation table.

Continuous random variable: A random variable that may theoretically assume any value between two points on the measurement scale; it can thus have an infinite number of possible values between those points.

Control group: A group of people who do not receive the experimental treatment; a group used for comparison purposes; those people to whom no experimental stimulus is administered but who resemble members of the experimental group in all other respects; in an experimental research design, a group in which the independent variable is left unchanged; serves as a reference to compare the effect of manipulating the independent variable in the experimental group(s).

Control variable: A variable, other than the independent variable(s) of primary interest, whose effects we can determine; an intervening variable that has been controlled for in the research design; a variable that is included in designs as an independent variable for the purpose of explaining (controlling) variation.

Correction for continuity: An additional step added to the formula for chi-square if there are only four cells (a 2-by-2 table) entailing the subtraction of .5 from the absolute difference between the expected and observed frequencies for each cell prior to squaring it. It is also known as the *Yates correction factor.*

Correlated *t* test: See dependent *t* test. See also *t* test.

Correlated variables: Variables whose values are associated; values of one variable tend to be associated in a systematic way with values in the others.

Correlational analyses: Statistical methods that allow us to discover, describe, and measure the strength and direction of associations between and among variables; include the various techniques of computing correlation coefficients and regression analyses.

Correlation coefficient: A single statistic that indicates both the strength and direction of the relationship between two ordinal-levels, interval-levels, or ratio-level variables; correlation coefficients have values between 11 and 21, with positive values indicating positive relationships and negative values indicating negative relationships; two commonly used correlation coefficients are Pearson's product-moment correlation coefficient (Pearson's *r*) and Spearman's rho.

Correlation matrix: A table used to display the correlations among three or more pairs of variables.

Covariance: The degree to which certain values of one variable tend to be found disproportionately with certain values of some other variable.

Criterion variable: The variable whose values are predicted from measurements of the predictor variable.

Critical region: A set of outcomes of a statistical test that leads to the rejection of the null hypothesis.

Critical value: A value of a test statistic that demarcates the region of rejection and that is thus used as a criterion for statistical significance in hypothesis testing; the value of the statistic that marks the significance level.

Cross-break table: See cross-tabulation table.

Cross-tabulation table: A table showing the joint frequency distribution of two or more nominal-level variables; presents how often each combination of values of each variable occurs; the entries in the table show the number of observations falling into the cells.

Cumulative frequency distribution: A frequency distribution that gives the number of scores that occur at or below each value of a variable.

Cumulative frequency polygon: A frequency polygon that shows how often scores occur at or below each value of a variable.

Cumulative percentage distribution: A table that shows what percentage of scores occurs at or below each value of a variable.

Cumulative proportion graph: A graph in which one axis represents values of a variable and the other represents the proportion of the distribution that falls below those values (i.e., their cumulative proportions); when the data have been grouped, each point on the graph is plotted over the upper true limit of the interval it represents; each point thus represents the proportion of the observations falling at or below that interval.

Cumulative proportion table: A summary table of a group of observations that has one column listing values of a variable and another column indicating the proportion of the distribution that falls at or below each value; when the data have been grouped, the table lists intervals on the measurement scale rather than individual values.

Curvilinear correlation: A relationship between variables that, if displayed using a scattergram, would form one or more curves; a relationship between two variables that is not linear.

Data: The numbers or scores generated by a research study; the word *data* is plural.

Datum: Singular of *data*.

Degrees of freedom: A characteristic of the sample statistic that determines the appropriate sampling distribution; the number of ways in which the data are free to vary; the number of observations minus the number of restrictions placed on the data; a number related to the sample size in a way that depends on the particular statistical technique employed; in many statistical tests, degree of freedom, or *df*, is needed in order to determine the *p*-value.

Dependent events: Events that influence the probability of occurrence of each other.

Dependent *t* test: A hypothesis-testing procedure used to decide whether two dependent samples could have occurred by sampling error; sometimes referred to as a dependent groups *t* test, correlated groups *t* test, paired groups *t* test, or matched groups *t* test.

Dependent variable: The variable that we do not directly introduce or manipulate; after the different levels of the independent variable have been administered, all research participants are measured, in the same way, on the same dependent variable; a variable in which the changes are results of the level or amount of the independent variable(s); also, the variable whose variations are of most interest to the researcher; when used with correlation or regression, it is referred to as the criterion variable.

Derived variable: The correlation between one criterion variable and a group of predictor variables.

Descriptive data analyses: Methods used for summarizing and describing data in a clear and precise manner; strictly speaking, descriptive analyses apply only to the people (or objects) actually observed; methods for data reduction.

Design bias: Any effect that systematically distorts the outcome of a research study so that the results are not representative of the phenomenon under investigation. Includes measurement bias and sampling bias.

Deviation from the mean: The distance of a single score from the mean of the distribution from which the scores come.

Deviation score: The difference between the mean of a distribution and an individual score of that distribution; deviation scores are always found by subtracting the mean from the score; a positive value indicates a score above the mean; a negative value indicates a score below the mean.

Dichotomous variable: A variable that can take on only one of two values.

Direct relationship: A relationship between two variables in which high values of one variable are found with high values of the second variable and vice versa; the status of the relationship between two correlated variables is either positive or negative.

Directional hypothesis: A hypothesis stated in such a manner that the direction of the relationship between variables is hypothesized for the results; it uses a statistical test with only one region of rejection, that is, a one-tailed test; a directional test is called for only when certain assumptions can be made; because the region of rejection is located entirely at one end of the distribution in a directional test, fewer deviant values of the observed statistic will lead to rejection of the null hypothesis than in the nondirectional test with the same rejection level.

Directional test: See directional hypothesis.

Discrete measurement: Measurement that can generate only certain values that are separated by discrete intervals.

Discrete variable: A variable that can assume only a finite number of values.

Discriminant analysis: A form of multivariate statistical analysis that is used to classify cases into two or more values of a nominal or ordinal criterion variable based on measurements of a group of interval or ratio predictor variables.

Discriminant function: A derived variable created in multivariate discriminant analysis that represents the weighted values of several independent variables.

Dispersion: The amount that values of a variable tend to cluster around a measure of central tendency within a data set. It is alternately referred to as spread or variability.

Distribution: The pattern of frequency of occurrence of scores; the total observations or a set of data for a variable; when observations are tabulated according to frequency for each possible score, we have a frequency distribution.

Distribution-free method: A method for testing a hypothesis or setting up a confidence interval, for example, that does not depend on the form of the underlying distribution.

Distribution-free tests: A term referring to a large family of statistical tests that, in general, do not require assumptions about the precise shape of the population distribution; the population distribution of a variable need not be normal in shape and data need not be at least interval level; also called nonparametric tests.

Dummy table: A cross-tabulation table that contains asterisks to reflect where disproportionately large frequencies will be found if a directional hypothesis is supported.

Dummy variable: A variable that is created by converting a qualitative variable into a binary variable.

Duncan test: A statistical procedure for identifying which subsample mean reflects a statistically significant difference from the other subsample means when using analysis of variance (*ANOVA*).

Effect size: The percent of variance in the dependent variable that can be explained by the independent variable. The predicted effect size is one consideration (along with rejection level) in choosing a sample size that will result in the optimal statistical power for data analysis.

Empirical frequency distribution: A frequency distribution tabulated from data that have actually been collected (as opposed to a theoretical frequency distribution, which is constructed from theoretical or mathematical considerations).

Empirical sampling distribution: A sampling distribution generated by actually taking random samples and measuring each sample's characteristics.

Error of estimation: Distance between an estimate and the true value of the parameter estimated.

Error of measurement: In measurement, the extent of its inaccuracy.

Estimate: Number computed from sample data used to approximate a population parameter.

Estimator: Rule that tells us how to compute an estimate based on data contained in a sample; an estimator is usually given as a mathematical formula, as in regression analysis.

Expected frequencies: In the chi-square test, the frequencies of observations in different categories (cells) that would be most likely to appear if the null hypothesis were true.

Expected value: The long-run average of a random variable over an indefinite number of samplings.

Expected value of a statistic: The mean of a statistic's sampling distribution.

Experiment: A research study in which we have control over the levels of the independent variable and over the assignment of people or objects to different conditions.

Experimental group: In an experimental research design, the group in which the independent variable is manipulated or introduced.

Extraneous variable: See intervening variable.

F-ratio: The between-group estimates of the variance of the sampling distribution of the mean divided by the within-group's estimate; the F- ratio can be viewed as a measure of the strength of a treatment effect.

F statistic: A test statistic that is used to compare variances from two normal populations; used in analysis of variance.

Factor analysis: A statistical method for identifying certain factors or dimensions that exist in a data set.

Factorial designs: Variations of analysis of variance (*ANOVA*) that are used to examine the relationship among two or more nominal or ordinal independent variables and one interval or ratio dependent variable.

Factorial experiments: Experimental research designs that look at the separate effects and interactions of two or more independent variables at the same time.

Factor rotation: A group of statistical procedures designed to develop more precise meanings of the factors created through a factor analysis.

Fisher's exact test: A nonparametric statistical test that can be used to examine the association between two dichotomous nominal-level variables when the size requirement for expected frequencies for using chi-square cannot be met.

Five-number summary: A concise description of the distribution of the values of a variable in a sample or population. It consists of the minimum value, the 25th percentile, the median, the 75th percentile, and the maximum value. It can be portrayed graphically in a box plot.

Frequency: Number of observations falling in a cell or value category of a specific variable.

Frequency distribution: A table or graph that presents the number of times (frequency) with which different values of the variable occur in a group of observations; a technique of descriptive statistics that shows how often each score occurs.

Frequency polygon: A graphic technique of descriptive statistics that uses the height of connected dots to display the shape of the distribution of a variable; graph of a frequency distribution in which the horizontal axis represents different values of a variable and the vertical axis represents frequencies with which those values occur; in constructing a frequency polygon, a dot is placed over each value of the variable at a height corresponding to the appropriate frequency; the dots are then connected with lines to form a polygon.

Frequency table: In its simplest form, a two-column table with one column listing values of a variable and the other column listing the frequency with which the different values occur in a group of observations. Columns for percentages, cumulative percentages, and cumulative frequencies may also be included.

Goodness-of-fit test: A method of data analysis used to decide whether a sample with a given frequency distribution could have occurred by chance from a population with a known frequency distribution (or known percentage composition); a nonparametric statistical test that allows us to decide whether observed frequencies are essentially equal to or significantly different from expected frequencies.

Grouped cumulative frequency distribution: An extension of a grouped frequency distribution that shows how often scores occur at or below each interval.

Grouped frequency distribution: Table or graph in which frequencies are not listed for each possible value of the variable; rather, a frequency is listed for each of a number of intervals on the measurement scale; each interval is a range of values; all observations falling within the limits of the interval add to the frequency count for that interval; grouped frequency distributions are used most often when data represent observations on a continuous variable.

Grouped frequency histogram: A histogram that shows how often scores occur at given intervals.

Grouped frequency polygon: A frequency polygon that shows how often scores occur at given intervals.

Histogram: A graphic representation of a frequency distribution in which the horizontal line represents values of a variable and the vertical line represents frequencies with which those values occur; a bar is constructed over each value of the variable (or the midpoint of each interval, if the data are grouped) and extended to the appropriate frequency; the term histogram usually refers to such a graph for interval or ratio data, whereas the term bar graph usually refers to such a graph for nominal or ordinal data; a graphic technique of descriptive statistics that uses the heights of adjoining bars to show how often each score occurs.

Horizontal axis: The horizontal dimension of a two-dimensional graph; it usually represents values of the independent variable in frequency distributions; sometimes called the x axis.

Hotelling's T^2: A statistical test used to examine the relationship among two or more independent variables and two or more dependent variables.

Hypothesis: See research hypothesis.

Hypothesis testing: A technique in inferential statistics in which we make a decision about the state of reality in the population; the decision consists of either accepting the state of reality proposed by the null hypothesis or rejecting the null hypothesis in favor of the research hypothesis; usually postulates a very specific set of conditions; a technique of inferential statistics that helps us decide whether research results are attributable to chance.

Hypothetical population: A statistical population that has no real existence but is imagined to be generated by repetitions of events of a certain type.

Independent samples design: An experiment in which people are assigned to different groups on a completely random basis; samples are drawn in such a way that the particular subjects chosen for one sample have no influence on which subjects are chosen for the other sample.

Independent t test: A statistical test used to decide whether two independent samples could have occurred by sampling error. See also t test.

Independent variable: The variable we believe to be associated with the different values of the dependent variable; the variable that is manipulated or introduced in a research study in order to see what effect differences in it will have on those variables proposed as being dependent on it.

Inferential statistics: Statistical methods that make it possible to draw tentative conclusions about the population based on observations of a sample selected from that population and, furthermore, to make a probability statement about those conclusions to aid in their evaluation.

Interaction: When the effect of one factor on a response depends on the level(s) of one (or more) other factor(s); the effect of one independent variable on another; the failure of one independent variable to remain constant over the levels of another; two treatments are said to interact if scores obtained under levels of one treatment behave differently under different levels of the other treatment.

Interquartile range: A statistic used as a measure of variability; the distance between the 75th and 25th percentiles; the interquartile range is more stable than the simple range and can be used with ordinal-level data; it does not, however, reflect the value of every observation in the group (as does the standard deviation); the median and interquartile range are often used together to describe the distribution of a variable, since both are based on percentiles.

Interval measurement: A measurement that, in addition to ordering scores, also establishes an equal unit so that distances between any two scores are of a known magnitude; a measurement in which objects, events, or processes are assigned to ordered categories that are separated by equal intervals; any measuring device that is capable not only of placing people (or objects) in their rank order on a characteristic but can also measure the differences between them in regard to that characteristic.

Intervening variable: A variable whose existence is inferred, but that cannot be manipulated; a variable that may affect just what influence (if any) an independent variable has on a dependent variable; also referred to as a confounding variable or an extraneous variable; when controlled for in a research design, it is known as a control variable. In its most specific usage, a variable that may have come between (in time) the introduction of the independent variable and the dependent variable and may thus have affected the latter.

Inverse relationship: A relationship between two variables in which high values of one variable are found with low values of the other variable and vice versa; sometimes referred to as a negative relationship or negative correlation.

Kendall's partial rank correlation coefficient: A nonparametric test designed to examine the correlation between two variables of at least ordinal level while controlling for a third variable of at least ordinal level.

Kendall's tau: A correlation coefficient showing the strength and direction of a relationship between ranks of two variables in a number of paired observations; it can thus be used when one or both variables produce data at the ordinal level or when interval or ratio data are badly skewed; it is sometimes used as a quickly computed substitute for Pearson's *r*.

Kolmogorov-Smirnov one-sample test: A nonparametric test that compares the overall distribution of a sample with another theoretical distribution in relation to an ordinal or skewed interval or ratio dependent variable.

Kolmogorov-Smirnov two-sample test: A nonparametric test that compares the overall distribution of two samples in relation to an ordinal-level or skewed interval-level or ratio-level dependent variable. It identifies the point at which the two samples reflect the greatest difference.

Kruskal-Wallis test: A nonparametric statistical test that can be used to examine the relationship between a nominal variable with more than two values and an ordinal-level or skewed interval-level or ratio-level variable. It is a common nonparametric alternative to simple, one-way *ANOVA*.

Kurtosis: A quality of the distribution of a set of data dealing with whether or how much the data pile up around some central point; the quality of peakedness or flatness of the graphic representation of a statistical distribution.

Least-squares criterion: The principle that the best regression line is one that would result in the smallest sum of squared deviations from the line.

Leptokurtic distribution: A relatively peaked frequency distribution; a frequency distribution that is more concentrated around the mean than the corresponding normal distribution.

Level of confidence: A term used in constructing confidence interval estimates of parameter values to specify our confidence that the inter-

val includes the parameter value; using procedures for constructing a 95 percent confidence interval, for instance, we would enclose the true parameter value within its limits on 95 percent of such attempts; the higher the level of confidence, the wider the interval.

Level of measurement: Refers to the degree to which characteristics of the data may be modeled mathematically; the higher the level of measurement, the more statistical methods are applicable.

Level of significance: See rejection level.

Limits of confidence intervals: The upper and lower values at the two ends of a confidence interval; in a symmetrical confidence interval, the limits are located one allowance factor above and below the sample statistic.

Linear correlation: A correlation between variables that if displayed using a scattergram would approximate a straight line.

Linear relationship: A relationship between two variables in which a straight line can be fitted satisfactorily to the points on the scattergram; the scatter of points will cluster elliptically around a straight line rather than around some type of curve.

Line of best fit: See regression line.

Lower confidence limit: Smaller of the two numbers that form a confidence interval; in frequency distributions where data have been grouped, it is the lower boundary of an interval on the measurement scale.

Mann-Whitney *U* test: A nonparametric test that is used to examine the relationship between a dichotomous nominal-level variable and an ordinal-level or skewed interval-level or ratio-level variable. It is a common alternative to the parametric independent *t* test.

***MANOVA* (multiple analysis of variance):** A form of multivariate statistical analysis used to compare the means of two or more interval-level or ratio-level dependent variables across the value categories of a nominal-level independent variable.

Marginals: The count of frequencies with which certain responses occur; in a cross-tabulation table, the row and column totals.

Matched pairs test: A statistical test for the comparison of two population means; the test is based on paired observations, one from each of the two populations; in the two-sample experiment, a procedure in which the entire subject pool is arranged in matched pairs, where pair members are similar (matched) on important characteristics; one member of each pair is then assigned to each group.

Matrix: A two-dimensional organization; each dimension is composed of several positions or alternatives; any particular score is a combination of the two dimensions as, for example, in a correlation matrix.

McNemar's test: A nonparametric test used to examine both the direction and amount of change in a group of cases in a pretest-posttest situation where the criterion variable is at the nominal level. It is sometimes called the *test for significance of changes.*

Mean: A term shared by several measures of central tendency (arithmetic mean, harmonic mean, geometric mean, and quadratic mean), all of which are computed using the value of every observation in the data set; in a general sense, the mean is equivalent to the average of all of the values within a data set.

Mean deviation: Measure of variability, that is, literally the mean (absolute value) of the deviations about the mean.

Measure of central tendency: A single number that describes the location, or relative magnitude, of a typical score in a sample or population; synonymous with the term *average;* the mode, median, and mean are examples of central tendency.

Measurement: In the most general sense, the assignment of labels to observations according to a rule or system; in statistics, measurement systems are classified according to level of measurement and may produce data that can be represented in numerical form or in words; the assignment of numerals to objects or events according to specific rules.

Measurement bias: A systematic source of measurement distortion that can occur because of any of a wide variety of phenomena.

Measure of variability: A single number that describes how spread out a group of scores is in a sample or population; the range, variance, and standard deviation are examples of variability.

Measures of association: Indicators of relationship magnitude or the actual strength of the relationship between variables. The level of measurement of the independent and dependent variables is used to determine which of several measures of association can appropriately be used.

Median: A measure of central tendency defined as the point on the measurement scale where 50 percent of the observations fall above it and 50 percent of the observations fall below it; it thus coincides with the 50th percentile; it is useful in skewed distributions because it is not as sensitive as the mean to the presence of a few outliers (extremely high or low values); it requires at least ordinal-level data.

Mesokurtic distribution: A frequency distribution that is neither excessively peaked nor excessively flat; the normal distribution is a mesokurtic distribution.

Midpoint of an interval: The value located halfway between upper and lower limits of an interval, found by adding upper and lower limits and dividing by two; when graphing or computing statistics from grouped data, the midpoint of each interval is sometimes used to represent all observations appearing in that interval.

Mode: A measure of central tendency; the most frequently occurring value in a distribution of scores (in grouped distributions, the midpoint of the interval with the highest frequency).

Moses test of extreme reactions: A nonparametric test designed for experimental situations in which it is believed that the introduction of the independent variable will produce extreme changes in the ordinal-level dependent variable in one direction among some research participants and extreme reactions in the opposite direction among others.

Most powerful test: The statistical test that has the smallest probability of producing a Type II error.

Multiple-group design: An experimental research design with one control group and several experimental groups.

Multiple linear regression: A multivariate statistical procedure that is used to predict the value of an interval- or ratio-level criterion variable using the values of two or more interval- or ratio-level predictor variables.

Multiple *R*:   A form of multivariate statistical analysis that determines the amount of variation in a criterion variable that can be explained by the combined variation of a group of predictor variables.

Multivariate analysis: A statistical analysis of the simultaneous relationship among three or more variables.

Mutually exclusive events: In applications of probability theory, two or more events that cannot both happen on a single trial; on a single flip of a coin, for example, the events heads and tails are mutually exclusive.

Negatively skewed distribution: See negative skew.

Negative relationship: The situation in correlational analysis in which high values of one variable tend to be associated with low values of another and vice versa; negative relationships are indicated by negative correlation coefficients.

Negative skew: A descriptive term applied to frequency distributions with many high values and few extremely low values; on a frequency polygon, negative skew produces a tail in the direction of low values—to the left; skewness in which the mean is less than the mode.

Nominal measurement: A measurement that simply classifies elements into two or more mutually exclusive categories, indicating that elements are qualitatively different but not giving order or magnitude; a measurement in which objects, events, or processes are assigned to categories having no inherent order; the level of measurement whose only requirement is that each observation falls in one, and only one, measurement category; also referred to as categorical measurement; it is the lowest level of measurement.

Nondirectional test: A statistical test with two regions of rejection, that is, a two-tailed test; the area under the sampling distribution curve equal to the rejection level is divided into two equal parts at each end of the distribution, creating two regions of rejection; an observed statistic in either region leads to rejection of the null hypothesis; a test used when we have

not predicted the direction of a relationship between two variables.

Nonparametric tests: Usually refers to statistical tests of hypotheses about population probability distributions, but not about specific parameters of the distributions; a test that does not require a normal population distribution; a method for testing a hypothesis that does not involve an explicit assertion concerning a parameter; hypothesis-testing procedures that do not make stringent assumptions about population parameters.

Normal distribution: A symmetrical bell-shaped curve that often arises when a trait is composed of a large number of random, independent factors; the curve possesses a specific mathematical formula.

Null hypothesis: A statement concerning one or more parameter(s) that is subjected to a statistical test; a statement that there is no relationship between the two variables of interest; the belief that any apparent relationship between or among variables in one or more research samples has been caused by sampling error; the hypothesis that is tested when seeking to gain statistical support for a research hypothesis.

Null research hypothesis: A relatively rare form of research hypothesis in which the researcher predicts that no statistically significant relationship between variables will be found. It is the third form that a research hypothesis can take (along with one-tailed or two-tailed research hypothesis).

Obscuring variable: A third variable that may cause a researcher to underestimate the true strength of the relationship between the independent and the dependent variables. Also called a *suppressor variable.*

Observation: An objectively recorded fact or item of datum; statistics are usually applied to collections of observations. Also referred to as a case.

One-sample *t* test: A hypothesis-testing procedure used to decide whether a sample could have occurred by sampling error.

One-tailed research hypothesis: A form of research hypothesis in which the researcher predicts that a statistically significant relationship between variables will be found and also predicts the direction of that relationship.

One-tailed test: See directional hypothesis.

One-way analysis of variance: See simple *ANOVA*.

Ordinal measurement: A measurement that classifies and ranks elements or scores; a procedure that is capable of rank-ordering individuals (or objects) on a particular characteristic but that cannot distinguish how different each is from the others; a measurement in which objects, events, or processes are assigned to ordered categories; the level of measurement above nominal but below interval; the data represent at least ordinal scale measurement if each observation falls into one, and only one, category and if observation categories can be rank-ordered.

Origin: The point of a graph at which the *x* axis and *y* axis intersect.

Outcome: A possible result of an experiment or observation; in probability applications, the result of an experimental trial; see also probability.

Outlier: An extreme value of a variable in a data set that is either larger or smaller than most other values in the variable's distribution.

Paired observations: An observation on two variables, where the intent is to examine the relationship between them; paired observations form the raw material of correlational analyses; recording both a person's height and weight and keeping both of those measurements associated with the same person constitute collection of a paired observation.

Parameter: A characteristic of a population determined from observations on every member of the population; population parameters of interest to us include the mean, range, median, standard deviation, and many others; also a characteristic of a mathematical relation whose value must be specified before the expression can be evaluated; a measure computed from all observations in a population.

Parameter estimates: Attempts to estimate the values of population parameters (e.g., the mean) from statistics computed on a sample selected from the population; estimates may

consist of a single value (a point estimate) or a range of values (confidence interval).

Parametric tests: Statistical methods for estimating parameters or testing hypotheses about population parameters; a statistical test in which the null and research hypotheses are stated in terms of population parameter values; an example is the test for the significance of the difference between two means; procedures that make relatively stringent assumptions about population parameters.

Pareto chart: A graph portraying the cumulative frequencies and cumulative percentages for a frequency distribution of a variable.

Partial *r*: A test of correlation in which the relationship between two variables is examined while holding a third potentially intervening or extraneous variable constant.

Pearson's product-moment correlation coefficient: A correlation coefficient that specifies the strength and direction of a relation between two interval- or ratio-level variables; it is the most commonly used statistic in correlational analyses; also called Pearson's *r*.

Percent: Synonymous with *in 100* or the number of cases out of 100.

Percentage distribution: A table that displays the percentage of cases that were found to have each of the respective measurements of a variable.

Percentile: A point on the measurement scale below which a specified percentage of the group's observations fall; the 20th percentile, for instance, is the value that has 20 percent of the observations below it.

Percentile rank: A transformed score that tells us the percentage of scores falling at or below a given score.

Perfect relationship: A relationship between two variables in which the value of one variable is known if the value of the other variable is specified; a relationship, either direct or inverse, in which there is a perfect predictability between the two variables; when all points in the scattergram lie exactly on the regression line.

Pie chart: A graph that displays the frequency distribution of a variable as portions of a circle reflecting percentages of the whole.

Platykurtic distribution: A frequency distribution that has a relatively flat shape; a distribution that is less concentrated around the mean than the corresponding normal distribution.

Point estimate: A single value, produced by application of inferential methods to observations on sample members, that is our best guess of a parameter value.

Population distribution: A distribution of all the scores in a population; a collection of all observations identifiable by a set of rules; a designated part of a universe from which a sample is drawn; the complete group of potential observations.

Positively skewed distribution: See positive skew.

Positive relationship: The situation in correlational analyses that exists when high values of the first variable tend to be associated with high values of the second variable, and low values of the first variable tend to appear with low values of the second.

Positive skew: A descriptive term applied to frequency distributions with many low values and a few extremely high values; on a frequency polygon graph, positive skew produces a tail in the direction of the positive values; skewness in which the mode is less than the mean.

Power of test: See statistical power.

Prediction: The estimation of scores on one variable from data about one or more other variables.

Predictor variable: The variable that, it is believed, allows us to improve our ability to predict values of the criterion variable.

Probability: A measure of likelihood; the number of outcomes in which an event can occur divided by the total number of possible outcomes; reported as a *p*-value.

Probability distribution: For discrete random variables, the probability distribution is a relative frequency distribution; the relative frequencies associated with values indicate the probabilities of their occurences.

Proportion: A fraction of one.

p-value: The mathematical probability that sampling error might have caused variables to be related in a research sample.

Quartile: A percentile that is an even multiple of 25; the 25th percentile is the first quartile, the 50th percentile is the second quartile (it is also the median), and so forth.

Random variable: A variable that can assume different values; there is a probability associated with occurrence of different values of the variable, and these probabilities constitute a probability distribution.

Range: Difference between the largest and smallest numbers of an array plus one; the distance between the highest and lowest values in a distribution (more accurately, the distance between the upper true limit of the highest value and the lower true limit of the lowest value); it is used as a measure of variability.

Ratio measurement: A measurement that, in addition to containing equal units, also establishes an absolute zero point within the scale; a measurement in which objects, events, or processes are assigned to ordered categories that are separated with equal intervals, and where the zero point is not arbitrary; the highest level of measurement; it is reached when each observation falls in one, and only one, category; when observation categories can be ordered; when there are equal intervals between adjacent categories on the measurement scale; and when a value of zero represents a zero quantity of the variable being measured.

Raw score: A numerical value assigned to an observation that is expressed in the original units of measurement; a score obtained directly by measuring some characteristic of a person, event, or process in a research study.

Regression analysis: A variation of a correlational analysis that makes possible prediction of the value of one variable from observations on another variable; these predictions are based on a collection of previously made paired observations on both variables; regression analyses require that the two variables be fairly strongly correlated and that the relation between them approximate a linear one.

Regression equation: A derived equation in the form of $Y' = a + b(X)$ that makes it possible to predict the value of a criterion value from a value of a predictor variable.

Regression line: A hypothetical line that goes through data points and that uses the method of least-squares; one of two least-squares lines through a scatter plot of paired observations;

each regression line constitutes the collection of predicted values for one of the variables; the straight line of best fit (usually according to the least-squares criterion) for a set of bivariate data; the line of best fit in a scattergram; mostly used to predict values of the *y* variable from values of the *x* variable.

Rejection level: The selected probability level at which the null hypothesis is rejected; the commonly used rejection level is .05; the probability of rejecting the null hypothesis when it is true; also called the alpha level.

Rejection region: A specific region of a normal curve that, when it contains a measurement from a sample, suggests that it is safe to reject the null hypothesis.

Relative frequency distribution: A table or graph that shows observation categories and the proportion of the group that falls within each value category—that is, the relative frequency of each category; the proportion of observations that falls in one category or interval; in probability applications, the relative frequency of an event is the proportion of trials on which the event occurs.

Reliability: The consistency of a measurement instrument.

Reliability coefficient: A measure of the consistency of a statistical test; there are several methods of computing a reliability coefficient, depending on the test and the specific situation.

Replication: Repetition of the same research procedures (usually by a second researcher) for the purpose of determining if earlier results can be duplicated; the collection of two or more observations under a set of identical experimental conditions.

Research hypothesis: A prediction that two or more variables will be found to be related; the hypothesis to be supported if the null hypothesis is rejected; also called the alternative hypothesis.

Rival hypothesis: Theoretical alternatives for explaining the apparent relationship between the independent (or predictor) variable(s) and the dependent (or criterion) variable(s); other variables that might explain variations in the dependent (or criterion) variable(s).

Robustness: Refers to the property that certain hypothesis-testing procedures have of yielding accurate results regardless of whether all assumptions for the test are strictly satisfied.

Sample: A subset of the population under study; a subset of a population often used synonymously with *group* and *condition* when discussing research designs; sometimes referred to as a research sample.

Sample distribution: The frequency distribution of all observations in a sample; when a number of different samples are selected from one population, each sample will probably have a sample distribution slightly different from other samples.

Sample statistic: Characteristics of samples; statistics computed from observations on sample members; the mean of a sample is a sample statistic because only members of the sample contribute to its value; the mean of a population is a parameter (rather than a statistic) because all members of the population contributed to its value.

Sampling: A method of selecting members of the population for inclusion in a research study; strictly speaking, proper sampling procedures must be used if inferences about the population are to be made from sample statistics; two broad categories of sampling procedures are random (probability) sampling and nonrandom (nonprobability) sampling.

Sampling bias: Refers to the systematic distortion of a research sample. It can occur for any of a variety of reasons and produces a sample that is not representative of its population. Not to be confused with sampling error.

Sampling distribution: A theoretical distribution that can be specified for any statistic that can be computed for samples from a population; it is the frequency distribution of that statistic's values that would appear if all possible samples of a specified size were drawn from the population; it is the foundation of inferential statistics because it allows us to specify the probability with which different values of the statistic appear; it is assumed that a statistic computed from sample observations is one value from such a distribution.

Sampling error: Refers to the natural phenomenon whereby sample statistics tend to differ from population parameters; the degree to which the sample can be predicted to vary from the population in relation to some variable based on this phenomenon. Sometimes referred to as chance. Not to be confused with sampling bias.

Scattergram: A graphic representation of the relationship between two interval- or ratio-level variables; a two-dimensional graph in which each axis represents values of a different variable; paired observations on both variables are represented as dots on the graph; it may be used as a preliminary step in a correlational analysis or to portray in graphic fashion the strength and direction of a relationship between two variables; sometimes referred to as a scatter plot.

Score: A numerical value assigned to an observation; a case value.

Score interval: In a grouped frequency distribution, the range of observed values is divided into a number of score intervals; the frequency distribution table lists the number of observations that fall into each score interval.

Semi-interquartile range: Half the interquartile range, sometimes used as a measure of variability.

Sign test: Nonparametric statistical test used to compare the same sample at two different times.

Simple *ANOVA*: A statistical test used to decide whether two or more samples could have occurred by chance from populations with equal means.

Simple linear regression: A statistical procedure that produces an equation that makes it possible to predict the value of the criterion variable for a given value of the predictor variable.

Skewed distribution: A distribution in which more observations fall on one side of the mean than on the other side.

Skewness: A quality of the distribution of a set of data dealing with whether the data are symmetrically distributed around a central point.

Spearman's correlation coefficient: A correlation coefficient showing the strength and direction of a relationship between ranks of two variables in a number of paired observations; it can thus be used when one or both variables produce data at the ordinal level or when interval or ratio data are badly skewed; it is sometimes used as a quickly computed substitute

for Pearson's *r*; also referred to as Spearman's rho.

Specifying variable: A third variable that can further explain a relationship between the independent and dependent variables that is statistically significant but that seems to exist in two different directions.

Spurious relationship: Occurring because of sampling error; not a real relationship that exists beyond the sample or samples in which it was identified.

Stability: The degree to which a statistic's value remains constant when it is computed for a number of different groups that are essentially alike but that differ in a few values; in inferential statistics, a stable statistic is one whose value remains stable from sample to sample when all samples are taken from the same population.

Standard deviation: A common measure of variability; it requires at least interval-level data and reflects the value of every observation in the distribution; like other measures of variability, it is a single number whose size indicates the spread, or dispersion, of the distribution; a measure of variability that is the square root of the variance; it represents a specified distance along the baseline of a distribution curve.

Standard error: An estimate of how well a regression equation can predict values of the criterion variable from known values of the predictor variable.

Standard error of a statistic: The standard deviation of the underlying (sampling) distribution of the statistic.

Standard error of estimate: In the regression situation, the standard deviation of observed values around the regression line; the smaller the standard error of estimate, the more precisely we can predict scores of the criterion variable.

Standard error of the difference: Refers to the standard deviation of the sampling distribution of the difference for independent samples.

Standard error of the mean: The standard deviation of the underlying (sampling) distribution of the mean. It is the square root of the variance of the mean.

Standard normal distribution: The normal distribution with a mean of 0 and a standard deviation of 1.

Standard score: A score stated in units of standard deviation from the mean of the distribution; a negative score indicates a score below the mean and a positive score indicates a score above the mean; an individual observation that belongs to a distribution with a mean of 0 and a standard deviation of 1; any distribution of raw scores can be transformed into a distribution of standard scores without changing the shape of the distribution or the relative order or distances between members because the transformation to standard scores is linear; also referred to as a *z* score.

Statistical decision: Choosing between states of possible reality on the basis of probability considerations; hypothesis testing involves a statistical decision in which we either accept or reject the null hypothesis.

Statistically significant: Judged too unlikely to have occurred by chance. A statistically significant relationship between variables within a sample or samples is probably not the work of sampling error. However, other variables or conditions may have produced it.

Statistical power: The ability of a statistical test to reject correctly the null hypothesis; a test's ability to detect a true relationship between or among variables.

Statistical power analysis: A procedure for determining the likelihood of committing a Type II error given the size of sample(s) used and the statistical test of inference employed.

Statistics: In comparison to the term *parameters,* statistics refers to the characteristics of a sample rather than to the characteristics of a population; in the context of descriptive statistics, measures taken on a distribution; in the context of inferential statistics, measures or characteristics of a sample; in a more general sense, the theory, procedures, and methods by which data are analyzed; the area of study that includes methods for producing and interpreting statistics; generally speaking, statistical methods are applied in an attempt to understand large masses of data, to discover and describe characteristics of the data that are not

apparent from casual observation, and to describe characteristics of a group of observations rather than single observations.

Stem-and-leaf plot: A graph consisting of numbers which reflect the actual case values of all cases in a frequency distribution.

Structural variables: In data analyses, those characteristics formed by combining units from lower levels of analysis.

Suppressor variable: A third variable that may cause a researcher to underestimate the true strength of the relationship between the independent and dependent variables. Also called an *obscuring variable.*

Symmetrical distribution: A distribution in which, for every observation on one side of the mean, there is another observation at an equal distance on the other side of the mean; in a symmetrical distribution, the left half of the polygon (or histogram) is a mirror image of the right half; a distribution with a frequency polygon whose left and right sides will coincide if it is folded in the middle along a vertical line.

Transformed standardized score: A score that allows us to tell at a glance where it falls in a distribution of scores; a standard score that has been transformed so that it now belongs to a distribution with any mean and standard deviation we wish; transformed scores are used most often in evaluating test scores.

Trimmed mean: A measure of central tendency calculated by first trimming a small percentage (usually 5%) of values off the upper and lower limits of an array of case values and then averaging the remaining values.

True limits of a number: The upper and lower points on the measurement scale that enclose all values of the variable actually represented by a number.

t **test:** A group of parametric tests that use the *t* distribution to examine the issue of inference; determines if there is a statistically significant difference between the means of two samples or between a sample's mean and its population's mean.

Two-tailed research hypothesis: A form of research hypothesis in which the researcher predicts that a statistically significant relationship between variables will be found but does not predict the direction of that relationship.

Two-tailed test: See nondirectional test.

Type I error: Error that occurs when the null hypothesis is rejected when a true relationship between variables does not exist; also called *alpha error.*

Type II error: Error that occurs when the null hypothesis is not rejected when a true relationship between variables exists; also called *beta error.*

Unbiased estimator: Estimator that has a probability distribution with the mean equal to the estimated parameter; an estimate of a parameter is said to be unbiased if its expected value is equal to the parameter.

Unbiased statistic: A statistic computed in a manner such that the mean of its underlying distribution is the parameter that the statistic estimates.

Underlying sampling distribution of a statistic: The distribution (usually theoretical) of all possible values of the statistic from all possible samples of a given size selected from the population.

Unimodal: Refers to a distribution with only one mode.

Univariate analysis: Statistical analysis of the distribution of values of a single variable.

Upper confidence limit: Larger of the two numbers that form a confidence interval.

Upper limit of an interval: In frequency distributions where data have been grouped, the upper boundary of an interval on the measurement scale.

Validity: The degree to which a measurement instrument accurately measures what it claims to measure.

Variability: Dispersion of a distribution; the extent to which values differ among themselves; variability is not the name of a specific statistic; rather, it is the term applied to the characteristic of dispersion.

Variable: A characteristic that takes on different values; any attribute whose value, or level, can change; any characteristic (of a person, object, or situation) that can change value or kind from observation to observation.

Variance: Measure of variability that is the average value of the squares of the deviations from the mean of the scores in a distribution; measure of data variation; the mean squared deviation from the mean; the squared standard deviation, sometimes called the mean square.

Variation: Sum of the squared deviations about the mean; in some applications, variation is useful in its own right as a measure of variability; also called sum of squares.

Vertical axis: The vertical dimension of a two-dimensional graph; it usually represents frequency in frequency distributions, relative frequency in relative frequency distributions, and cumulative proportion in cumulative proportion graphs; when experimental results are graphed, it usually represents values of the dependent variable.

Weighted mean: The average of a group of scores that are weighted to reflect their different levels of importance. The weighted mean is widely used to compute student final grades when different graded exercises or examinations have been assigned different percentages of the course grade.

Wilcoxon sign: A nonparametric statistical test that examines the relationship between two "ordinal plus" variables in two matched case samples.

x **variable:**   The variable plotted on the *x* axis of a scattergram and the predictor variable (used to predict the *y* variable) in regression; usually the independent variable in a research study.

Yates' correction factor: In computing the obtained chi-square statistic, a mathematical correction that should be applied when $df = 1$.

Yule's *Q*:   One of several easily computed statistical tests often used for exploratory data analysis, that is, to determine if relationships between variables are sufficiently promising to examine, using more powerful forms of analysis.

y **variable:**   The variable plotted on the *x* axis in a scattergram and the predicted variable (predicted from the *x* variable) in regression; usually the dependent variable in a research study.

Zero relationship: The situation that exists when values of one variable are not related in any way to values of another variable; with a zero relationship, knowing the value of one variable gives us no indication of the value of the other; perfect zero relationships are represented by correlation coefficients of 0.

z **score:** A transformed score that tells us how many standard deviations a score lies away from the mean in a distribution.

Z **test:** A hypothesis-testing procedure used to decide whether a given sample could have occurred by chance from a population with a given mean and known standard deviation.

Index

Abscissa, 29
Absolute frequency distributions, 22
Absolute zero point, 14
Accuracy, 33
Alpha levels, 88–90
Analysis of variance
    multiple, 240–241
    simple, 238–240
Arrays, 21
Association. *See also* Chi-square test of association
    measures of, 93
Assumptions, 125
Average. *See* Mean

Bar graphs, 30, 36
Beta weights, 157–158
Bias
    design, 77–78
    measurement, 77–78
    sampling, 78
Bimodal variables, 40, 47
Binary variables, 15
Bivariate analysis, 16
    of correlation, 134–155
Box plots, 55–56

Canonical correlation, 158–159
Causation, correlation versus, 145–146
Central limit theorem, 110
Central tendency, 39–47
    mean. *See* Mean
    median, 42–43, 47, 49
    mode, 40–42, 45, 47
    uses of, 40, 45–47
Chi-square goodness-of-fit test, 221–223
    described, 221–222
    examples of application, 222–223

Chi-square test of association, 187–214
    computation of chi-square, 194, 196
    critical values of chi-square, 195
    degrees of freedom, 193–195
    examples of application, 202–206
    expected frequencies, 191–193, 207–208
    Fisher's exact test as alternative to, 202
    interpreting results of, 197–198
    McNemar's test, 209–211
    meaningfulness of, 198–200
    median test, 211–213
    multivariate, 206–209
    nature of, 188
    observed frequencies, 189–191, 193
    in one-tailed research hypothesis, 188–189,
        197–198
    popularity of, 187
    presentation of chi-square, 197
    related indicators of strength of relationship,
        200–201
    restrictions on use of, 201
    sample size and, 198–200
    special applications of, 209–213
Cluster analysis, 161–162, 182
Coefficient of determination, 144–145
Cohen, Jacob, 123–124
Conceptualization
    defined, 5
    levels of measurement and, 9
Concurrent validity, 144
Confidence level
    defined, 111
    95 percent, 112
    99 percent, 112–114
Confusion matrix, 183
Constants, defined, 4

Continuous variables, 14
Correction for continuity, 196
Correlation, 7, 134–162. *See also* Regression analysis
   bivariate, 134–155
   causation versus, 145–146
   cluster analysis, 161–162, 182
   covariance and, 134
   defined, 134
   factor analysis, 159–161
   interpreting linear, 137–138, 142–146
   multiple *R*, 156–159
   multivariate, 155–162
   nonparametric alternatives, 154–155
   nonperfect, 140–142
   partial *r*, 155–156
   Pearson's *r*, 146–153, 169
   perfect, 138–140
   uses of, 135–138
Correlational groups *t* test, 224–227
Correlation coefficient, 93, 142–146
   coefficient of determination, 144–145
   computation of, 147
   correlation versus causation, 145–146
   interpreting very strong correlation, 143–144
   maximum values of, 149
   in prediction process, 165
   range of, 143
Correlation matrix, 146
Council on Social Work Education (CSWE), 1–2
Covariance, 134
Cramer's *V*, 200–201
Criterion variables, 9, 134, 137, 167
Critical values
   of chi-square, 195
   of Pearson's *r*, 150
   of *t*, 219
Cross-tabulation. *See* Chi-square test of association
Cumulative frequency distributions, 22–23,
   25–28, 237
Cumulative percentage frequency distributions, 24,
   25, 26–27

Data
   defined, 3
   information versus, 3
   misrepresentation of, 28–29
Data analysis
   frequency distributions in, 26–28
   levels of measurement, 15–16
Data reduction, 16–17

Degrees of freedom (df)
   in chi-square analysis, 193–195
   defined, 193
Dependent *t* test, 224–227
   nonparametric alternative, 225–227
   with one sample measured twice, 224–225
   with two connected samples measured once, 224
   Wilcoxon sign test, 225–227
Dependent variables
   defined, 8–9
   level of measurement of, 120
   in parametric tests, 125, 128
Derived variable, 158
Descriptive analysis, 16–17, 135
Design bias, 77–78
Dichotomous variables, 14–15
Directional research hypothesis. *See* One-tailed
   research hypothesis
Discrete variables, 14
Discriminant analysis, 182–183
Dispersion. *See* Variability
Dummy tables, 188–189
Dummy variables, 15, 181
Duncan test, 239

Effect size
   statistical significance and, 92–94
   and strength of relationships between variables,
      121, 123
Expected frequencies, in chi-square analysis,
   191–193, 207–208
Extraneous variables, 9

Factor analysis, 159–161
Factorial designs, 240
Factor rotation, 160
Fisher's exact test, 202
Five-number summary, 55
Frequency
   in chi-square analysis, 189–193, 207–208
   defined, 4
   of value categories and values, 4–5
Frequency distributions, 20–29
   absolute, 22
   cumulative, 22–23, 25–28, 237
   cumulative percentage, 24, 25, 26–27
   in data analysis, 26–28
   grouped, 24–26
   misrepresentation of data and, 28–29
   percentage, 23–24
Frequency polygons, 32–34

Goodness-of-fit test, 221–223
    described, 221–222
    examples of application, 222–223
Graphs, 29–36
    bar, 30, 36
    common mistakes in displaying data, 35–36
    frequency polygons, 32–34
    histograms, 32
    Pareto charts, 34
    parts of, 29–30
    pie charts, 30–32
    scattergams, 135–142
    stem-and-leaf plots, 34–35
Grouped frequency distributions, 24–26

Histograms, 32
Hottelling's T^2, 241
Hypothesis testing, 76–114. *See also* Statistical tests
    design bias in, 77–78
    errors in drawing conclusions about relationships,
        90–92
    in one-sample *t* test, 220–221
    probability in, 79–82
    refuting sampling error in, 82–83
    research hypotheses in, 83–85
    rival hypotheses in, 77
    sampling distributions and, 98–114. *See also*
        Sampling distributions
    sampling error in. *See* Sampling error
    statistical significance in, 88–90, 92–95,
        131–132, 200
    steps in, 130–132
    testing null hypothesis, 85–88, 130–131

Independent *t* test, 227–238
    described, 227–228
    examples of application, 228–235
    nonparametric alternatives, 235–238
Independent variables, 8–9
    defined, 8
    level of measurement of, 120
Inferential analysis, 17, 81–82, 87, 98, 117, 131, 135
    Pearson's *r* for, 148–153, 169
    sampling distributions and, 100–102
Information
    data versus, 3
    defined, 3
Interquartile range, 49–50, 55
Interval-level data, 32
    normal distributions and, 61, 66, 69

skewed distributions and, 119
Interval-level measurement, 13, 81, 120, 125, 128,
    182, 217, 239
Intervening variables, 9

Kendall's partial rank correlation coefficient, 156
Kendall's tau, 154, 156
Kolmogorov-Smirnov (K-S) two sample test, 236–238
Kruskal-Wallis test, 240

Lambda, 200
Least-squares criterion, 171, 172–174
Levels of measurement, 9–16
    and analysis of data, 15–16
    interval, 13, 81, 120, 125, 128, 182, 217, 239
    nominal, 10–11, 45, 47, 126, 129, 182
    ordinal, 11–13, 45, 47, 126, 128–129, 182
    ratio, 13–14, 120, 125, 128, 182, 217, 239
    in selecting statistical tests, 120, 125–126, 128
Linear correlations, 137–138, 142–146
Linear regression
    multiple, 180–182
    simple, 164, 167–169
Line diagrams, 30
Logistic regression, 183–184

Mann-Whitney *U* test, 235–236, 240
Matched groups *t* test, 224–227
McNemar's test, 209–211
Mean, 43–45, 46–47
    comparing sample mean to population mean, 218–220
    normal distribution and, 62–64, 66
    in prediction process, 165
    sampling distributions of, 102–110
    with skewed distributions, 119
    trimmed, 43, 47
    weighted, 44–45
Mean deviation, 50–51, 52, 55
Measurement bias, 77–78
Measures of association, 93
Median, 42–43, 47, 49
Median test, 211–213
Misrepresentation of data, 28–29
    example of, 28–29
    risk of, 28
Mode, 40–42, 45, 47
Multiple analysis of variance (MANOVA), 240–241
Multiple linear regression, 180–182
Multiple *R*, 156–159
    example of application, 157–158

in multiple linear regression, 180–182
variations of, 158–159
Multivariate analysis, 16, 126–127
chi-square, 206–209
cluster analysis, 161–162
of correlation, 155–162
factor analysis, 159–161
multiple *R*, 156–159
partial *r*, 155–156
of regression, 180–182

National Association of Social Workers (NASW), 1–2
Negatively skewed distributions, 60
Nominal-level measurement, 10–11, 45, 47, 126, 129, 182
Non-directional research hypothesis. *See* Two-tailed research hypothesis
Nonparametric tests, 125–126, 128, 154–155
dependent *t*, 225–227
example of application, 154–155
independent *t*, 235–238
Kendall's tau, 154, 156
Spearman's rho, 154
Nonperfect correlations, 140–142
Normal distributions, 58–74
areas of, 68
deriving raw scores from percentiles, 72–74
example of application, 70–72
for interval-level variables, 61, 66, 69
nature of, 60–64
percentiles, 65–66, 72–74
for ratio-level variables, 61, 66, 69
samples drawn from, 105–110
skewed distributions versus, 42, 58–60
standard deviations in, 62–64, 66
z scores, 64–72
Null hypothesis, 85–88. *See also* Sampling error
in chi-square test of association, 188–189
described, 85
as sampling error, 79
testing, 85–88, 130–131

Obscuring variables, 208–209
Observed frequencies, in chi-square analysis, 189–191, 193
One-group pretest-posttest research design, 224–225
One-sample *t* test, 218–223
chi-square goodness-of-fit test, 221–223
comparing sample mean to population mean, 218–220

critical values of *t*, 219
hypothesis testing, 220–221
presentation of findings, 221
One-tailed research hypothesis
chi-square test of association and, 188–189, 197–198
described, 84
rejection levels, 107–110, 122, 123
testing, 85–86, 105, 130
z scores, 108–109
Operationalization
defined, 5–6
levels of measurement and, 9
Ordinal-level measurement, 11–13, 45, 47, 126, 128–129, 182
Ordinate, 29

Paired groups *t* test, 224–227
Parameter estimation, 111–114
defined, 111
from statistics, 111–114
Parameters, defined, 17
Parametric tests, 125, 128
Pareto charts, 34
Partial *r*, 155–156
Pearson's product moment correlation, 93
Pearson's *r*, 146–153, 169
computation of, 146, 147
correlation matrix and, 146
critical values, 150
example of application, 149–153
for inference, 148–153
Percentage frequency distributions, 23–24
Percentiles
converting raw scores to, 65–66
deriving raw scores from, 72–74
Perfect correlations, 138–140
direction of, 139–140
strength of, 139
Phi, 200–201
Pie charts, 30–32
Point of origin, 29–30
Population
comparing experimental sample with, 100–101
comparing nonexperimental sample with, 101–102
defined, 17
distribution of variables in, 119–120
Population mean, comparing sample mean to, 218–220
Positively skewed distributions, 59
Power. *See* Statistical power

Predicted *Y*, 175–176, 177
Prediction, 164–167
Predictor variables, 9, 134, 137, 167
Probability theory, 79–82
    inferential analysis and, 17, 81–82, 87, 98, 100–102,
        117, 131, 135, 148–153, 169
    laws of, 80
    sampling error and, 80–81
    p-values, 88, 200

Range, 48–50
    of correlation coefficient, 143
    interquartile, 49–50, 55
    reporting, 55
    semi-interquartile, 50, 55
    standard deviation versus, 121
Ratio-level data, 32
    normal distributions and, 61, 66, 69
    skewed distributions and, 119
Ratio-level measurement, 13–14, 120, 125, 128, 182,
        217, 239
Raw data, 16, 21
Raw scores
    converting to percentiles, 65–66
    converting to *z* scores, 64–72
    deriving from percentiles, 72–74
Regression analysis, 164–185
    computation of regression equation, 169–172
    discriminant analysis, 182–183
    examples of application, 177–179
    interpreting results of, 176–177
    logistic regression, 183–184
    multivariate, 180–182
    prediction and, 164–167
    regression line, 172–176
    simple linear regression, 164, 167–179
Regression coefficient, 174
Regression equation, 167–172
    computation of, 169–172
    least-squares criterion, 171, 172–174
    in simple linear regression, 167, 168, 169–172
Regression line, 139, 172–176
    interchanging *X* and *Y* variables, 176
    least-squares criterion, 171, 172–174
    predicted *Y*, 175–176, 177
    regression coefficient, 174
    y-intercept, 174–175
Rejection levels, 88–90, 106–110, 122, 123, 131, 149
    for one-tailed research hypothesis, 107–110, 122, 123
    for two-tailed research hypothesis, 106–107, 122, 123

Relationships between variables
    errors in drawing conclusions about, 90–92
    strength of, 121, 123, 200–201
    surprising, 94–95
Reliability, 7, 135
Replication, 82–83
Research hypothesis, 8–9, 83–85
    conceptualization of, 5
    dependent variables in, 8–9
    independent variables in, 8–9
    null hypothesis, 84, 85–88
    one-tailed. *See* One-tailed research hypothesis
    two-tailed. *See* Two-tailed research hypothesis
Rival hypotheses, 77
Robustness, 124–125
Rule of the instrument, 117

Sample mean, comparing population mean
        to, 218–220
Sample size
    in chi-square test of association, 198–200
    choice of, 124
    sampling distributions and, 91, 98–100, 104
    sampling error and, 98–100, 122–123
Sampling bias, 78
Sampling distributions, 98–114
    characteristics of, 102–103
    defined, 100
    estimating parameters from statistics, 111–114
    inference and, 100–102
    of means, 102–110
    sample size, 91, 98–100, 104
Sampling error, 79, 149. *See also* Null hypothesis
    as function of variability, 122, 123
    probability theory and, 80–81
    refuting, 82–83
    sample size and, 98–100, 122–123
    statistical significance and, 93
Sampling method, in selecting statistical tests,
        118–119
Scattergrams, 135–142
Secondary data analysis, 3
Semi-interquartile range, 50, 55
Simple analysis of variance (one-way ANOVA),
        238–240
    computation of, 239–240
    nonparametric alternative, 240
Simple frequency distributions, 22
Simple linear regression, 164, 167–172
    formulating research question for, 167–168

Simple linear regression, *(continued)*
   limitations of, 168–169
   uses of, 167
Skewed distributions, 42, 58–60
   nature of, 58–59
   negatively skewed, 60
   positively skewed, 59
   samples drawn from, 110
   use of mean or standard deviation with, 110, 119
Spearman's rho, 154
Standard deviation, 51–54
   computation of, 52
   normal distribution and, 62–64, 66
   pictorial representation of, 54
   in prediction process, 165–166
   range versus, 121
   reporting, 55
   with skewed distributions, 110, 119
   of standard error of the mean, 104
Standard error, 177
Standard error of the mean
   defined, 103
   standard deviation of, 104
Standard scores. *See z* scores
Statistical analysis, 83
   categories of, 16–17
   data analysis in, 3, 15–16, 26–29
   general methodological terms, 3–9
   getting help with, 129–130
   importance to social workers, 1–2
   levels of measurement, 9–14. *See also*
     Levels of measurement
   other measurement classifications, 14–15
   uses of, 2
Statistical power, 121–124
   analysis of, 123–124
   avoiding Type II errors, 121–123
   defined, 121
   of nonparametric tests, 126
   strength of relationship between variables, 121,
     123, 200–201
   Statistical Power Analysis for the Behavioral
     Sciences (Cohen), 123–124
Statistical rejection level, 88–90, 122, 123, 131, 149
Statistical significance, 88–90, 131–132
   alpha levels, 88–90
   complex interpretations of, 95
   defined, 92
   effect size and, 92–94
   p-values in, 88, 200

   rejection levels in, 88–90, 122, 123, 131, 149
   surprising relationships in, 94–95
Statistical tests, 116–132
   data analysis for, 129–130
   factors to consider, 118–125
   importance of using correct, 116–118
   levels of measurement, 120, 125–126, 128
   multivariate, 126–127. *See also* Multivariate
     analysis
   nonparametric, 125–126, 128, 154–155
   parametric, 125, 128
   selection guidelines, 127–129
   steps in hypothesis testing, 130–132
Stem-and-leaf plots, 34–35
Step-down procedure, 158
Sum of squares, 51
Suppressor variables, 208–209

Trimmed mean, 43, 47
t tests, 215–238
   dependent, 224–227
   independent, 227–238
   one-sample, 218–223
   use of, 216–217
Two-tailed research hypothesis
   described, 84–85
   rejection levels, 106–107, 122, 123
   testing, 85–86, 130
   z scores, 106
Type I errors, 90–92, 131
   avoiding, 91–92
   nature of, 90
   statistical power analysis and, 123–124
Type II errors, 120
   avoiding, 121–123
   nature of, 90–91
   statistical power analysis and, 123–124

Univariate analysis, 16

Validity, 7, 144
Value categories
   defined, 4
   frequencies of, 4–5
Values of variables
   defined, 4
   frequencies of, 4–5
Variability, 48–56
   defined, 48
   interquartile range, 49–50, 55
   mean deviation, 50–51, 52, 55

range, 48–49
reporting measures of, 55–56
sampling error as function of, 122, 123
standard deviation, 51–54
variance, 51, 52
Variables, 3–5
bimodal, 40, 47
binary, 15
continuous, 14
criterion, 9, 134, 137, 167
defined, 4
dependent, 8–9, 120, 125
derived, 158
dichotomous, 14–15
discrete, 14
distribution in population, 119–120
dummy, 15, 181
extraneous, 9
frequencies of value categories and values, 4–5
independent, 8–9, 120
intervening, 9
number analyzed, 16
obscuring, 208–209
operationalization of, 5–6

predictor, 9, 134, 137, 167
relationships between, 90–92, 94–95, 121, 123, 200–201
strength of relationships between, 121, 123
value categories of, 4–5
values of, 4–5
Variance, 51, 52

Weighted mean, 44–45
Wilcoxon sign test, 225–227
Within-groups variance, 239

Yates correction factor, 196
Yule's Q, 200

z scores
converting raw scores to, 64–72
defined, 65
example of application, 70–72
negative, 67
for one-tailed research hypothesis, 108–109
positive, 67
practical uses of, 69–70
for two-tailed research hypothesis, 106

page 63 Uptown Tall
flat one..

Question 4
_____

Normal curve.

Narrow lines close together.

Middle one
_____
pg 61
on left
positively
skewed

U